MICHAEL SOLOMONOV

ZAHAV

• A WORLD OF ISRAELI COOKING •

AND

STEVEN COOK

MICHAEL SOLOMONOV

ZAHAV

• A WORLD OF ISRAELI COOKING •

AND
STEVEN COOK

PRODUCED BY **DOROTHY KALINS INK**
PHOTOGRAPHS BY **MICHAEL PERSICO**
DESIGN BY **DON MORRIS DESIGN**

A RUX MARTIN BOOK
HOUGHTON MIFFLIN HARCOURT
BOSTON NEW YORK 2015

For information about permission to reproduce
selections from this book, write to Permissions,
Houghton Mifflin Harcourt Publishing Company,
215 Park Avenue South, New York, New York 10003.

www.hmhco.com

Library of Congress Cataloging-in-Publication Data
Solomonov, Michael.
  Zahav : a world of Israeli cooking / Michael Solomonov
and Steven Cook ; produced by Dorothy Kalins ;
photography by Mike Persico.
      pages cm
  "A Rux Martin book."
  ISBN 978-0-544-37328-0 (hardcover) —
  ISBN 978-0-544-37329-7 (ebook)
1. Cooking, Israeli. I. Title.
  TX724.S65 2016
  641.595694 — dc23
  2015004346

Produced by Dorothy Kalins Ink, LLC

Design by Don Morris Design

Recipe Editor: Joy Manning

Printed in China
C&C 10 9 8 7 6 5 4 3 2 1

DEDICATION

This book is for my brother,
David Ben-Zion Solomonov.

You are with me always.

CONTENTS

INTRO
• An Improbable Journey •
10

TEHINA
• The Secret Sauce •
24

SALATIM
• Vegetables Are Everything •
74

3

MEZZE
• Hospitality Incarnate •
116

4

BEYOND CHICKEN SOUP
• The World in a Bowl •
156

CONTENTS

GRANDMOTHER'S BOREKAS

• *Tradition Was My Teacher* •
192

LIVE FIRE

• *As Close to Magic as I'll Come* •
232

BEN-GURION'S RICE

• *Rice Is Easy, Perfection Is Hard* •
264

MESIBAH
• *It's Party Time* •
290

MILK & HONEY
• *A Glimpse of the Divine* •
316

INTRO

• An Improbable Journey •

IT TAKES MORE than a restaurant to move a person to write a cookbook. For that matter, it takes more than being a cook to move a person to open a restaurant. This book is the chronicle of a journey—physical, emotional, personal. As inevitable as it likely seems now, since you are holding this book in your hands, nothing in my life happened the way it was supposed to.

FAMILY PORTRAIT
I am about ten years old in this picture taken about 1988 at our house in Pittsburgh, with my little brother David, my dad, Big Solo, and my mother, Evelyn.

"Along the way I share the story of my life. It's inextricable, the life and the food."

No one event followed logically from one point to the next. Luck, coincidence, hard work, even tragedy have shaped me, have led me to a life, a restaurant—quite a few of them now—a true working partnership, a marriage, and my two sons.

I wrote this book to celebrate those things, of course. But something stronger motivates me. I am compelled, driven even, by the need to share what I have learned about the cooking of Israel and how I interpret it for others to experience and enjoy. To me, it is urgent that the flavors of Zahav reach a wider audience. I want you to fall hard for the warm spices of baharat, the lemony tang of sumac, the powerful peppery punch of the condiment called schug, and see how those things can enhance not just your cooking, but your understanding, too. I want you to know the mellow excitement of a bowl of Yemenite soup and appreciate how that bowl contains a world. Sure, I'll show you how I make fluffy matzo balls, but I want you to love other dumplings, too, like the stuffed kubbe, ghondi, and kofte that can float your soup.

I want to celebrate the vegetable classic that we know as Israeli salad, but then I want to show you how I make it in the dead of winter using persimmons and mangoes instead of out-of-season tomatoes. I learned so many things from my Bulgarian grandmother, Savta Mati, especially the flaky borekas she taught me to make as a young boy. We shared no common language, but we communicated just the same.

I would love to see you filling your dining table—or kitchen table—with many delectable little plates—mezze. To me, mezze is hospitality incarnate: Dishes like Fried Cauliflower, Lamb Basturma, Chicken Pastilla, and "Baked" Kibbe helped me fall in love with the intense flavors of Israeli cooking. And sure, I want to celebrate real tehina, the essential paste made from the purest sesame seeds. It is what makes the hummus you probably bought this book for (and that probably put Zahav on the map). But I want you to know, too, the sweeter side of tehina, how it easily becomes the confection halva, or a crumbly cookie, or that almost–ice cream semifreddo. I have cooked all this food in front of Mike Persico's camera to demystify the methods and

ingredients, to help you make it yours. I want to get you as close as a book can get you to the true experience of cooking this food.

I want you to taste how Twice-Cooked Eggplant combines char and creaminess to become almost another vegetable. You will come to appreciate the Zen of making rice and the utter joy of coming ever closer to perfection with every pot you make. I want you to share the inner thrill I get each time I turn a piece of meat over live fire, feeling an ancient connection to this primitive ritual. I want you to experience Mesibah, party time: how a tableful of friends and family enhances the lives of cooks and eaters, too. I want you to make the braised lamb shoulder that's launched a thousand dinners at Zahav, and I'll reveal all its secrets, down to the last chickpea infused with pungent pomegranate. Along the way I'll share the story of my life. It's all inextricable, the life and the food. How could it be otherwise?

OVED'S SABICH
On a trip to Israel in 2008 with the Zahav staff just before we opened, we stop in Givatayim on the outskirts of Tel Aviv for Oved's famous pita stuffed with fried eggplant, eggs, and hummus.

Previous spread: **On the beach at Caesarea, near Haifa, 2008.**

I WAS BORN IN ISRAEL, in a small town called G'nei Yehuda, south of Tel Aviv, but my family moved to the United States when I was two, and I grew up in the Squirrel Hill neighborhood of Pittsburgh, feeling mostly American. My brother, David, was born when I was three. One of my clearest childhood memories is standing next to my father in the hospital and screaming, "That is my brother, David, and HEEE is Jewish!" When I was fifteen, my parents decided to move back to Israel. To say I went grudgingly is an understatement. I returned to the U.S. as soon as I could. David stayed behind. And while I was learning how to julienne, brunoise, and make (and break) hollandaise sauce, David was graduating from high school and, like every other young Israeli, preparing for military training. In October 2001, he entered an Israeli Defense Forces infantry unit.

Culinary degree in hand, I weaseled my way into a job at Marc Vetri's eponymous restaurant in Philadelphia. After I nearly broke all the kitchen equipment, and finally learned how to keep the chocolate polenta soufflé from collapsing, Marc offered me the sous chef position. I was terrified but over the moon with excitement. I signed on for the two-year commitment right before Vetri closed for its three-week summer break. A three-week break? Super Italian, I know. So it happened that in the summer of 2003, I

LAST TIME
With David in the backyard of our half-sister's house in Hadera in 2003. On that trip, I first saw Israel through the eyes of a chef.

"We were talking and laughing like we'd never been apart; not only brothers but friends."

returned to Israel for the first time since I'd graduated from culinary school in Florida two years earlier. My mom had bought me the plane ticket on the condition that I cook for her and her friends. Dave had a month's leave from the military, and my mother wanted us to spend time together. It was also Savta Mati's eightieth birthday. The whole family would be there to celebrate.

Dave and I had been close growing up, but the move to Israel created a wedge in our relationship. Our parents had divorced soon after they'd returned there. Dave was still young enough to make a relatively easy transition to his new life, but I felt betrayed and angry. When I returned to the U.S., we drifted further apart. By 2003 we rarely spoke and hardly knew each other. But all that changed on that trip to Israel. We spent three weeks together, hanging out at the beach, partying. We visited Savta Mati together, and we did a lot of eating. Dave had the inside scoop on all the best places, so we traveled up and down the country, eating. I cooked two dinners for my mother and her friends, and Dave served them. I bought foie gras from a bicycle delivery man, shopped for produce and spices in the open-air markets, and sorted through fish caught in local waters. For the first time, I saw the country through the lens of a chef, and it was amazing! There were so many ethnic influences, so many different styles of eating. But the best part was being able to reconnect with my brother. By the end of the trip, we were talking and laughing like we had never been apart. We were not only brothers but friends.

Right before I left for the airport to return home, I embraced David, squeezed the shit out of him, and kissed him on the cheek. I told him that I loved him and that I was proud of him. We said our goodbyes while he shook me off. I returned to Vetri, and Dave went back to the army for his final month of service. I remember wondering when I would see Dave next, if he would try college in Philly or go back to Pittsburgh.

A few weeks later, it was Yom Kippur, the holiest day on the Jewish calendar. Vetri was closed, so I went to Pittsburgh for the night to drive my father's old car back to Philly the next day: My brother would need it when he returned to the U.S. I was heading east on the Pennsylvania Turnpike, just outside of Lancaster, when I got a call from my Aunt Ava. She could barely get the words out. "You need to call me the moment you get home," she said. "It's very important. Do you understand?" I pulled over and got out of the car. I made my aunt tell me what was going on. "It's David," she said. "He is dead. He was killed today in the North." The words rang in my head.

He.
Is.
Dead.

How could this be? David was supposed to be out of the army. I had just seen him. This had to be a mistake. But it wasn't. David had volunteered to cover a patrol shift on Yom Kippur for one of his religious comrades. He was holed up behind a boulder in an apple orchard in Metula, at the top of a hill overlooking Lebanon. He was a spotter, charged with locating Hezbollah fighters across the valley and relaying their locations back to his unit. A trap was set to draw David out of cover, and he was shot by three Hezbollah snipers.

LITTLE DAVID
Ten years later, in 2013, with another David, my two-year old son, we have a simple memorial service for my brother in Moshe Fine's apple orchard in Metula, 100 yards from the Lebanese border.

WE BURIED MY BROTHER right after I landed in Israel, and I stayed for the next seven days, in my mom's little apartment, mourning with friends and family and what felt like the entire country. When I returned to Philadelphia, I was somewhat relieved that I could put all my energy into work and cooking and my new position. From the outside, it looked like I was hanging in there, working hard and coming to terms with Dave's death, but truthfully, my tendency toward addiction reared its head the moment I returned from his funeral. I broke up with my longtime girlfriend and ended up sleeping on a futon in Vetri's office. I was becoming increasingly difficult to be around, and even my attitude at work became spotty. Everyone around me attributed my behavior to Dave's death. I played that card for years.

MARIGOLD
Steve opened his restaurant in 2004. That's him in the kitchen a year before I took over.

"Slowly my destiny revealed itself. I had to translate this food for the American palate."

Since my two-year stint as sous chef at Vetri would soon be coming to an end, it was time to figure out the next step. For a moment, I considered joining the Israeli Army myself. I wanted to live Dave's life (and probably die his death) to get closer to him and to his memories. Thankfully, Marc and my new girlfriend, Mary, talked me out of it. One night at Vetri, Marc came down from the office and said that a chef that he knew who owned a little BYOB in West Philly was looking for a cook in the kitchen. Marc thought I should consider it.

A few days later, I got a call from Shira, an old Pittsburgh friend. Shira's family and mine were friends. My mom had been Shira's teacher in middle school. Shira, it turned out, was engaged to Steven Cook, who happened to be the restaurant guy who'd called Marc looking for a chef. We all met for coffee and talked for a while. Steve explained that he was looking for someone to take over for him in his kitchen at Marigold, which was already getting tons of great press. He said I could cook whatever I wanted. I left the coffee shop quite enthusiastic and the following day, while driving with Mary (by this time my fiancée), we saw Shira and Steve on the street and gave them a ride to the movies. A week later, as I was leaving my apartment in the Italian market, I literally ran into Shira on her way from getting sandwiches at Sarcone's.

Of course, I assumed all of this was a sign from the restaurant gods. And after working in the kitchen of Steve's restaurant one Saturday night, I felt that the gods were correct. I began as the chef of Marigold Kitchen in October 2005. It was clear from the beginning that Steve and I were onto something. Our strengths and weaknesses seemed to complement each other, and in addition to growing as business partners, we became friends.

I began to appreciate Steve's business sense (he was a graduate of Wharton as well as the French Culinary Institute), and I tried to absorb as much as I could. I focused on making great food and for the first time, I set free the Israeli influences that had begun to seep into my consciousness. The Yemenite soup that I had fallen in love with at boarding school found its way onto the menu in the form of braised monkfish with apple, celery root, and Yemenite spices; grilled kebabs became lamb kofte, wrapped in cabbage and served in a pool of lentil soup.

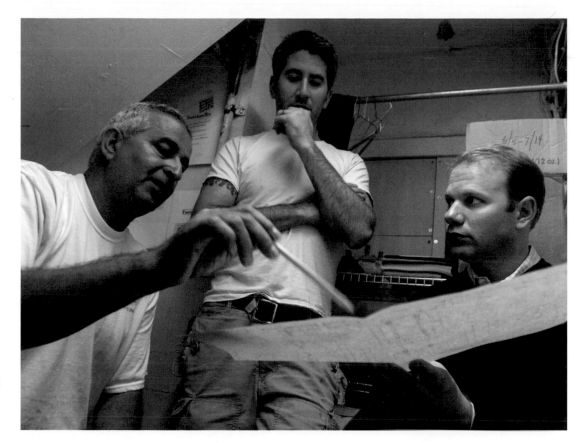

The more my menu at Marigold leaned toward Israel, the more passionate I became about cooking. I had loved making Northern Italian food at Vetri (and serious French at the Striped Bass before that), but now I was beginning to develop my own style—a style that because of David's death took on deeper meaning. My brother had died fighting for Israel, and nothing I could do would change that. But for the first time, I began to see cooking as a powerful way to honor David's memory.

BIG PLANS
If it looks like we have no idea what we're doing, in the winter of 2007, that's because it's true. The early days of Zahav were a mystery to us. Thankfully we had our contractor Ofer (see Yemenite Soup, page 160).

I could expose people to a side of Israel that had nothing to do with politics and didn't ever make the evening news. After a couple of trips to Israel together, Steve and I began discussing opening an "Israeli" restaurant. There was something magical about eating in Israel, we agreed, something that you just could not find back home, and certainly not in an upscale restaurant. In Israel, the meal always began with pita and hummus and other dips, followed by a dizzying array of bright vegetable salads, plate after plate of intensely flavored mezze, and ended with skewers of kebabs and shishlik grilled over live charcoal. It was all delicious and soulful, vibrant and elemental. It was rich but healthy. It was old but new.

Slowly my destiny seemed to reveal itself. Someone had to translate all of this for the American palate, and I knew then that it should be me. When Zahav opened in May 2008, it was the first restaurant of its kind in America. Today, people assume that the success of Zahav was a foregone conclusion. But in fall 2008, things looked very different. What most people knew about Israeli food began and ended with hummus and falafel. Even the two of us didn't quite know what it meant to be an Israeli restaurant. During our first year, we were forced to make painful staffing cuts. Steve and I stopped taking paychecks. At one point, we were a month away from turning out the lights.

Zahav began to turn around when we embraced the notion that Israeli food is not a static collection of traditional recipes. It is an idea. Israel is only sixty years old, a barely melted pot of cultures from all over the world. There aren't really Israeli restaurants in Israel, as strange as that sounds. There are Bulgarian restaurants and

Arabic restaurants and Georgian restaurants and Yemenite restaurants—and many, many more. What connects them, what makes them Israeli, is an approach to dining and hospitality that is shaped by a shared experience.

May 9, 2011, was Zahav's third anniversary. A few days later, on Israeli Memorial Day, I sat in a synagogue in Philadelphia and thought about my brother and everything that had happened since he died almost eight years earlier. The very next day was Israeli Independence Day, and I found myself in an auditorium at New York City's Lincoln Center for the James Beard Awards, where my name was called as Best Chef: Mid-Atlantic. The presenters even pronounced it correctly. For that, and for all the awards and accolades that came before and after, my greatest pride still comes from welcoming our guests to Zahav every single night. From my position at the bread

station, covered in flour and with the heat of our wood-burning oven at my back, I can look out at the entire dining room in front of me. For me, it never gets old.

You won't find all of the dishes in this book at a single restaurant in Israel. Together, though, they make an impression of a cuisine that is evolving even as I write this. I hope that you will explore these recipes and, in them, find some of the magic that Steve and I found in Israel. Better yet, go to Israel and see for yourself.

So yes, Zahav is a restaurant. But it is also an idea, one I happily wrestle with every day on our gentle hillside in Philadelphia—the City of Brotherly Love.

WELCOME.

SECRET GARDEN
Zahav today is a happy, buzzing place, much like the courtyard in the old city of Jerusalem that inspired it. Even the floors are outdoor stone pavers.

WHAT KOSHER MEANS TO ME

JEWS WHO KEEP KOSHER do not mix milk and meat in the same dish or even the same meal. This is actually an extremely difficult way to cook great food. I was trained in classic French technique, which was built on large quantities of butter. When I worked in an Italian restaurant, it seemed like the whole kitchen was covered in a light dusting of Parmigiano-Reggiano. Israeli cooks may not have some of these things that we take for granted in the kitchen, but tehina is the great equalizer.

Plenty of Israelis eat treyf these days. Pork is sold as "white steak" and the beautiful shellfish from the Mediterranean would test the faith of Job. But at Zahav, and in this book, we choose to honor the spirit of a few fundamental rules of kosher cooking. We don't serve pork or shellfish, and we don't use milk and meat in the same dish. The reason is simple: Kosher rules help define the boundaries of Israeli cuisine. The second you add pork or shellfish to a dish, it can become Greek or Turkish. When you add yogurt to lamb, it can become Lebanese or Syrian. Without the influence of kosher rules, the notion of Israeli cuisine itself begins to fray.

I'll be honest. I'm eating a bacon cheeseburger as I write this. And sometimes when I'm cooking in the restaurant, I'll say to myself, "Man, I wish I could baste this piece of meat with butter, or add lobster to this dish." I don't keep kosher at home, nor am I asking you to do so. Some of the recipes in this book would be great with shellfish or pork; for example the tarator sauce (page 48) is amazing with fried mussels. And I'm not going to stop you from grinding bacon into kofte (page 180). Sometimes, I'll make suggestions for nonkosher variations of recipes. Otherwise, I'll leave it up to you to figure out how to disappoint your Jewish relatives.

SAY CH …
A GUIDE TO
PRONUNCIATION

THE RECIPES AND INGREDIENTS in this book are straightforward, but sometimes the spelling and pronunciation are not. The Hebrew language has sounds for which there are no English equivalents, so the spelling I use here is as close as I can get. There are no official transliterations; the spellings I tend to prefer are the ones my family used when I was growing up.

Fortunately, spelling has nothing to do with flavor. And just because an ingredient sounds unfamiliar or exotic doesn't mean it's hard to find or difficult to use. The word hawaij, pronounced CHA-waj (or hawaj, hawayej, hawayij, chawage), for example, may look like a monkey got ahold of a keyboard. But it really just refers to a spice blend of black pepper, cumin, and turmeric, three ingredients found in every supermarket in America. In cases where a particular ingredient may be trickier to find, I ask you to see Resources (page 359), where we've made a list of our favorite vendors. (I promise, none of these recipes call for eye of newt, but if you know where to find some, please let me know.)

The food will taste the same no matter how you pronounce it, but if you want to impress your friends, you'll need to master the "ch" sound that is prominent in Hebrew. This is not the soft sound in cheese, but a hard, guttural sound that comes from the roof of your mouth, like you're clearing your throat. It is the sound of the letter "h" in words like hummus and tehina. To practice, channel your inner Jewish grandfather and repeat the following sentence: On Chanukah, I dip my challah in hummus-tehina.

"Spelling has nothing to do with flavor; an ingredient may look unfamiliar, but that doesn't mean it's difficult to use."

1

TEHINA

• *The Secret Sauce* •

I LIKE IT on eggplant with pomegranate. I like it with walnuts on fish. I like it with beets. I like it with garlic on roasted lamb. I like it with date molasses on foie gras. I like it with harissa on kofte. I like it on a schnitzel sandwich with Iraqi mango pickles. I like it on ice cream. I like it straight from the jar.

"Tehina is the same as 'tahini,' the Greek spelling for the pure, unctuous sesame seed paste."

Israelis love tehina like Americans love Doritos and wrestling—unconditionally and a little bit irrationally. The country doesn't run without it. Israelis eat it raw and use it as a dip. They put it on sandwiches and salads. They sauce fish and meat with it. They use it in sweets. They add it to hummus by the truckload. Although I was born in Israel, my family moved to Pittsburgh when I was two. Growing up, my entire Israeli identity was limited to a few Hebrew phrases, usually shouted by my father: *Maspeek!* (enough!), pounding the table for emphasis when I misbehaved, which was often; *hazak* (hard), encouraging me to blow my nose; *kvissa* (laundry chute), reminding me not to leave my clothes all over the place.

But part of our household identity was the can of tehina that was always on our kitchen table. Not as much for my Bulgarian father, who lived most of his life in Israel; he couldn't have been happier in the land of the hamburger. But for my American mother, who had fallen in love with Israel and left for the States before she was ready, that can of tehina represented her adopted home. I didn't touch the stuff as a child. My idea of a three-Michelin-star meal was peas and rice—served on separate plates. I remember watching my father pull sizzling lamb chops off the grill, dripping with fat and juices, and proceed to smother them with tehina. All I could think was, why the hell would you ruin a beautiful piece of meat like that?

I know I'm not the only one to view tehina with suspicion. As an American, I understand this. As an Israeli, I feel that it's my duty to act as a spokesman for the tehina lobby. First, let's start with some terminology. Tehina is the same thing as 'tahini,' which is the typical (and more recognizable) Greek spelling. Tehina is how Israelis refer to the identical product. It's the word I grew up with, so it's what I use in this book. When I say tehina, I generally mean pure sesame paste, made from toasting and grinding raw sesame seeds. If you see a jar of tehina that has more than one ingredient, drop it and run. When I say prepared tehina, I am referring to my Basic Tehina Sauce (page 32) made from blending tehina with garlic, lemon, water, and salt.

Until very recently, it was hard to find great tehina here in the States, and what was available could be quite bad. Tehina was either considered a health food—sentenced to dusty shelves in the natural foods aisle—or an ethnic product exiled to Middle Eastern

PAPRIKA stands in totemic columns in the Jerusalem market, ready to be dusted on a plate of hummus, *below.* Soom tahini, *left.*

Previous spread: **Pressing toasted sesame seeds into tehina.**

27

• INGREDIENT •

SOOM TAHINI

THIS IS A DELIGHTFUL, IMPROBABLE STORY, but nonetheless true: Three sisters from Philadelphia have set out to revolutionize the tahini business in America: Shelby Zitelman Stamm (above left), Jackie Zitelman Horvitz with her Israeli husband, Omri Horvitz (middle), and Amy Zitelman Hersch (far right) first brought me Soom Tahini to taste. Now, between Zahav, Federal Donuts, and our new hummus place, Dizengoff, we buy almost 1,400 pounds of the stuff a month! The Zitelman sisters are evangelists. "Americans have been stuck with hard and oily tahini. We come in at the top of the market with pure and delicious sesame butter," says Amy. Soom's tahini (*soom soom* is Hebrew for sesame seeds) is made from white seeds grown in Ethiopia's abundant sunshine in its northwestern Humera district. The seeds are shipped to Israel for processing, overseen by Omri and Jackie, who then send the jars to us. (See Resources, page 359.)

markets. That can on our kitchen table growing up was full of separated tehina, with a greasy slick on top and a thick layer of sludge stuck to the bottom. These were signs that our tehina was old and poorly made. But for the longest time, that orange and brown can was practically the only brand readily available in the States. It was not a great advertisement for tehina. I didn't appreciate how good tehina could be until I started cooking. Like most ingredients, there is the mass-produced stuff and then there is the artisanal product that reminds you what the fuss is about. I remember standing on the floor of a tehina-processing workshop in Nazareth, inhaling the rich and heady aroma of toasted sesame seeds and watching a stream of fresh tehina pour from the

COOKIES
The sweeter side of tehina shines in desserts like Tehina Shortbread Cookies (page 66) and in the famous Halva candy (page 68).

"Great tehina is creamy, nutty, and rich, with a delicate sweetness. Roasting gives it a slight smokiness."

grinder into a vat below. I felt a strong urge to stick my head under the tap; we did warm shots instead. The taste of properly roasted, high-quality sesame seeds (the best come from Ethiopia), still warm from the grinding stone, is like a slap in the face compared to the stuff in a can. In a good way.

The key to making great tehina is to drive away as much water and fibrous material from the sesame seeds as possible, until you're left with the pure fat. At the Al Arz workshop in Nazareth, first they remove the hulls from the sesame seeds. The seeds are then slow roasted in an open steel drum with a rotating arm that keeps them in constant motion. The drum is heated from beneath using steam, effectively creating a giant double boiler. This is the gentlest possible method and it eliminates any scorched flavors that can result from unevenly roasted seeds.

Great tehina is creamy, nutty, and rich, with a delicate sweetness. Roasting the sesame seeds gives the sauce its earthy and slightly smoky backbone. The mouthfeel is unctuous, with a finish that's long and smooth. Used properly, tehina can bring back wayward dishes by balancing out sweetness and softening acidity. And it's great at smoothing out rough edges (like Israelis, who are famous for being a bit prickly). When people tell me they don't like tehina, they usually say it tastes bitter. American children aren't generally exposed to bitter flavors. In Israel, on the other hand, a popular after-school snack is a slice of bread slathered with tehina and date molasses. It is the peanut-butter-and-jelly sandwich of Israel. Bitterness is an underappreciated but powerful tool in developing flavor. Great flavors rely on a balance of tastes, like the sweet and salty perfection of a Reese's Peanut Butter Cup. Without the bitter, there would be no coffee or chocolate or beer. The economies of Brooklyn and Portland would crash and burn. And there would be no tehina.

Tehina is especially important in the traditional Israeli kosher kitchen because it can enrich savory dishes without using cream or butter and it can create satisfying desserts, too. It's the Israeli mother sauce. But kosher or not, tehina is one of the most important and versatile staples in my kitchen. It might be the least sexy ingredient (it's the color of wet sand; it sticks to the roof of your mouth), but I haven't seen many culinary problems that tehina couldn't solve.

SESAME SEEDS

SINCE ISRAELIS LOVE tehina so much, I always assumed that the sesame seeds it's made from were grown in Israel. Although in ancient times sesame seeds were a major crop in the Middle East, this is no longer true. The majority of sesame seeds that make the rich and nutty tehina we love are now imported. The best come from Ethiopia, where the far-reaching fields of sesame plants thrive, *above*. There the plants are given the altitude, rainfall, and sunshine they require. The plants bear many lobed seed pods that split when ripe, revealing their miraculous tiny seeds, *left*.

Sesame seeds come in white and black; the white seeds are used to make tehina, the black are most often sprinkled over savory dishes. Of course the tehina made from sesame seeds is foundational to my cooking, but I depend on the seeds themselves to finish a savory dish, or scatter over borekas (page 206), and challah (page 210) before baking. Think of these plants growing in these fields the next time you bite into a sesame bagel and brush off the seeds that fall into your lap!

BASIC TEHINA SAUCE

Makes about 4 cups

THIS SIMPLE SAUCE is one of my basic building blocks and is so versatile that once you master it, there are a million things you can do with it. The important step here is to allow the garlic and lemon juice to hang out for 10 minutes after blending but before adding the jarred tehina. This step helps stabilize the garlic and prevents it from fermenting and turning sour and aggressive, which is the problem with a lot of tehina sauces (and therefore the hummus made from them).

Because you're making an emulsion (oil-based tehina incorporated into water and lemon juice), the tehina sauce can sometimes separate or seize up. Don't panic! That's why you keep a glass of ice water nearby and add a few tablespoons at a time to the lemon juice–tehina mixture while you're whisking, until your creamy emulsion returns.

> 1 head garlic
> ¾ cup lemon juice (from 3 lemons)
> 1½ teaspoons kosher salt
> 2 generous cups tehina
> ½ teaspoon ground cumin

● Break up the head of garlic with your hands, letting the unpeeled cloves fall into a blender. Add the lemon juice and ½ teaspoon of the salt. Blend on high for a few seconds until you have a coarse puree. Let the mixture stand for 10 minutes to let the garlic mellow.

● Pour the mixture through a fine-mesh strainer set over a large mixing bowl, pressing on the solids to extract as much liquid as possible. Discard the solids. Add the tehina to the strained lemon juice in the bowl, along with the cumin and 1 teaspoon of the salt.

● Whisk the mixture together until smooth (or use a food processor), adding ice water, a few tablespoons at a time, to thin it out. The sauce will lighten in color as you whisk. When the tehina seizes up or tightens, keep adding ice water, bit by bit (about 1½ cups in total), whisking energetically until you have a perfectly smooth, creamy, thick sauce.

● Taste and add up to 1½ teaspoons more salt and cumin if you like. If you're not using the sauce immediately, whisk in a few tablespoons of ice water to loosen it before refrigerating. The tehina sauce will keep a week refrigerated, or it can be frozen for up to a month.

BLEND
a whole head of garlic
and the lemon juice
into a coarse puree.

STRAIN
the crushed garlic
and lemon juice.

POUR
tehina into the strained
lemon/garlic juice.

WHISK
ice water bit by bit
into the stiff tehina.

TASTE
as you go for
salt and cumin.

CONSISTENCY should be creamy, light, and fluffy.

"The most comfortable place for me in the kitchen, and where you'll find me most nights, is turning out hot laffa from the taboon."

HUMMUS

I SOMETIMES WONDER where my career would be without hummus. More than anything, it's the dish that brings people to the restaurant in the first place. And more often than not, it is what brings them back. There's something transcendent about the perfect bowl of hummus that tells our guests they're in the right place. I often imagine that somewhere beneath the restaurant is an engine room with two guys shoveling hummus into a giant furnace that keeps the stoves lit and the lights on. Without hummus, Zahav would be a cold, dark shell.

Hummus originated in the Middle East long before Israel, but Israelis have adopted it as their own. There is an entire genre of restaurants dedicated to it. Step into a *hummusiya* and you'll see a cross-section of Israeli society—politicians, construction workers, doctors, lawyers, bus drivers. Israelis eat hummus for breakfast, lunch, and dinner, with nothing more than great pita, sliced onion, a few pickles and olives, a bowl of Israeli salad, and some harif, or hot sauce. A cold beer doesn't hurt. That's what we had in mind when we opened our own hummusiya, Dizengoff, in center city Philadelphia in 2014.

Please note that great hummus is never refrigerated. The best places make a big batch each morning and close the doors when it runs out, usually by midafternoon.

When Israelis eat hummus, they say, "Let's go wipe some hummus," which refers to the action of scooping up hummus with pita, and also makes it clear that eating hummus is a social activity. It does not involve standing at the kitchen counter, dipping factory-shaped baby carrots into a cold, stiff tub of store-bought hummus by the light of the refrigerator. In the U.S., the market for hummus has exploded. American farmers can't plant chickpeas fast enough, and major snack food companies are snapping up small manufacturers to get in on the action. And while I am gratified to see such widespread acceptance of something so close to my heart, I fear that the real product is getting lost in translation.

Hummus in Israel is pure luxury. The texture is smooth and creamy, and the flavors are nutty, rich, and satisfying in a completely wholesome way. The problem with even the best-quality store-bought hummus is that it requires certain additives to make it shelf-stable—most likely citric acid. These additives turn hummus sharp and sour—light years away from the dreamy qualities of fresh hummus.

Fortunately, great hummus could not be easier to make at home. All it requires is a food processor, cooked chickpeas, and my Basic Tehina Sauce (page 32). Some people will tell you that canned chickpeas are useless. Unfriend them immediately. While I'd prefer that you soak and cook dried chickpeas as we do at the restaurant, fresh hummus made from canned chickpeas is a hundred times better than anything you can buy at the grocery store. And it takes less than 5 minutes. Hummus follows the rule that simple things are often the hardest to do well. Our hummus at Zahav has only five ingredients, but it took us longer to develop than any other recipe. I can still remember our manager (and native Israeli) Eilon's expression when we finally nailed it. A smile came across his face and he closed his eyes and didn't speak for two full minutes.

> *"Israelis say, 'Let's go wipe some hummus,' scooping it with pita."*

CHICKPEAS
Dried, canned, soaked, and cooked.

HUMMUS TEHINA

Makes 3½ cups

BY NOW, YOU'LL NOT BE SURPRISED to learn that the secret to great Israeli-style hummus is an obscene amount of tehina, as much as half of the recipe by weight, so it's especially important to use the best quality you can find. Unlike Greek-style hummus, which is heavy on garlic and lemon, Israeli hummus is about the marriage of chickpeas and tehina. In fact, there are no other ingredients, just a dash of cumin. The only lemon and garlic involved is in my Basic Tehina Sauce. There are countless variations, but I'm not talking about black bean, white bean, or edamame hummus. Those might be perfectly nice dips, but since hummus is the Arabic word for chickpeas, that's what we use.

Remember to leave time for the dried chickpeas to soak overnight.

1   cup dried chickpeas

2   teaspoons baking soda

1½   cups Basic Tehina Sauce
      (page 32), plus a bit
      more for the topping

1   teaspoon kosher salt

¼   teaspoon ground cumin
      Paprika
      Chopped fresh parsley
      Olive oil, for drizzling

● Place the chickpeas in a large bowl with 1 teaspoon of the baking soda and cover with water. (The chickpeas will double in volume, so use more water than you think you need.) Soak the chickpeas overnight at room temperature. The next day, drain the chickpeas and rinse under cold water.

● Place the chickpeas in a large pot with the remaining 1 teaspoon baking soda and add cold water to cover by at least 4 inches. Bring the chickpeas to a boil over high heat, skimming off any scum that rises to the surface. Lower the heat to medium, cover the pot, and continue to simmer for about 1 hour, until the chickpeas are completely tender. Then simmer them a little more. (The secret to creamy hummus is overcooked chickpeas; don't worry if they are mushy and falling apart a little.) Drain.

● Combine the chickpeas, tehina sauce, salt, and cumin in a food processor. Puree the hummus for several minutes, until it is smooth and uber-creamy. Then puree it some more!

● To serve, spread the hummus in a shallow bowl, dust with paprika, top with parsley and more tehina sauce if you like, and drizzle generously with oil.

HUMMUS PITRYOT

HUMMUS MASABACHA

**HUMMUS WITH FRESH
BEANS AND LAMB**

HUMMUS TEHINA

HUMMUS FOUL

TURKISH HUMMUS

JERUSALEM HUMMUS

HUMMUS WITH FRESH BEANS AND LAMB

ONE OF MY FAVORITE THINGS about summer is the arrival of shell beans. I can never eat enough English peas, fava beans, or fresh chickpeas. I'll take a giant bowl of buttered English peas over an ounce of white truffles any day. There is just something luxurious about being able to eat large quantities of even the most humble ingredients when they are at their peak and available in abundance.

This recipe is my reimagined mashup of the Masabacha, Foul, and Jerusalem hummus traditions. I replace dried favas and chickpeas with their fresh counterparts and fold them into a stew of braised lamb. Ladled into the center of a bowl of hummus and accompanied by fresh pita, this is a complete and extremely satisfying meal.

(As a line cook, I used to dread coming face to face with a bushel of fresh fava beans that needed to be shelled and peeled, but I've actually come to enjoy the Zen of it. Pour yourself a glass of whatever you're drinking and get lost in the repetition.)

● Combine 1½ cups shredded meat and ½ cup sauce left over from The Zahav Lamb Shoulder (page 302) or other braised meat with 1 cup shelled fresh fava beans (boiled for 1 minute and peeled), or green chickpeas, in a saucepan. Warm the mixture over medium heat until the meat is heated through and the fava beans are tender. Fold 2 tablespoons chopped fresh mint and a squeeze of lemon juice into the meat. Serve over 1 recipe Hummus Tehina (page 39).

HUMMUS PITRYOT

EVERY ONCE IN A WHILE, a guy arrives at the restaurant with a wrinkled brown paper sack full of the most enormous clusters of Hen-of-the-Woods mushrooms I've ever seen. We don't call to place an order; he just shows up. He's a part-time ski instructor who spends some of his time foraging in the mushroom-rich woods of the Brandywine Valley, just outside of Philadelphia. Pitryot, mushrooms in Hebrew, are a classic hummus accompaniment and a great way to ratchet up the earthy and meaty flavors while still keeping it vegan. Hen-of-the-Woods work well because their "petals" get crispy when roasted, adding a nice textural contrast to the hummus. (The name of this mushroom came from its resemblance to the ruffled tail feathers of a hen. It is also referred to by its Japanese name, maitake.) Any mushroom will do, even the lowly but underrated white button mushroom, as long as you use a screaming-hot skillet and don't crowd the pan.

● Break up 1½ cups Hen-of-the-Woods mushrooms into 1- to 2-inch pieces. Film the bottom of a large skillet with canola oil and heat over medium-high heat. Add the mushrooms along with 2 slivered garlic cloves. Cook, stirring, until the mushrooms are brown and crisp in places, about 8 minutes. Add 1 tablespoon chopped fresh dill and toss. Serve over 1 recipe Hummus Tehina (page 39) and top with chopped fresh parsley, paprika, and olive oil.

HUMMUS FOUL

FOUL MEDAMES, or simply foul, is a dried fava bean stew that is a staple in Middle Eastern cuisine, especially in Egypt. Interestingly, the dish is thought to have Jewish roots. Foul means fava beans and medames means buried, referring to the practice of burying pots of fava beans in the embers of the fires, a common practice when cooking for the Jewish Sabbath: The dish could be left to gently cook overnight and be ready for lunch on Saturday without further tending—the ancient equivalent of the modern-day slow cooker.

Foul is a common breakfast dish, often as a topping for hummus with hard-boiled eggs. I like to use haminados (see page 308); hard-boiled eggs slow-cooked in a stew, or hamin, which gives them a beautiful caramel color, a creamy texture, and a deep flavor. (We get a similar effect by long-simmering the eggs in a coffee-based brine.) I love the contrast of the long-cooked, deep-flavored fava beans against the fresher, brighter hummus.

● Soak 1 cup dried fava beans overnight, then drain and rinse. Quickly boil the fava beans to soften them, then drain and peel away the outer skin. Cook the peeled fava beans in boiling salted water with a few garlic cloves and a pinch each of ground cumin, coriander, and cardamom until tender, about 1 hour. Let the beans cool in their cooking liquid. Drain, reserving a little cooking liquid, then toss the beans with the cooking liquid.

● Top 1 recipe Hummus Tehina (page 39) with the warm fava beans. Season with lemon juice, salt, and additional cumin, coriander, and cardamom. Top with chopped fresh parsley, olive oil, and ground Urfa pepper (see page 48). Serve with slow-cooked eggs (haminados) on the side.

HUMMUS MASABACHA

MASABACHA IS A DISH of whole or coarsely mashed chickpeas dressed with tehina that's been thinned out with a little lemon juice or water—sort of like deconstructed hummus. Often it's simply eaten on its own, but I prefer it spooned into the center of a bowl of Hummus Tehina. I like the temperature and textural contrast between the warm, chunky chickpeas and the room-temperature creamy hummus. It's hummus two ways, from a time way before that sort of thing was fashionable.

● Mix 1 cup cooked or canned chickpeas with ¼ cup Basic Tehina Sauce (page 32) and the juice of ½ lemon. Warm this mixture gently in a small saucepan and spoon into the center of 1 recipe Hummus Tehina (page 39). Top with chopped fresh parsley, paprika, and olive oil.

TURKISH HUMMUS

I RIPPED OFF THIS DISH from my friend Ana Sortun, the great chef of Oleana restaurant in Cambridge, and it has become one of the most popular variations we prepare at Zahav. As the name indicates, it's not Israeli, and it involves butter. We blend melted butter (in place of the tehina) with chickpeas and roasted garlic and then bake the hummus in a cast iron dish. When it comes out of the oven, we douse it with some great Israeli olive oil and sprinkle on a bit of ground Urfa pepper—a smoky and fruity Turkish variety (see page 48)—and serve it warm.

● Cut the top off a head of garlic, drizzle it with olive oil, and roast it in a 350°F oven until brown and very soft. Squeeze out the roasted garlic into a medium saucepan and add 4 tablespoons (½ stick) butter. Melt the butter slowly with the garlic. Combine the cooked chickpeas from the Hummus Tehina recipe (page 39), the butter-garlic mixture, and the juice of 1 lemon in a food processor and puree until smooth. Salt well. Transfer to an ovenproof dish and sprinkle some whole cooked chickpeas on top. Bake until the top is golden brown, about 5 minutes. Garnish with olive oil and ground Urfa pepper and serve.

JERUSALEM HUMMUS

THIS TYPICALLY REFERS to hummus that is garnished with hot, spiced ground beef, often with the addition of pine nuts. The appeal of this dish is obvious, with the hot beef fat exerting a "bad" influence on the normally wholesome hummus. To my knowledge, the name isn't geographically precise, but eating a bowl of it on a winter's night in Jerusalem is one of the best things ever.

● Heat 1 tablespoon canola oil in a large skillet over medium-high heat. Add 1 cup chopped onion and cook, stirring occasionally, until it begins to soften, 5 to 8 minutes. Add 1 pound ground beef, 2 slivered garlic cloves, and 2 tablespoons pine nuts. Cook, stirring, until the beef is browned, about 10 minutes. Add ½ teaspoon baharat (see page 54) and season with salt. Garnish with chopped fresh parsley. Serve over 1 recipe Hummus Tehina (page 39).

CHICKPEAS

HUMMUS IS THE ARABIC WORD for chickpeas (or garbanzos). Americans are going nuts for hummus, the chickpea puree with a base of tehina, and for good reasons. It's absolutely delicious, and chickpeas are so healthy and an excellent source of dietary fiber and vegetable protein. They're grown in vast fields, like soybeans, and the fresh green peas in their fuzzy pods are sometimes available at farmers' markets. At Zahav, our dried chickpeas come from Turkey, Mexico, or Canada, although American farmers seem to be planting them in record amounts. Make sure to buy them from a source whose inventory turns over quickly; old dried chickpeas will never get tender. I prefer smaller ones when I can find them—they cook evenly, resulting in a uniformly creamy and tender bean. Soaking the chickpeas in water overnight before cooking helps produce beans that retain their integrity. When cooking dried chickpeas for hummus, we always add a bit of baking soda to both the soaking and cooking water. This turns the water alkaline, helping the beans cook faster. It also breaks down the texture of the beans, which is desirable for hummus (but not for serving them whole). Some advance planning is needed to properly cook dried chickpeas; in most cases, canned organic chickpeas will also work.

BLACK BASS WITH WALNUT TARATOR

Serves 4

***TARATOR* CAN MEAN** different things, depending on whom you ask. In parts of the Middle East, the term is synonymous with prepared tehina sauce. In Bulgaria, it's yogurt soup with cucumbers and dill (page 217). When I think of tarator, I'm generally referring to the Turkish and Balkan variety, which is a sauce made from almonds or walnuts that is enriched with tehina. I first encountered this version somewhere on the European side of Istanbul. The street vendor handed me a hot dog bun slathered with almond-based tarator and stuffed with crispy fried mussels. Incredibly good!

Tarator is a most satisfying accompaniment to seared fish. We get great black bass from New Jersey, less than an hour's drive from Philadelphia, and sear the skin so it's super crisp. As the base for our sauce, we use the fish bones to make fumet, a simple fish stock, and then incorporate the walnuts and tehina. Because walnuts are so robust, you need a hearty fish to stand up to them, like salmon, sturgeon, or black bass. For milder fish, replace the walnuts with almonds or pine nuts to mellow the sauce and achieve a Zen-like balance between the fish and the tarator.

4 *(6-ounce) skin-on black bass fillets*
 Kosher salt
 Canola oil, for frying
3 *garlic cloves, unpeeled*
 A few sprigs dill
 Walnut Tarator (page 48)

● Season the bass fillets with salt. Heat ¼ inch oil in a large cast iron skillet over medium-high heat. Lightly crush the garlic cloves on the counter with the palm of your hand and add them to the oil. When the oil begins to shimmer but before it begins to smoke, and working in batches to avoid crowding, add the fish fillets to the pan, skin side down. Shake the pan so the skin doesn't stick. Lower the heat to medium and let the fish cook undisturbed until the flesh turns opaque halfway up the sides of the fillets, about 5 minutes. While the fish is cooking, tilt the pan to pool the oil and use a spoon to baste the fish with the hot garlic oil.

● With a spatula, carefully flip the fish (the skin will release easily when it is ready) and cook for an additional 2 minutes on the flesh side. Transfer the fillets to a warm platter and top with the dill sprigs. Serve immediately with the walnut tarator.

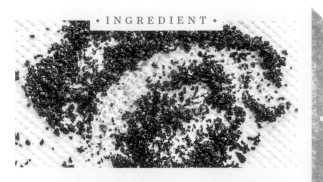

• INGREDIENT •

GROUND URFA PEPPER

URFA PEPPERS ARE MEDIUM SPICY Turkish peppers that are sun-dried during the day and wrapped tightly at night, yielding a rich, oily, pepper with notes of chocolate and smoky raisins. Urfas are sold ground. They work with duck and lamb, but also with such sweets as cinnamon and white chocolate. I love to bloom ground Urfa in brown butter as a dressing for cooked vegetables. If you can't find ground Urfa pepper, use ground anchos. (See Resources, page 359.)

WALNUT TARATOR
Makes about 1 cup

- ½ cup walnut pieces
- ½ cup Basic Tehina Sauce (page 32)
- ¼ cup Fish Fumet (recipe follows)
- 2 tablespoons lemon juice
  Kosher salt
- 1 teaspoon ground Urfa pepper
  or ground Aleppo pepper (optional)

● Place half the walnuts in a food processor and pulse until very finely ground, but stop before they turn into a paste. Hand-chop the remaining walnuts into pea-size pieces. Transfer the ground walnuts to a large bowl and add the chopped walnuts, tehina sauce, fumet, and lemon juice. Whisk in salt and Urfa or Aleppo pepper.

FISH FUMET
Makes about 2 ½ cups

THIS IS THE PART OF THE BOOK where I tell you to ask your fishmonger to scale, fillet, and pin-bone the bass and save the bones. And then you say to yourself, "Does this guy actually think I have a fishmonger?" To which I respond, "No, but it sounds cool." In a perfect world, we'd all have a fishmonger. But in the meantime, just ask the guy behind the counter wherever you buy your fish for some fish bones and to make sure that the bones are really neutral and fresh. Nothing is worse than going to the trouble of making fumet and having it smell like low tide.

- 2 tablespoons canola oil
- 1 onion, sliced
- 1 celery rib, sliced
- ½ teaspoon kosher salt

FED NUTS
Steve and I opened
our first shop on
"Two" Street in 2011,
and still hang out there.

*Head and bones from 1 black bass
or other firm white fish*

1   *teaspoon coriander seeds*

1   *teaspoon peppercorns*

2   *cardamom pods*

4   *sprigs parsley*

½   *cup dry white wine*

● Warm the oil in a wide, shallow saucepan over low heat. Add the onion, celery, and salt. Cook the vegetables, covered and stirring occasionally, until they are translucent and softened but not brown, about 10 minutes.

● Cut out the gills and eyes from the fish head and chop the bones into a few large pieces. Add the head

and bones to the pot, along with the coriander seeds, peppercorns, cardamom, and parsley. Cook, stirring occasionally, until the flesh around the bones turns opaque, about 10 minutes.

● Add the wine and just enough water to barely cover the bones, about 2 cups, and bring to a boil over high heat. Skim off any foam that rises to the top with a large spoon. Lower the heat and gently simmer the fumet for 15 minutes.

● Strain the fumet through a fine-mesh strainer into a bowl, pressing on the solids to extract as much liquid as possible. Cover and refrigerate for up to 2 days. You can freeze leftover fumet for up to 2 months.

ZA'ATAR

ZA'ATAR IS BOTH THE WILD HERB that grows in the Galilee (and elsewhere) and the spice mix that blends this wild herb with sesame seeds, sumac, and salt. Za'atar, the herb, tastes like a cross between marjoram and savory, but nothing comes that close to the real thing (believe me, I've tried). The spice mix has the same place on Israeli tables that salt and pepper do here. Israelis put za'atar on everything, but it's especially fine with dairy (labneh with za'atar and olive oil), bread, and grilled meat. (See Resources, page 359.)

CHICKEN SCHNITZEL WITH PASSION FRUIT AND AMBA TEHINA
Serves 4

SCHNITZEL GETS A BAD RAP. If you've ever been on a bus tour of Israel or spent time in an Israeli prison, you know what I am talking about. Limp, greasy, and warmed over, it's a deep-fried staple of the cafeteria steam table with a pool of ketchup. This is a shame, because great chicken schnitzel is a thing of beauty. It was one of my dad's specialties growing up, so I've always had a soft spot for it. Sandwiched between two pieces of white bread, schnitzel took me to my happy place where all the food was beige and crunchy.

Schnitzel was first brought to Israel by European immigrants in the late nineteenth century. Most people didn't have ovens in their homes, so this pan-fried dish quickly became a staple. Since the country was so poor, a piece of chicken that could be pounded out to look like twice as much meat was a valuable thing. The secret to great schnitzel is patience. Cooked slowly in plenty of fat in a wide enough skillet, the crust will be browned and crispy by the time the chicken is cooked through. The other key is well-seasoned bread crumbs, perked up with a handful of za'atar, the ubiquitous Israeli spice blend.

Chicken and tehina have a beautiful affinity for each other. The tehina adds richness to the lean meat without overpowering its delicate flavor. Here I bump it up with passion fruit puree and the Iraqi mango pickle called *amba* that's a staple at falafel stands all over Israel. Passion fruit is just sweet and sour enough to keep it from being cloying, and the amba is super-savory and funky, if a little too pungent on its own. Together, they become an incredible accompaniment to crispy schnitzel, making it completely reminiscent of Israeli street food, perhaps the highest compliment I could give. This recipe will not, apparently, guarantee you a win on *Iron Chef America,* so you may want to keep that ketchup handy. (Not that I'm bitter.)

• INGREDIENT •

AMBA (MANGO PICKLE)

AMBA IS GREEN MANGO that has been pickled with fenugreek, turmeric, garlic, and about a hundred other things, depending on the style you buy (in a jar). Indian amba is usually chunky and spicy—more relish than sauce and used like a chutney. The Arabic version is smoother and a little viscous from the fenugreek. Amba came to Israel via Iraq but, like fiery Yemenite schug (see page 169), amba has become an essentially Israeli condiment, especially on falafel. Sometimes we use amba as a puree. To make it, just put a jar of chunky amba in a blender and puree until smooth. (See Resources, page 359.)

AMBA TEHINA

1 cup Basic Tehina Sauce (page 32)

2 tablespoons passion fruit puree

2 heaping tablespoons amba

    Kosher salt

SCHNITZEL

2–3 slices stale challah, roughly chopped

¼ cup sesame seeds

2 tablespoons za'atar

4 boneless, skinless chicken breasts

    Kosher salt

¾ cup all-purpose flour

2 large eggs, beaten

    Canola oil, for frying

● **FOR THE AMBA TEHINA:** Whisk the tehina sauce, passion fruit puree, and amba in a mixing bowl until combined. If the sauce seems too thick, thin with a few tablespoons of ice water. Taste and add salt.

● **FOR THE SCHNITZEL:** Pulse the challah in a food processor until it turns to crumbs. Mix 1 cup challah crumbs with the sesame seeds and za'atar in a shallow bowl and set aside.

● Keeping the blade of a sharp knife parallel to the cutting board, slice each chicken breast in half to create 2 thin cutlets. Lightly pound out and salt.

● Place the flour and eggs in separate shallow bowls. Dredge each cutlet first in the flour, shaking off any excess, then the eggs, and finally in the challah-za'atar mixture.

● Heat about ¼ inch oil in a large cast iron skillet over medium heat until shimmering but not smoking. Add the breaded cutlets and cook until golden brown on each side, about 2 minutes per side. Work in batches if needed to avoid crowding the skillet.

● Serve the hot schnitzel with the amba tehina.

CRUDITÉS WITH GREEN TEHINA

Makes about 1⅓ cups

ONE OF MY FIRST JOBS in a professional kitchen was at a resort on Shelter Island, between the North and South Forks of Long Island. I experienced a lot of things for the first time that summer, including weekend traffic on the Long Island Expressway and being a migrant worker. But once I looked past the Hampton crowds and the deadly heat in the kitchen (I'm talking 120 degrees; cooks would regularly pass out during service and we'd be so busy, we'd just keep on cooking), I realized that I had never worked with such amazing ingredients before. We got the freshest Montauk striped bass, and from local farms some of the best produce I have ever tasted—produce harvested minutes from where I was cooking it.

The crudité platter on the menu really bothered me, though. I was an arrogant and immature line cook, and I couldn't understand how the chef could serve just plain raw vegetables. What was he getting paid for? As I've matured in the kitchen, I've come to realize that a perfect carrot doesn't need my help. Nor must I vaporize a cucumber to prove myself as a chef. I've come to love minimally prepared vegetables plunged into a tangy dip and eaten with gusto! For a vegetable like fennel, simply salting it in advance brings out its essential fennel-ness. Other vegetables, like broccoli or cauliflower, might need a brief steam to show off their best side. A couple minutes under the broiler can give asparagus a slight char that brings out its meaty flavor. It doesn't take much effort if you start with great vegetables, and you can apply the same simple techniques to whatever is in season or looks particularly good.

Tehina is my dip of choice when it comes to crudités. Its richness is a great foil to the vegetables' austerity. I like to blend lots of herbs, especially parsley, chives, and dill, into tehina sauce for this dip. The herbs act like grace notes to the vegetables and turn the tehina the most beautiful green color. Thinned out with water and lemon juice, this dip easily becomes a great salad dressing.

1 cup Basic Tehina Sauce (page 32)
2 tablespoons chopped fresh parsley
1 tablespoon chopped fresh chives
1 tablespoon chopped fresh dill
1 teaspoon chopped fresh mint
1 teaspoon chopped fresh cilantro
   Salt
   Seasonal vegetables,
   cut into dip-friendly pieces

● Place the tehina sauce and herbs in a food processor and blend until thoroughly combined. If the sauce seems too thick, thin with a few tablespoons of ice water. Taste for salt and transfer to a bowl. If not using immediately, cover and refrigerate for up to 3 days. Serve surrounded with the freshest vegetables for dipping.

SEARED CHICKEN LIVERS WITH CARAMELIZED ONION TEHINA

Serves 4

AS A CHILD, you couldn't pay me enough to eat chicken livers (my mother became pretty good at sneaking them into stir-fries, masking the taste with plenty of soy sauce). Then, all of a sudden, I was the guy who'd dive into the mountain of chopped liver on the bar mitzvah buffet table. It's an acquired taste.

Liver and onions is a classic combination for good reason. Slowly cooked and deeply browned onions develop a complex sweetness that keeps the funkiness of the livers in check. Here, I puree the onions and fold them into my basic tehina sauce to create a condiment that is sweet, savory, and rich enough to stand up to the meaty livers.

I cure the livers with salt and the spice mix baharat overnight. Baharat's warm flavors accentuate the livers' natural sweetness. Once they're cured, I sear the livers quickly in a big skillet over high heat so they develop a great crust on the outside but remain creamy inside. I like to serve the livers with the rice and lentil dish called Mujadara (page 286).

   1 *pound chicken livers*
  ¾ *teaspoon kosher salt*
      Big pinch baharat
  ½ *cup Basic Tehina Sauce (page 32)*

  2 *tablespoons pureed caramelized onions*
      (see page 287)
  2 *tablespoons date molasses (see page 64)*
  2 *tablespoons lemon juice*
  2 *tablespoons canola oil*
      Simple Sumac Onions (page 97)
      Celery leaves

● Dry the chicken livers on paper towels to remove as much surface moisture as possible. Season the chicken livers with the salt and baharat. Arrange on a plate, cover with plastic wrap, and allow the livers to cure overnight in the refrigerator.

● Stir together the tehina sauce, caramelized onions, date molasses, and lemon juice and set aside.

● Heat the oil in a large skillet over high heat until shimmering but not smoking. Add the livers in a single layer and cook until dark brown on the outside but still pink in the middle, about 2 minutes per side. (Larger livers will take a little longer.)

● Spread a layer of the tehina sauce on a platter and arrange the livers on the sauce. Top with the sumac onions and celery leaves and serve.

• I N G R E D I E N T •

BAHARAT

BAHARAT (the word is Arabic for spices) most commonly refers to a Middle Eastern spice blend of warm flavors that I think of as Turkish pumpkin pie spice. It has all the usual suspects, such as cinnamon, allspice, nutmeg, and cloves, but with hints of cardamom, coriander, and cumin that lend an exotic quality. Baharat is available at good spice shops or Middle Eastern markets. (See Resources, page 359.)

SWEETBREADS WRAPPED IN CHICKEN SKIN WITH BLACK GARLIC TEHINA

Serves 8

THIS WAS ONE OF THE FIRST signature dishes I created when I became the executive chef at Marigold Kitchen in Philadelphia in 2005. *Sweetbreads* is a pleasant word—until you realize we're talking about the thymus gland of a baby animal. Sweetbreads are, however, one of the mildest organ meats; some people say they taste like chicken. So, I thought, why not wrap them in the best part of the chicken: the skin. Once wrapped, I sear the sweetbreads in a hot skillet until the skin is crisp and well rendered, and the interior is just cooked through. Well-cooked sweetbreads are firm but not bouncy; they retain a slightly creamy interior that makes them luxurious to eat.

I serve these little nuggets with tehina sauce enriched with black garlic. Sweetbreads have a very delicate flavor, and the mellow tehina does not drown it out. But they are also very rich (especially when wrapped in the chicken skin), so the zip of the black garlic provides a needed counterpoint. This preparation takes a bit of effort (the package is held together with meat glue, which you'll need to order). But when the sweetbreads are sizzling and crisp and dipped in the black garlic tehina, I swear to God, they taste just like an Israeli barbecue on the beach.

> Skin from 8 chicken breasts
> 1 pound sweetbreads
> Kosher salt
> 2 tablespoons transglutaminase
> (aka meat glue; see Resources, page 359)
> Canola oil, for frying
> 1 cup Basic Tehina Sauce (page 32)
> 4 black garlic cloves (see left)
> Ground sumac (see page 97)

● Rinse the chicken skins and sweetbreads separately under cold running water for 10 minutes each. Dry everything thoroughly with paper towels.

● Lay the chicken skins on a cutting board, skin side down. Using a paring knife, scrape away the fat from the inside of the skin. Trim each piece into a rough rectangle, about 3 by 4 inches.

● Trim away excess gristle and connective tissue from the sweetbreads and cut into 8 rectangular pieces. (It's okay if they're not uniform—wrapping hides irregularities.) Season the sweetbreads with salt.

● Put a square of plastic wrap on a clean cutting board and lay a piece of chicken skin on top, inside up. Lightly season the inside of the chicken skin with salt and, using gloves (to protect your fingers

· INGREDIENT ·

BLACK GARLIC

BLACK GARLIC ISN'T ISRAELI, but it might as well be for the amazing way it blends with tehina sauce. We buy ours already prepared, and its popularity has made it increasingly available. Black garlic is made by heating heads of garlic for a long time at a low temperature until the sugars in the garlic are deeply caramelized. The resulting garlic is mellow, sweet, and fruity—not unlike tamarind. Black garlic adds a savory (and meat-free) backbone to everything it touches. It's great pureed with olives and ground Urfa pepper as a sauce for lamb. And I love it in Matzo Ball Soup (page 174). (See Resources, page 359.)

from the meat glue), sprinkle liberally with the transglutaminase. Place a piece of sweetbread on top of a wide edge of the chicken skin. Roll the chicken skin around the sweetbread, tucking in the bottom. Trim away excess skin. Wrap the roll tightly in the plastic wrap, twisting both ends to create a uniform sausage shape. Repeat to make 8 rolls. Refrigerate the rolls overnight to allow the transglutaminase to work its magic.

● Heat about ¼ inch oil in a large skillet over medium-high heat until the oil is shimmering but not smoking. Remove the plastic wrap from the rolls. Working in

batches, arrange the rolls in a single layer in the skillet and pan-fry, turning as they brown, until they are just cooked through and the chicken skin is crisp, about 8 minutes.

● For the black garlic tehina, combine the tehina sauce and black garlic in a food processor. Puree until smooth, adding ice water a couple tablespoons at a time if the sauce seems too thick.

● Serve the sweetbreads immediately, dusted with sumac and with the tehina for dipping.

GREEN BEANS AND MUSHROOMS WITH TEHINA, LENTILS, AND GARLIC CHIPS
Serves 4

I CREATED THIS DISH for a Chanukah meal at Zahav in 2013, the year that the first day of Chanukah coincided with Thanksgiving. Since this hadn't happened in over 100 years (and won't happen again for another 77,000), we decided to have fun and merge some of our Israeli flavors with traditional American Thanksgiving casseroles. This is our riff on the classic green bean casserole, with tehina standing in for the cream of mushroom soup.

Kosher salt

¼ teaspoon ground cinnamon

¼ cup beluga lentils

2 shallots, one chopped, one thinly sliced

¼ cup tehina

¼ cup cider vinegar

Pinch black pepper

Pinch ground fenugreek (see page 172)

¼ cup olive oil

4 cups green beans, trimmed and cut into 1-inch pieces

1½ cups quartered button mushrooms

¼ cup canola oil

4 garlic cloves, thinly sliced

2 teaspoons lemon juice

2 tablespoons chopped fresh dill

● Bring 2 cups water to a boil in a medium saucepan. Add a pinch of salt, the cinnamon, and lentils. Partially cover and lower the heat to medium. Simmer until the lentils are tender but not mushy, 17 to 20 minutes. Drain and set aside to cool.

● Combine the chopped shallot with the tehina, vinegar, black pepper, fenugreek, and a pinch of salt in a food processor and puree. Be careful not to let the tehina overheat—add ice water, 1 tablespoon at a time, if the mixture seizes up. Season with more salt if you like. Set the tehina sauce aside.

● Heat the olive oil in a large skillet over medium heat. Add the green beans and a pinch of salt and cook, stirring, until the beans start to soften, about 3 minutes. Add the sliced shallot and the mushrooms to the skillet and continue cooking until the green beans are tender and lightly browned, about 10 minutes more. Transfer to a bowl with a slotted spoon, discarding any excess oil. Set aside and keep warm.

● In a small saucepan over high heat, combine the canola oil, garlic, and reserved lentils. Cook, stirring constantly, until the garlic begins to brown and the lentils start to swell, about 7 minutes. When the garlic and lentils are golden brown, drain them onto a plate lined with paper towels and season well with salt.

● To assemble, mix the tehina sauce with the green beans and mushrooms and spoon the mixture onto a serving platter. Drizzle with the lemon juice and top with the crispy garlic and lentils, and then the dill.

FRIED POTATOES WITH HARISSA TEHINA

Serves 4

THIS DISH HAPPENED by serendipity. At Zahav, our Israeli pickles come packed in huge cans with a ton of excess pickle juice. One day, in a passion for brining, I decided to throw some peeled potatoes into that leftover pickle juice. A day later, I drained and fried the potatoes, ending up with the most amazing French fries ever. The potatoes were seasoned from within with a garlicky tang from the pickle juice.

Deep-frying can be an undertaking, so when I make this dish at home, I just slice the potatoes into rounds and pan-fry them on both sides in a cast iron skillet until they're nice and crispy.

I serve the potatoes with tehina augmented with harissa, the North African condiment based on dried chiles that's a staple on the Israeli table. In my harissa, I use ground Aleppo pepper from Syria, which has a fruity flavor and is not screamingly hot, so you can appreciate the pepper's earthy undertones. I thin the sauce with a little more pickle juice to cut through the richness and echo the flavor of the potatoes. I'll bet there's a jar in your fridge, with a lonely pickle or two bobbing in a sea of brine. This recipe is the perfect way to put those pickles out of their misery.

> 3   Yukon Gold potatoes,
>   peeled and cut into ¼-inch rounds
>
> 2   cups plus 2 tablespoons pickle brine
>   Canola oil, for frying
>
> 1   cup Basic Tehina Sauce (page 32)
>
> ¼   cup harissa

● Combine the potatoes and the 2 cups pickle brine in a large bowl. Cover with plastic wrap and refrigerate overnight. When you're ready to cook the potatoes, drain them well and pat dry with paper towels.

● Heat ¼ inch oil in a large skillet over medium heat until shimmering but not smoking. Working in batches to avoid crowding the skillet, add the potatoes in a single layer and fry until brown and crisp on the outside and tender within, about 3 minutes per side.

● To make the harissa tehina, whisk together the tehina sauce and the 2 tablespoons pickle brine. Stir in the harissa—I like it when the sauce looks a bit broken and streaky. Serve the potatoes with the tehina sauce.

• INGREDIENT •

HARISSA

HARISSA IS THE FAMOUS North African red pepper sauce that's most commonly used to spice up couscous and is so essential to my cooking. Excellent versions are available in jars and tubes. (See Resources, page 359.) Here's our Zahav recipe if you'd like to master your own. We call it by its Hebrew name *harif,* which means spicy.

Combine ½ cup ground Aleppo pepper, 1 garlic clove, 1½ tablespoons red wine vinegar, 1 teaspoon ground cumin, a pinch each of ground coriander and ground caraway, and ¼ teaspoon kosher salt. Blend in a food processor to a coarse puree. Add ¼ cup canola oil and process for another few seconds. Stop short of making it perfectly smooth. Refrigerated, harissa will keep 2 weeks.

FRIED EGGPLANT WITH TEHINA AND POMEGRANATE SEEDS

Serves 6

SOMETIMES I FEEL like my mission in life is to make people fall in love with eggplant. But eggplant doesn't always make it easy. It can be bitter and make your lips pucker. When prepared properly, however, eggplant can be sweet, robust, creamy, and absolutely delicious (see Twice-Cooked Eggplant, page 106). It is an excellent vehicle for spiced meat and smoke and makes a fantastic pickle. These basic fried slices take on a few exotic ingredients that make the eggplant pop. The eggplant is seared until very dark brown, then dressed with tehina sauce (think deconstructed baba ganoush) and carob molasses, which offers just enough acidity to cut through the richness of the tehina and just enough sweetness to counter the bitter edge of the eggplant. A handful of pomegranate seeds makes the plate look like a million bucks.

> 2 *large eggplants*
> *Kosher salt*
> *Canola oil, for frying*
> 1/3 *cup Basic Tehina Sauce (page 32)*
> 3 *tablespoons carob molasses (see page 65)*
> 1/2 *cup pomegranate seeds (see below)*
> 1/4 *cup shelled pistachios*

● Remove 4 vertical strips of skin from each eggplant with a peeler, leaving the remaining skin attached. Trim the ends and cut the eggplants into 3/4-inch-thick rounds. Generously season both sides with salt and place on a cooling rack set over a baking sheet to catch any drips. Refrigerate overnight.

● Heat 1/2 inch oil in a large skillet over medium-high heat. Wipe both sides of each eggplant slice with a paper towel to remove surface moisture and excess salt. When the oil is shimmering but not smoking, add the eggplant slices in a single layer, working in batches to avoid crowding the skillet. Fry the eggplant on each side until dark brown, about 5 minutes per side. You want the eggplant to be seriously dark on the outside and creamy on the inside, so be patient. When the skillet starts to seem dry, add more oil as needed. Remove the eggplant slices from the skillet and drain on paper towels.

● Place the eggplant on a platter and spoon the tehina sauce on top. Drizzle with the carob molasses and scatter the pomegranate seeds and pistachios on top.

• INGREDIENT •

POMEGRANATE SEEDS

TO REMOVE THE SEEDS from a pomegranate, place a deep bowl in your kitchen sink and roll up the sleeves of a shirt you dislike. Cut the pomegranate in half crosswise. Place one half of the pomegranate in your palm, cut side down. Hold your hand over the bowl and, using a wooden spoon, beat the back of the pomegranate to loosen the seeds. Keep whacking and let the seeds fall out of your hand into the bowl below. Discard any white membrane that may fall into the bowl. Set aside 1/2 cup of the seeds for the eggplant and store any extra in the refrigerator.

DATE MOLASSES
Best eaten with tehina and toast, it's my peanut butter and jelly.

DATE MOLASSES

WHEN THE BIBLE refers to Israel as the land of milk and honey, the honey in question is likely date molasses. Dates are so important to Middle Eastern cooking that a majority of Israeli dates are exported to countries that don't openly trade with Israel. Israel's original date palms were destroyed during Ottoman rule; the revival of the modern industry was spurred by a daring smuggling operation in the 1950s that brought 75,000 date palm saplings to Israel from Iraq and Iran. Date molasses is a natural, thick sweetener extracted from dates with good natural acidity; it's used in both savory and sweet dishes. (See Resources, page 359.)

· INGREDIENT ·

CAROB MOLASSES

CAROB IS BEST KNOWN for disappointing people by not being chocolate. But I think this does a disservice to its unique qualities. Carob is a pod that grows wild on trees all over the north of Israel, and it has been used as a sweetener since biblical times. But it also has enough depth to take on savory ingredients. Carob molasses, available in jars as in the Galilee shop above, is made by cooking the fruit of the carob pod in water and reducing it until it is thick and glossy. The result is a "chocolaty" syrup that's wonderful with sharp cheese, spooned over grilled meats, or drizzled over ice cream. (See Resources, page 359.)

TEHINA SHORTBREAD COOKIES
Makes about 30 cookies

IT MAY COME AS A SURPRISE, but tehina is perfect in desserts because, in addition to adding nutty flavor, it helps modulate sweetness and leaves you wanting more. For me, there's nothing as comforting as these shortbread cookies enriched with tehina. They are ridiculously easy to make and extremely satisfying. Because the tehina replaces some of the butter in a traditional shortbread, they are actually quite light. (Or at least that's how I rationalize eating ten of them in one sitting.) I love to crumble them on Turkish Coffee Ice Cream (page 354) or layer them with Tehina Semifreddo (page 72) to make the ultimate ice cream sandwich. But these cookies are perfectly delicious simply dusted with confectioners' sugar and served with coffee.

1¾ sticks (7 ounces) unsalted butter, at room temperature
1 cup sugar
1 cup tehina
2 cups all-purpose flour
1 teaspoon baking powder
Pinch kosher salt

● Combine the butter and sugar in a stand mixer on medium speed or in a large bowl with a hand mixer and mix until light and fluffy, about 2 minutes. Add the tehina and continuing mixing until well incorporated.

● Combine the flour, baking powder, and salt in a mixing bowl and whisk together. Transfer to the tehina mixture and beat until just incorporated. Cover the bowl with plastic wrap and refrigerate for at least 1 hour or overnight. (The dough keeps well in the freezer for a few months.)

● Preheat the oven to 350°F. Line two baking sheets with parchment paper. Drop the batter by heaping tablespoons onto the prepared baking sheets. Bake until the cookies are light brown around the edges and set, about 15 minutes. Let cool on the baking sheets for 10 minutes, then transfer to a wire rack to cool completely. The cookies can be stored at room temperature in an airtight container for 1 week.

COFFEE BREAK
We were about to spend thousands of dollars on restaurant equipment that would soon break, but you can't do business in the old city of Jerusalem without a cup of coffee.

SWEETS
Racks and racks of halva in
every market and in every flavor
from almond to chocolate chip.

HALVA

Makes one 8-inch square pan

HALVA IS A CONFECTION made from raw tehina and sugar, sometimes stabilized with additives. I am addicted to halva in all of its forms and flavors—it is the perfect balance of sweet and savory. When I first became the chef at Marigold Kitchen in Philadelphia in 2005, I used to keep a secret tub of halva stashed in my desk drawer. During stressful times (there were a few), I would dip into that tub to calm my nerves and comfort myself. I suppose it was healthier than chain-smoking cigarettes, except that I did that, too.

Typically a commercial product, halva is possible to make at home with the help of a candy thermometer and stand mixer. This gives you the chance to customize the flavors; halva takes extremely well to mix-ins.

When you walk through the *shuk* (market) in Israel, you'll see halva stalls with huge slabs in every imaginable flavor, from rose water to pistachio to chocolate to coffee. I like to flavor my halva with vanilla and lemon zest, even though I've never actually seen that combination in Israel. Halva makes an excellent "truffle" candy when cut into cubes and dipped into melted chocolate.

> 2 cups sugar
> ½ vanilla bean, scraped
> Zest of 1 lemon
> 1½ cups tehina
> Pinch kosher salt

● Line an 8-inch square baking pan with parchment paper. Have ready another sheet of parchment paper.

● Combine the sugar, vanilla seeds, and lemon zest with ½ cup water in a saucepan over medium heat, stirring to dissolve the sugar. Then cook, without stirring, until the mixture registers 245°F on a candy thermometer.

● While the sugar syrup is cooking, place the tehina and salt in the bowl of a stand mixer fitted with the paddle. Beat on medium speed.

● When the sugar syrup reaches 245°F, carefully stream it into the tehina with the mixer running. Mix until the syrup is incorporated and the mixture begins to pull away from the sides of the bowl, but no longer.

● Working quickly with a flexible heatproof spatula, transfer the mixture to the prepared pan. Press the top of the halva flat with the sheet of parchment paper and your hands. Let cool completely to room temperature. Cut into squares and store at room temperature, well wrapped in plastic wrap, for a week.

HALVA MOUSSE

Makes 3 ½ cups, serves 6

CREATED BY ACCIDENT, this dessert is now a staple on the Zahav menu during the summer months. I was originally trying to make halva ice cream, but ended up instead with a frozen block resembling hardened cement. Disgusted with the result, I left the frozen hunk on the counter and went out for a walk. When I returned a few hours later, the mixture had thawed into the most delicious and ethereally textured mousse I'd ever tasted. I like to serve it with fresh fruit compote, and chickpea brittle, which sounds a little weird but is actually delicious. When your guests are complimenting you by licking their plates,

tell them they're eating a dessert made with hummus ingredients; you'll get a chuckle and maybe a polite clap. I like to layer the mousse, compote, and brittle in parfait glasses, but you can serve it in bowls. Or just spoon it into a teacup.

> 3½ cups roughly chopped Halva (page 68)
> ½ cup milk
> Big pinch kosher salt
> ⅔ cup heavy cream, well chilled
> Huckleberry Compote (recipe follows)
> Chickpea Brittle (recipe follows)

HUCKLEBERRY COMPOTE
Makes about 1 cup

> 2 cups huckleberries or blueberries
> 1 cup sugar
> ½ teaspoon rose water (see page 351)
>   Peel of 1 orange
>   Juice of ½ lemon (if using blueberries)

● Combine the berries with the sugar, rose water, and orange peel in a lidded container. Cover and let macerate overnight in the refrigerator.

● Transfer the berry mixture to a medium saucepan and simmer over medium heat until the mixture has thickened to a jam-like consistency, about 10 minutes. If using blueberries, stir in the lemon juice off the heat.

CHICKPEA BRITTLE
Makes about 3 cups

> 2 cups cooked or canned chickpeas, rinsed
> 1 tablespoon canola oil
> ¾ cup packed light brown sugar
> 3 tablespoons butter
> 3 tablespoons heavy cream

● Preheat the oven to 450°F. Line a baking sheet with parchment paper and set aside.

● Combine the halva, milk, and salt in a food processor and puree until smooth. Transfer to a large bowl.

● In the bowl of a stand mixer with the whisk attachment (or use a hand mixer and a big bowl), whip the cream until soft peaks form. Stir about one third of the whipped cream into the halva mixture until completely incorporated. Gently fold half the remaining cream into the halva mixture until just a few streaks remain. Continue folding in the rest of the cream until just incorporated. Serve with the compote and brittle.

● Toss the chickpeas with the oil, transfer to another baking sheet, and roast until crisp, 25 to 30 minutes.

● Combine the brown sugar, butter, and cream in a saucepan over medium heat. Cook, stirring, until the mixture darkens in color slightly and large, lava-like bubbles cover the surface, about 10 minutes. Add the chickpeas and stir to combine. Working quickly and using a flexible heatproof spatula, spread the mixture out in an even layer on the prepared baking sheet. Let cool to room temperature. Break into 2-inch pieces to serve. The brittle will keep for 1 week in a sealed container.

TEHINA SEMIFREDDO

Serves 8

BECAUSE TEHINA IS ESSENTIALLY the oil from sesame seeds, it keeps frozen desserts firm without ever getting icy, even if your freezer has a mind of its own. This softly frozen dessert is the next best thing to ice cream and is absolutely therapeutic to make. You don't need an ice cream machine, and it will keep in your freezer for at least 3 days, so semifreddo is a great recipe for entertaining. The idea behind any mousse, frozen or unfrozen, is to fold the ingredients together so that the mixture is homogenous but doesn't deflate from being overworked. This requires a bit of a delicate touch, so sip a little chamomile tea and practice some deep breathing before you start. You want the texture of each ingredient to be as similar as possible before bringing them together, so it's important to mix the tehina thoroughly before adding it to the mousse.

Tehina semifreddo is superb with seasonal fruit such as strawberries, rhubarb, and rose water in the summertime and passion fruit and lime in winter. And it's not half bad drenched in chocolate sauce with bananas and whipped cream. Here, I crumble Tehina Shortbread Cookies (page 66) on top.

2 cups heavy cream, well chilled
7 large egg yolks
1 cup sugar
½ cup tehina

● In the bowl of a stand mixer with the whisk attachment (or use a hand mixer and a big bowl) whip the cream to medium peaks. Refrigerate.

● Combine the yolks and sugar in a small metal bowl set over a saucepan with ½ inch of gently simmering water on the bottom. Whisk constantly until the sugar is dissolved and the yolks have lightened in color, about 2 minutes. Remove from the heat.

● Transfer about one third of the whipped cream to another large bowl and pour in the yolk mixture. Stir together until well combined. Add half the remaining cream and fold gently with a rubber spatula until just incorporated. Repeat with the remaining whipped cream.

● In another large bowl, combine ½ cup of the whipped cream–yolk mixture with the tehina and stir until well combined. Carefully fold in the rest of the whipped cream–yolk mixture with a rubber spatula. Divide among eight 4- to 6-ounce bowls or ramekins, cover with plastic wrap, and freeze for up to 3 days.

2

SALATIM

• *Vegetables Are Everything* •

THERE WERE CARROTS dressed with lemon and cumin from Morocco, potatoes and peas in mayonnaise from Russia, sweet peppers with white beans from Bulgaria, eggplant with pomegranate and walnuts from Iran, and pickled onions with sumac from Lebanon. The flavors were vivid and distinct and the vegetables were absolutely perfect.

I was in my twenties and already a professional cook before I really discovered salad. When I visited family in Israel in 2006, my father had taken me to eat at Busi, a restaurant in South Tel Aviv. South Tel Aviv is not the part of the city that appears on postcards. It has long been a first stop for new immigrants coming from Morocco and Iraq and Ethiopia and Russia, and the scruffy neighborhood looks the part. Although rising real estate prices and redevelopment have recently spurred a wave of gentrification, South Tel Aviv still maintains the character of a place where people are engaged in a daily struggle for the basic necessities of life. This makes it a perfect place to observe the ebb and flow of Israeli cuisine as each new wave of immigrants brings a new culinary vernacular and, in turn, absorbs the flavors and customs of the Israeli character.

Busi is a typical (and kickass) *shipudiya*—essentially a restaurant that serves meat on sticks grilled over charcoal. The waiter asked if we wanted salatim. *"Betach,"* my father replied in Hebrew, which means "of course," but with the proper Israeli inflection can also mean "of course, you idiot." What followed were seventeen (yes, seventeen!) little dishes filled with vegetables treated in every imaginable way: cooked and raw, dressed and marinated, pickled and spiced, roasted and stewed. I don't know which was more impressive—the sheer number of the salads or the fact that they represented a dozen or more ethnic cuisines. They almost made me forget about the grilled meat.

VEGETABLE SALADS begin each meal at Zahav, *left.* Many have been on the menu since day one. On Sundays, we often shop the Headhouse farmers' market, *above and previous spread,* close to the restaurant.

77

"The custom of starting the meal with fresh salads originated with the Palestinians."

Before that awakening, the salad I knew was the thing served at the beginning of every single dinner during my childhood: iceberg lettuce, a rubbery cucumber, a mealy tomato, some sliced onion, a few dry carrots, maybe some black olives from a can. Salad dressings were bottled. "Homemade" vinaigrette was a seasoning packet you mixed with oil and vinegar (in the cruet that came with the seasoning packet from the supermarket). When I started cooking for a living, I was introduced to the entrée salad: essentially some greens drowning in a "Caesar" dressing or Asian vinaigrette and invariably overwhelmed by grilled chicken, blackened mahi, or shrimp. The vegetables? The vegetables were an afterthought. In Israel, vegetables are not an afterthought. In Israel, vegetables are the whole thing.

Eating salatim at Busi was part of what inspired me to cook Israeli food. I loved the way that the meal began with so many different tastes and textures. It was completely stimulating without weighing down the palate, or me. (Every time I visit Israel, I manage to eat five meals a day and still lose weight!) And I love the way these vivid little dishes tell the story of Israel.

The custom of starting the meal with salatim originated with the Palestinians. Early Jewish settlers adopted this practice for the same reasons—they were poor and fresh vegetables were readily available and cheap. There were always cucumbers and tomatoes and cabbage and eggplant. From a few perfectly ripe vegetables, you could make dozens of salads. Over time, this multitude of preparations came to define the abundant hospitality that the region is famous for. Through salatim, you can see how each immigrant culture has become woven into the fabric of the country over time. Even Busi, founded by a Yemenite family just two generations ago, feels more Israeli than Yemenite at this point. A layman walking into a Georgian restaurant or a Bulgarian restaurant in Israel might think that all the salads are the same. And he would be right! There will be eggplant. There will be beets. There will be carrots. There will be cucumbers and tomatoes. On the other hand, if you know what to look for, you can tell where you are just by the way a particular salad is dressed. Or spiced. Or mixed. Is the tabbouleh ridiculously acidic and composed of 80 percent parsley? You're probably in a Palestinian restaurant. Does the dish of pickles include whole vegetables or huge wedges of watermelon or cabbage? Your host is most likely from the Balkans. Are there a suspicious number of eggplant salads on the table? You must be in northern Israel near the Galilee. Do the tomatoes taste like they're salted from the inside? You're probably down south in the Negev.

This balance between authenticity and adaptation has helped to shape my own approach to cooking. When we opened Zahav, I knew I wanted to share the pleasures of Israeli-style salatim service with our customers. At first, we tried to be super-authentic and faithfully re-create some of the most traditional Israeli dishes. But we couldn't get great tomatoes in Philadelphia in January. And importing them from Israel struck me as perhaps the most inauthentic thing we could do. The restaurant struggled a bit in its early days as we tried to find our identity: a modern Israeli restaurant in Philadelphia. What did that even mean? The answer, it turned out, was right underneath us. Literally. Here in eastern Pennsylvania, we're a stone's throw from some of the most fertile farmland in this country. We can't get tomatoes in winter, but we can use mangoes or pickle the persimmons we do get in winter to make an Israeli salad that tastes both familiar and exotic at the same time. We could make a tabbouleh with kale and apples that you'd never find in Israel, but still seems authentic. We could do what the Israelis do—adapt to our surroundings using tradition as our guide.

HEADHOUSE
Steve and I sometimes shop at the weekly market set on cobblestones under brick arches that date back to Revolutionary times.

When you sit down to dinner at Zahav today, you're served six little dishes (because seventeen would be crazy, right?) of bright and flavorful vegetable salads to start your meal. Some of them never change. If I ever took the Beets with Tehina (page 104) or the Twice-Cooked Eggplant (page 106) off the menu, our customers might riot. But the other salads represent the best of what's being harvested in our region. Sometimes I'll walk out the kitchen door and find hundreds of dollars' worth of local asparagus dropped off by a "helpful" farmer. There is no better motivation to create a new dish than having too much of a perishable product on your doorstep. I love all the recipes in this chapter, but please interpret them freely. Find great-looking green beans at the supermarket? Use them instead of okra in the Bamya (page 103). If a recipe calls for parsley and you like cilantro, hey, I like cilantro, too. Focus on the technique, not the ingredients, and adapt it to your kitchen. Just close your eyes and think like an Israeli.

ISRAELI PICKLES

Makes 6 cups

PICKLES ARE A TRADITIONAL WAY to preserve the harvest, especially important for Israeli pioneers, who could not rely on imported food for their tables. Not surprisingly then, pickles fit incredibly well into the Israeli preference for eating tons of salatim, mezze (an array of appetizers), and small plates. Pickles refresh your palate and whet your appetite for the next bite. At Zahav, our fried cauliflower mezze is so popular that we go through nearly 250 heads a week. This leaves us with an abundance of cauliflower hearts (what's left over after you remove the florets). Instead of trashing them, which most people do, we thought like an Israeli: "We can pickle that!"

Cauliflower hearts, along with celery and carrots, are the basis of the pickle plate on every table at Zahav. And there are a million vegetables that take well to this treatment. We flavor the pickles with turmeric and a little schug, for a zesty, absolutely addictive (and inexpensive) bite. Make these pickles as part of a salatim spread or as a briny counterpoint to glistening kebabs straight off the grill.

  4 celery ribs, cut into 1-inch chunks (about 2 cups)

  ½ head cauliflower, cut into 1-inch chunks (about 2 cups)

  3 carrots, peeled and cut into 1-inch chunks (about 2 cups)

  2 cups white vinegar

  ¼ cup kosher salt

  ¼ cup sugar

  1 tablespoon ground turmeric

  1 tablespoon schug (see page 169)

● Arrange the celery, cauliflower, and carrots in a deep baking dish.

● Combine 1 cup water, the vinegar, salt, and sugar in a saucepan over high heat and bring to a boil. Continue cooking, stirring, until the salt and sugar are dissolved, about 1 minute. Stir in the turmeric and schug. Pour the liquid over the vegetables and let cool.

● Transfer the cooled vegetables in their brine to containers, cover, and marinate in the refrigerator for at least 2 days before serving. They'll keep for another several days refrigerated in their brine.

ISRAELI SALAD

"Early Israeli pioneers literally made the desert bloom and helped establish the country as a powerhouse in agricultural technology."

ALTHOUGH IT'S TECHNICALLY a misnomer (the salad's origins are Arab), to me there is no dish that represents Israel better than Israeli salad—not just in its preeminence in Israeli cuisine, but as a symbol of the state's agricultural roots. In the very old days, all Jewish mothers wanted their sons to grow up to be farmers (or high priests). A few thousand years later, as waves of Jewish immigrants returned to Palestine, they sought a return to this agrarian way of life. These turn-of-the-century settlers established kibbutzim, collective farms that combined a utopian, socialist ideal with the pragmatic reality of settling in a politically and geographically hostile land.

The kibbutz became an icon of self-reliance and industriousness that helped shape Israeli culture for a hundred years. These pioneers literally made the desert bloom and helped establish Israel as the powerhouse in agricultural technology and productivity it is today. Not bad for a bunch of med school dropouts.

As anyone who has spent a night in a kibbutz guesthouse can attest, kibbutz dining halls are not earning any Michelin stars. But the kibbutz does give us one culinary legacy—the Israeli breakfast. Although it was long ago co-opted by Israeli hotels, this hearty brunch-like meal originated as sustenance for kibbutzniks returning from a long morning in the fields. The meal did not contain meat, for reasons related to kosher laws, but offered a rich spread of cheeses, yogurts, pickled and smoked fish, eggs, and, of course, Israeli salad.

In Israel, this cucumber and tomato salad is referred to as Arabic salad, chopped salad, or vegetable salad. There is no meal where Israeli salad is out of place at the table. I could eat it three times a day for the rest of my life. I can't think of a more perfect and balanced dish—it is refreshing and substantial at the same time, with great acidity from the fresh lemon, richness from the generous dose of olive oil, sweetness and umami from the tomatoes, and a slight bitterness from the herbaceous parsley. Israeli salad is wonderful because the more you eat, the better you feel.

This salad makes sense in Israel all year round. Tomatoes and cucumbers are cheap and plentiful. And they are the most amazing tomatoes and cucumbers I've ever tasted. The Persian cucumbers used there (and plentiful here) were perfected on a kibbutz in Israel in 1939 and called Beit Alpha. I often crave this salad during the long Northeastern winters, but its simplicity requires perfect ingredients to really sing—out-of-season tomatoes don't cut it. So we've adapted this salad to our seasonal environment. When tomatoes are not perfect, we use stand-ins like mangoes, pickled persimmons, passion fruit, or even grapes for a salad that's Israeli in spirit. Remember to season the salad with lots of salt, lemon, and olive oil. With so few ingredients, it's important to make the most of those you have.

TRADITIONAL ISRAELI SALAD

Serves 4 to 6

    3 *cups chopped tomatoes*
    3 *cups chopped cucumbers*
  ¼ *cup chopped fresh parsley*
    2 *tablespoons olive oil*
    2 *teaspoons lemon juice*
    1 *teaspoon kosher salt*

● Combine all the ingredients in a large bowl.
Toss well to combine and serve.

MANGO, CUCUMBER,
AND SUMAC-ONION
ISRAELI SALAD

TRADITIONAL
ISRAELI SALAD

ISRAELI SALAD MARTINI

Serves 1

WE ORIGINALLY INVENTED this cocktail at Zahav as a way to use the accumulated juices at the bottom of a bowl of Israeli salad—it seemed such a shame to let all that flavor go to waste. The olive oil from the salad can be a little weird in a cocktail, so now we prepare a separate mixer of tomato and cucumber water seasoned with parsley and lemon. It pairs incredibly well with the botanicals in gin for a summery riff on a martini. The same approach also works great with vodka and a bit of schug (see page 169) for a lighter, Israeli version of a Bloody Mary.

> 2 ounces gin
>
> 1½ ounces Israeli Salad Water (recipe follows)
>
> 1½ teaspoons lemon juice

● Pour the gin, salad water, and lemon juice into a shaker filled with ice. Shake vigorously and strain into a chilled martini glass. Add a slice of cucumber, tomato, and a twist of lemon and serve.

ISRAELI SALAD WATER

● Blend 1 cucumber and 1 tomato in a food processor with a sprig of parsley and a pinch of kosher salt. Transfer to a cheesecloth-lined strainer set over a deep bowl and strain in the refrigerator for several hours or overnight. Allow the sediment to settle to the bottom of the liquid and strain again through cheesecloth.

MANGO, CUCUMBER, AND SUMAC-ONION ISRAELI SALAD

Serves 4 to 6

> 2 mangoes, peeled and cut around the pit into small cubes (3 cups)
>
> 1 cucumber, diced (3 cups)
>
> ¼ cup Simple Sumac Onions (page 97), plus more for topping
>
> 3 tablespoons chopped fresh mint
>
> 3 tablespoons olive oil
>
> 2 teaspoons lemon juice
>
> 1 teaspoon kosher salt

● Combine all the ingredients in a bowl, toss to combine, and serve with additional sumac onions on top.

"When tomatoes are not perfect,
we use stand-ins like mangoes,
pickled persimmons,
passion fruit, or even grapes."

PICKLED PERSIMMONS

PICKLED PERSIMMONS

Serves 8

PERSIMMONS SEEM TO SHOW UP at the market at just the right time. When tomatoes are gone just long enough that we miss them and the whole winter is still ahead of us, persimmons appear like a lifeline. We use them in Israeli Salad (page 85) instead of tomatoes and pickle them. You'll see two varieties of persimmon in the market, both in gorgeous shades of orange and gold. The Hachiya persimmon is tapered at one end and must be fully ripe before you eat it. Underripe, they're so astringent they threaten to turn your mouth inside out. As Hachiyas become soft and ripe, their custard-like flesh can be spooned right out of the skin. The Fuyu persimmon, on the other hand, is squatter in shape, like a tomato, with a crisp texture that is great sliced for salads or pickles as I do here. My favorite persimmon is the Sharon fruit, an Israeli-developed hybrid that's closely related to the Fuyu.

The flavor of persimmon has notes of tropical fruit like mango and papaya, as well as a floral sweetness that reminds me of honey and brown sugar. This sweetness makes them a natural candidate for pickling. Pickled persimmons make an excellent snack or are great as part of a salad spread; their sweet-and-sour balance makes them a match for strong cheeses as well as gamy meats like Lamb Basturma (page 146).

    1 pound Hachiya or Fuyu persimmons,
       cut into quarters

    6 pitted dates, halved

    1 dried lime, crushed

    1 tablespoon black peppercorns

 1½ teaspoons mustard seeds

 1½ teaspoons coriander seeds

 1½ teaspoons poppy seeds

  ½ teaspoon ground cinnamon

    5 garlic cloves

    3 cardamom pods

    2 cloves

 1¾ cups white wine vinegar

    2 tablespoons sugar

  ½ teaspoon kosher salt

● Arrange the persimmons and dates in a baking dish. Sprinkle evenly with the crushed dried lime, peppercorns, mustard seeds, coriander seeds, poppy seeds, cinnamon, garlic, cardamom pods, and cloves.

● Combine 1 cup water with the vinegar, sugar, and salt in a saucepan and bring to a boil over medium-high heat. Pour the liquid over the persimmons and let cool to room temperature. Cover with plastic wrap and marinate in the refrigerator for 2 days before serving. Refrigerated, the pickles will keep perfectly for 2 weeks.

• INGREDIENT •

DRIED LIMES

SOMETIMES CALLED BLACK LIMES or *limu omani*, dried limes are commonly used to flavor soups and stews, rice, and fish dishes in Iran and the Persian Gulf region. They're made by treating whole limes with salt and letting them dry in the sun for several weeks, so they turn a dusty brownish black and take on an earthy, fermented quality. Retaining their sourness and fragrance, they gain a pungency that adds acidity and complexity to dishes. Unlike fresh lime, that acidity doesn't dissipate as it cooks.

To use, you can either poke a few holes in a whole dried lime and drop it into your cooking pot or grate dried lime into a powder with a rasp. At Zahav, we get amazing specimens from Lior Lev Sercarz. Dried limes are not expensive and are widely available in Middle Eastern markets and online. Although you can buy powdered dried lime, it's already lost much potency. Better to buy the whole fruit and grate it as you need it. (See Resources, page 359.)

TRADITIONAL TABBOULEH

Serves 4 to 6

HERE IN THE U.S., tabbouleh is generally made with bulgur wheat, parsley, and chopped tomatoes. But in Israel it is very unlikely that you will find it made the same way in two different kitchens. In the Galilee, tabbouleh is nearly all parsley, seasoned with an ungodly amount of lemon juice. The great thing about parsley is that it doesn't wilt from all that acid, so you can prepare the salad in advance and the flavor will improve over time. Kale has the same advantage and is an excellent alternative to parsley. The bulgur wheat provides a nutty and neutral canvas that lets you take this salad in a million different directions. I find quinoa to be an excellent medium for these flavors, too. When pomegranates are in season, I mix in their jewel-like seeds for a special treat. During the fall, I add apples and crushed walnuts, which mimic and can even replace the bulgur for a wheat-free version.

½	cup bulgur wheat
2	cups chopped fresh parsley
1	cup chopped tomato
¼	cup chopped red onion
3	tablespoons lemon juice
3	tablespoons olive oil
½	teaspoon kosher salt

● Cover the bulgur with cold water by several inches in a large bowl and let stand for 30 minutes. Drain well and return to the bowl. Add the parsley, tomato, onion, lemon juice, oil, and salt. Toss to combine and serve.

KALE, APPLE, WALNUT, AND SUMAC-ONION TABBOULEH

Serves 4 to 6

2 cups (packed) shredded stemmed kale leaves

¾ cup finely chopped walnuts

½ cup diced apple

¼ cup Simple Sumac Onions

¼ cup pomegranate seeds (see page 62)

3 tablespoons lemon juice

3 tablespoons olive oil

½ teaspoon kosher salt

● Combine all the ingredients in a large bowl. Toss to combine and serve.

· INGREDIENT ·

SUMAC

SUMAC IS A CLUSTER OF RED-SEEDED berries that you see on the feathery bushes that line our highways. The berries were ground and used to add sour flavors to food in the Middle East before the Moors introduced lemons. The Pennsylvania Dutch still make pink lemonade with our staghorn sumac, which is related to the Middle Eastern varieties. I love using ground sumac to add a sprinkle of tartness to dishes without using acid or liquid, perfect for such delicate things as raw fish. (See Resources, page 359.)

SIMPLE SUMAC ONIONS

Makes about 1 cup

1 red onion, thinly sliced

1 tablespoon red wine vinegar

1 teaspoon ground sumac

½ teaspoon kosher salt

● Combine all the ingredients in a bowl and toss to combine. Serve immediately.

QUINOA, PEA, AND MINT TABBOULEH

Serves 4 to 6

½ cup quinoa

1 cup fresh peas or thawed frozen peas

1 cup chopped fresh parsley

¼ cup diced red onion

3 tablespoons lemon juice

3 tablespoons olive oil

2 tablespoons chopped fresh mint

  Pinch ground Aleppo pepper

  Kosher salt

● Cook the quinoa in 1 cup boiling, salted water in a small saucepan, covered, for 15 to 20 minutes, until all the liquid has been absorbed. Bring a pot of salted water to a boil and cook the peas until tender, about 2 minutes. Drain, submerge in ice water to cool quickly, and mash with a fork.

● Combine the quinoa and mashed peas with the parsley, onion, lemon juice, oil, mint, Aleppo pepper, and a big pinch of salt in a medium bowl. Toss to combine and serve.

MOROCCAN CARROTS

Serves 4 to 6

I HAVE SAMPLED WHAT FEELS LIKE a hundred versions of Moroccan carrots, and we have served several versions at Zahav. To qualify as Moroccan carrots, the dish needs, at a minimum, cumin, lemon, mint, and a bit of chile. I like to use ground Aleppo pepper for its heat, plus garlic and orange juice. My favorite approach involves poaching whole, peeled carrots until they are just tender. I reduce the seasoned poaching liquid, which then becomes part of the dressing. Incorporating the cooking liquid into the dish means that it retains every drop of carrot flavor. When the carrots have cooled, they are sliced and dressed. Slicing them after cooking rather than before may seem backward, but they hold up better in the dressing when prepared this way.

6 large carrots, peeled
  Kosher salt
1 garlic clove, minced
¼ cup olive oil
¼ cup orange juice
2 tablespoons lemon juice
¼ cup chopped fresh cilantro
1 tablespoon chopped fresh mint
1 teaspoon ground Aleppo pepper
1 teaspoon ground cumin

● Put the carrots in a large deep skillet and just barely cover with water. Add a pinch of salt. Cook over medium-high heat until the carrots are just beginning to soften, 10 to 12 minutes. Remove the carrots with a slotted spoon and set aside; reserve the cooking liquid. When they are cool enough to handle, cut the carrots into half-moons and set aside.

● Simmer the carrot-cooking liquid until reduced and almost syrupy, about 10 minutes. Add the garlic and cook for about 1 minute more. Off the heat, add the oil, orange juice, lemon juice, cilantro, mint, Aleppo pepper, cumin, and 1 teaspoon salt. Whisk well to combine. Toss the carrots in the mixture and refrigerate before serving.

BAMYA (ROASTED OKRA)

Serves 6

BAMYA, A TRADITIONAL DISH of okra in tomato sauce, should be served either hot or cold, depending upon whom you ask. My great uncle Shmuel, for example, grew up believing that it was a hot dish. When his new bride, Erna, my grandmother's sister, served it to him for the first time—cold—the fallout left my great aunt in tears and nearly derailed the marriage.

Bamya is Bulgarian for okra, a name change that's helpful in getting people who would otherwise shun this vegetable to try it. Okra has a reputation for being unpleasantly slimy. The long, slender seedpods, sometimes called lady fingers, contain mucilage that develops when the okra is heated, especially when it is sliced or agitated. These properties are put to good use in classic dishes like gumbo, where the long cooking helps thicken the stew. An alternative is to neutralize the okra by leaving the pods whole and cooking them quickly over high heat, as in the breaded, deep-fried okra of the American South.

This recipe uses both approaches. The okra is first roasted in the oven to develop its flavor and dry it out a bit. Then it's served with a tomato sauce spiked with plenty of dried lime and cilantro.

We serve bamya cold at Zahav in the summer when local okra is abundant. High-quality IQF (individually quick frozen) okra, often available in supermarkets, is an option in other seasons. If you're totally opposed to okra, this recipe is great with blanched and shocked green beans and/or yellow wax beans. I am happy to report that Shmuel and Erna learned to put their differences aside and are still married after 60 years. And sometimes, their bamya is served hot.

6 *cups small whole okra*

5 *tablespoons olive oil*

⅓ *cup Basic Tomato Sauce (page 222)*

1 *tablespoon lemon juice*

½ *teaspoon grated dried lime (see page 92)*

½ *teaspoon kosher salt*

Handful fresh chopped cilantro

● Preheat the oven to 400°F. Toss the okra with 2 tablespoons of the oil and arrange on a baking sheet. Bake until the okra turns dark brown, about 25 minutes. Transfer to a bowl and toss the okra with the remaining 3 tablespoons oil, the tomato sauce, lemon juice, dried lime, and salt. Top with the cilantro. Serve hot or chilled.

BEETS WITH TEHINA
Makes 4 cups

BEET SALADS ARE FREQUENTLY paired with something acidic to cut through the sweetness of the vegetable: goat cheese, yogurt, or a bright, citrusy vinaigrette. This recipe takes a different approach, using the slight bitterness of tehina to tame the sugar and heighten the earthiness of the beets. The combination is magical, capable of casting a spell on people who normally don't like beets. This beet salad is one of a handful of dishes that have been on the Zahav menu every day since we opened—we should post a sign that says, "Over half a million served."

> 5 cups plus ½ teaspoon kosher salt
>
> 8 medium beets
>
> ½ cup Basic Tehina Sauce (page 32)
>
> ½ cup olive oil
>
> ¼ cup lemon juice
>
> ¼ cup chopped fresh dill, plus more for topping
>
> 2 tablespoons chopped fresh mint, plus more for topping

● Preheat the oven to 375°F. Spread 1 cup of the salt in an ovenproof skillet or baking dish. Put the beets on the salt and cover with the remaining 4 cups salt. Bake until the beets are tender, about 90 minutes.

● When they are cool enough to handle, remove the beets from the salt and peel. Set them aside to cool completely.

● Grate the beets into a mixing bowl using the coarse holes of a box grater. Add the tehina sauce, oil, lemon juice, dill, and mint and season with ½ teaspoon salt. Mix well to blend. Top with more chopped dill and mint and serve at room temperature or cold.

TWICE-COOKED EGGPLANT

Makes 5 cups, serves 4 to 6

THIS IS PROBABLY MY FAVORITE eggplant preparation of all time. First, I pan-fry the slices to char and sweeten the flesh, then I cook them again with tons of vinegar. The result is a sweet, sour, and smoky salad that converts unsuspecting eggplant haters into passionate fanboys with a single taste. As a bonus, this recipe flouts all conventions of French technique by charring the eggplant until just before it's burnt. Most of the chefs I've worked for would have made me throw it out if they saw it on my station. But by taking the eggplant to the edge, you can develop rich, deep, and almost chocolaty flavors that make this one of the punchiest bites there is. The flavor intensity of the salad makes it a great complement to roasted lamb, and it's out of control as a sandwich addition.

2 medium eggplants, cut into thick rounds

2 tablespoons kosher salt
   About 6 tablespoons olive oil

1 cup chopped red bell pepper

1 cup chopped onion

1 tablespoon ground coriander

1 teaspoon sweet paprika

¼ cup sherry vinegar

½ cup chopped fresh parsley

1 tablespoon lemon juice

● Sprinkle the eggplant slices with the salt and let stand for 30 minutes on paper towels or a rack.

● Film the bottom of a large nonstick skillet with oil and set over medium-high heat. When the oil is shimmering but not smoking, and working in batches if necessary to avoid crowding, add the eggplant slices in a single layer. Cook until almost black on the first side, about 10 minutes. Turn and repeat on the other side, adding more oil as needed. Remove the cooked eggplant to a plate.

● Add 2 tablespoons olive oil, the red pepper, onion, coriander, and paprika to the skillet. Cook, stirring occasionally, until the vegetables are very soft but not brown, about 12 minutes. Add the eggplant and vinegar to the pan, breaking up the eggplant and mashing it coarsely with a wooden spoon until well combined. Cook until the vinegar has evaporated, about 8 minutes. Off the heat, stir in the parsley and lemon juice. Serve warm or at room temperature.

TWICE-COOKED
eggplant salad,
page 106.

CHARRED EGGPLANT SALAD
Serves 8 to 10

PERHAPS THE ONLY THING Romanians like better than eggplant is garlic, so it's easy to see why this simple dish is so iconic. Eggplant is cooked over charcoal and then the scooped-out flesh is minced with raw garlic and salt. That's it. You can also roast the eggplant over a gas burner, under a broiler, or on a grill, turning it until the skin is blackened on all sides and the flesh is very tender. This creamy salad is ubiquitous in Israel as part of a spread of salatim.

> 2 *large eggplants, halved*
> 2 *garlic cloves, minced*
> ¼ *cup olive oil*
> 1 *teaspoon kosher salt*
> ½ *cup chopped fresh parsley*

● Cook the eggplant halves, either cut side up under a broiler or down on a hot grill, until the exterior is charred and the flesh is like pudding in texture. Let cool, then scrape off and remove the charred skin and put the flesh in a large bowl.

● Add the garlic and oil and stir vigorously, breaking up the eggplant, until the mixture is creamy and smooth. Season with the salt, stir, top with parsley, and serve.

VARIATION: For Baba Ganoush (below), add 1 cup Basic Tehina Sauce (page 32) and mix very well.

RED PEPPER SALAD
Serves 8

THIS RECIPE COMBINES two staples of the Bulgarian table—sweet pepper salad and beans stewed in tomato sauce—into one dish that can be served hot or cold. Big hunks of sweet red peppers are caramelized in a pan with onions, vinegar, grated carrots, and a bit of sugar. When the peppers are fully cooked, everything is pulsed in a food processor so that it comes together but is still very chunky—this is not a smooth puree. Red Pepper Salad can be served as a dip, or eaten by itself as a salad: I like to fold in cooked white beans. Heated, it's a great accompaniment to Bulgarian Kebabs (page 240). To serve it cold, bump up the vinegar and sugar a bit so that it tastes really vibrant. The cilantro is completely non-traditional, but I like the contrast to the sweet and sour flavors of the salad.

¼ cup olive oil

2 cups chopped onions

1 tablespoon sweet paprika

1 tablespoon red wine vinegar

5 cups roughly chopped red bell peppers (about 4 large)

1 cup peeled, grated carrots (about 2 carrots)

½ bunch cilantro (½ cup chopped)

1 tablespoon sugar

¼ teaspoon kosher salt

1 cup cooked white beans (optional)

2 tablespoons chopped fresh chives or garlic scapes

● Warm the oil in a large skillet over medium heat. Add the onions and cook, stirring occasionally, until softened but not browned, about 10 minutes. Add the paprika and stir, cooking for another minute. Add the vinegar and red peppers and continue cooking until the peppers are very tender, about 10 minutes. Add the carrots, chopped cilantro, sugar, and salt and stir to combine.

● Transfer the mixture to a food processor and pulse until coarse. Stir in the white beans, if you like. Serve hot or chilled. Before serving, top with the chives or scapes and the remaining cilantro leaves.

POTATO SALAD WITH PICKLED PEPPERS

Serves 4 to 6

SHIFKAS ARE BABY PICKLED PEPPERS, like the
Middle Eastern equivalent of pepperoncini. They
come in various sizes, some only as big as your
fingernail that are so goddamned cute. They can get
really hot and spicy, which makes them a perfect
match for fried food. I particularly like them with
falafel, and I alternate a bite of shifka for each bite
of falafel.

Because they're pickled, shifkas also work well
with starchy foods like potatoes.

For this salad, I boil potatoes and coarsely mash
them while they're warm, mixing in the pickled
peppers, olive oil, cilantro, and salt. The pepper-
pickling liquid is a great way to spark up the
seasoning for a zestier salad. Cooked potatoes never
do too well in the refrigerator, so I prefer to serve this
salad at room temperature on the day it's made.

6 *Yukon Gold potatoes (about 2 pounds)*

6 *tablespoons olive oil*

2 *garlic cloves, thinly sliced*

½ *cup chopped fresh cilantro*

½ *cup shifka or other pickled peppers,
    sliced into thin rings*

1 *teaspoon kosher salt*

● Put the potatoes in a pot and cover with water by
several inches. Bring to a boil. Cook until the potatoes
pierce easily with a paring knife, 15 to 20 minutes.
Drain and let cool. Peel and mash coarsely with a fork.
Transfer to a bowl.

● Warm 2 tablespoons of the oil in a large skillet
over medium heat. Add the garlic and cook, stirring,
for about 3 minutes. Pour the oil and garlic over the
mashed potatoes. Add the remaining ¼ cup oil, the
cilantro, pickled peppers, and salt and mix to combine.

SPICY FENNEL SALAD

Makes 4 cups, serves 4 to 6

EATING FENNEL RAW is my favorite way to appreciate its subtle licorice flavor and crisp, juicy texture. My spice guy Lior Lev Sercarz (see page 132) does a fennel salad with harissa, reflecting his family's Tunisian lineage. Here, I pair it with schug, whose fresh green chiles and cilantro pump up the bright flavors. The salad is best dressed and left to sit overnight in the refrigerator. It will keep a few days longer, but will become a bit less vibrant as the salt and acid in the schug go to work on the fennel. Fennel is a classic accompaniment to fish, but this spicy salad works well with roast chicken or even a grilled steak.

2 *fennel bulbs, thinly sliced on a mandoline (about 4 cups)*

1 *cup chopped fresh cilantro*

2 *tablespoons olive oil*

1 *tablespoon schug (see page 169)*

1 *teaspoon kosher salt*
  Chopped fennel fronds, for topping

● Combine all the ingredients in a bowl. Toss to combine and top with fennel fronds to serve.

ROASTED ZUCCHINI WITH ANCHOVIES, FETA, AND HAZELNUTS

Serves 4 to 6

WHAT'S COOL ABOUT THIS SALAD is that there is absolutely no waste. We start by roasting the trimmed zucchini in our wood-burning oven, but at home you can broil or grill them. We cut the roasted zucchini into bite-size pieces and dress them with lemon juice, salt, and herbs. The zucchini ends, which would normally be thrown away, are cooked, too, in our wood-burning oven, but for much longer, until they are almost burnt. When they're cool, we puree them with our Basic Tehina Sauce and—voila!— zucchini baba ganoush. This method works for other vegetables, too, like pumpkin or even tomatoes. To

serve, we spoon the salad over some of the zucchini baba and sprinkle a generous amount of feta cheese on top, along with chopped hazelnuts, which is a very Egyptian combination.

4 *zucchini, thickly sliced*

1 *tablespoon olive oil*

4 *teaspoons lemon juice*

2 *teaspoons chopped fresh parsley*
   Big pinch kosher salt

1 *cup Basic Tehina Sauce (page 32)*

2   anchovy fillets

¼   cup crumbled feta

2   tablespoons chopped toasted hazelnuts

● Position an oven rack 3 inches beneath the broiler heating element. Preheat the broiler to high.

● Toss the sliced zucchini with the oil, 2 teaspoons of the lemon juice, the parsley, and salt and arrange on a baking sheet. Broil until the zucchini is charred and blackened in spots, 10 to 20 minutes, depending on the heat of your broiler. Trim the ends from the zucchini, set the zucchini aside, and return the ends to the oven to broil until almost blackened, about 5 minutes more.

● Combine the blackened zucchini ends, tehina sauce, anchovy fillets, and remaining 2 teaspoons lemon juice in a food processor and puree until smooth. Spread this mixture on a serving platter and top with the broiled zucchini pieces. Scatter the feta and toasted hazelnuts over the zucchini and serve.

MEZZE

• Hospitality Incarnate •

I HAD BEEN EATING in Israel for as long as I could remember, but my honeymoon with my wife, Mary, was different. Everywhere we went—from hole-in-the-wall cafés to friends' homes to fancy restaurants—a parade of small dishes—mezze—would arrive at the table in waves that seemed to never end. It was as if time had stopped and would not start up again as long as we stayed at the table.

> *"My palate was never fatigued; just before I tired of one dish, there was a a new bite to try."*

The appeal of mezze was so simple: The more different dishes we sampled, the more likely we would eat something great, and the more we would enjoy the meal overall. Wasn't this the ultimate hospitality?

My first year as executive chef at Marigold Kitchen was an important year for me. I was in charge of my own kitchen for the first time and responsible for a restaurant that had already received considerable acclaim. I didn't want to fuck that up. When I took over the kitchen in the fall of 2005, my menu was solidly New American, in step with what Steve had been doing since he opened the restaurant in October 2004. But I could feel something else starting to happen in my cooking. By the following summer, I was serving leg of lamb with Turkish coffee, bass steamed in grape leaves, and rose water and pistachio donuts. Almost unconsciously, the experiences of growing up Israeli—the very experiences I had dismissed as irrelevant to a career as a serious chef—were somehow creeping into my cooking.

Mary and I were married during that first year, in June 2006. The wedding was on her family's farm on the Eastern Shore of Maryland—an outdoor ceremony that took place right after a monsoon. The catering truck rolled over in a ditch on the way to the farm. Thanks to the large number of Israeli guests (and my future father-in-law's inexplicable collection of several dozen pairs of galoshes), ditches were dug and the field was drained. By early afternoon, the ankle-deep mud under the tent was covered with sheets of plywood and old doors, and Mary's uncle married us in an interfaith ceremony on the shore of the Chesapeake. The humidity melted the buttercream on our wedding cake, and we danced until our clothes and shoes were ruined.

At the end of that summer, we closed Marigold for a few weeks and Mary and I flew to Israel. We arrived three days after the ceasefire that ended the Second Lebanon War. For the first time in a long while, I experienced time off not as a chef, but as a guest. Back home, I was lucky if I had five minutes for dinner before the restaurant started to fill up. I ate mostly on my feet, shoveling down leftovers from a stainless steel bowl or plastic deli container. In Israel, as in most countries in the region, the tradition of mezze is practically synonymous with warm and generous hospitality. And seeing it all through Mary's eyes was like experiencing it for the first time: so many flavors

AFTER THE DELUGE Our 2006 wedding on the Eastern Shore of Maryland, *left*. Typical Israeli street food, *above:* Yemenite pan-fried bread, harif, tomatoes, and za'atar.

Previous spread: Spices galore in Tel Aviv's Carmel Market.

OLIVE HEAVEN
A staggering array of choices at the richly aromatic Levinsky market in Tel Aviv.

"Our guests had no idea what (or how much) to order. They left hungry, confused, and unimpressed."

and temperatures and textures. My palate was never fatigued—just before I tired of one dish, a new one arrived. There was always a new bite to try, a new flavor to stimulate my appetite. And no matter how many meals we ate in a day, I never felt uncomfortably full. Despite the Israeli influences that had worked their way into my cooking, I suddenly knew that there was nothing Israeli about the dining experience at Marigold. I wanted people to experience the pleasures of eating this food in context. I wanted to welcome our guests with freshly baked laffa and the best hummus they had ever tasted. I wanted them to share such a variety of salads and mezze that each new plate would make them forget the last. I wanted them to appreciate the simple perfection of meat grilled over hardwood live fire. And I wanted to do it all according to the high standards that had been drilled into me in French and Italian kitchens.

When I got back to Philadelphia, I laid out my vision to Steve. We agreed that these ideas wouldn't work in a traditional appetizer and entrée dining format. It would have to be a new restaurant, one that really had never been done before. We sat on the back steps outside the kitchen door at Marigold. The landing overlooked the top of the garage next door, where we grew tomatoes and parsley in large pots. Summer was turning into fall and our leafy residential block of West Philly looked like a postcard. As we basked in the last warmth of the setting sun, in the dreamy calm before another dinner service at Marigold, an Israeli restaurant not only seemed possible, it felt like it was our duty. It even seemed like a good idea.

We spent the better part of the next two years drawing up plans for the restaurant that would become Zahav. The budget for the project was more than twice what our previous restaurants cost to open, and we scratched and clawed our way to raise the money from family and friends and friends of friends. We borrowed more money from the bank and signed for it personally. And then we borrowed some more. We were all in. People thought we were crazy (although many of them waited until after we opened to tell us). A cousin who invested with us told me years later that he had expected to lose it all. A real estate advisor was convinced we had chosen a terrible location,

ANCIENT GROVES
Venerable olive
trees, many still
productive, grow in
the Judean Hills
and, for that matter,
all over the North.

perched on a hill above street level in a sort of no-man's-land between the Society Hill and Old City neighborhoods of Philadelphia. In the first few months, it looked like they were right. Although we were generally well received by the critics, we were not connecting with customers. The restaurant had 100 seats but many nights we were lucky to fill thirty of them. Something had been lost in translation.

Our opening menu had eight separate sections, crammed with foreign words and no descriptions. The salad section alone listed seventeen options and asked diners to choose four, six, or eight for the table. Our guests had no idea what (or how much) to order. They left hungry, confused, and unimpressed. Steve and I cut our salaries in half, then eliminated them entirely. We had to make some very painful decisions to let go a few key employees we simply couldn't afford. Even so, we were dangerously close to not being able to make payroll. Zahav almost didn't make it to its first birthday.

We spent hours every day talking about ways to jump-start the restaurant. We cut our costs to the bare minimum and piled on additional responsibilities—Steve took over the beverage program, and I worked lunch and dinner—to keep things running with a skeleton crew. Our first break came when we participated in Philadelphia's restaurant week four months after we opened. This meant we had to consolidate our absurdly complex menu to fit the restaurant-week format. That constraint forced us to

UZBEKI APRICOTS and an astounding array of intensely flavorful dried fruit greet shoppers at every Israeli market.

think about what we wanted the essential Zahav experience to be. For one price, we laid out a meal that reminded us of eating in Israel: hummus and laffa, salads, mezze, grilled meats, and dessert. Walking through the dining room that week, I was surprised by the happy vibe. Instead of confusion and stress, I saw relaxed smiles. We had given our guests a clear blueprint that provided the right amount of choice and the right amount of food at the right value. It was a revelation! When restaurant week ended, we consolidated our menu from eight sections to three and kept the restaurant-week option. Today, about two thirds of our customers choose this fixed-price route. Still, a table of four could conceivably share twenty-four different dishes over the course of a meal!

Next, we turned our attention to the food itself. From day one, I had strived to make the menu as authentic as possible. I somehow thought that operating an Israeli restaurant required me to be faithful to tradition. The trouble was that our American audience lacked the context to give a shit. Sure, I could make the most authentic stuffed grape leaves, but what was anyone comparing them to? The guests only cared whether a dish was good in absolute terms. And even if it was authentic, would it be good enough to get excited about? On yet another slow night, Steve and I were standing on either side of the counter that separates the bread oven and the dining room. I was struggling with a dish of cured mackerel that had Balkan origins. I could see that our customers weren't enjoying it, and I worried about how to improve it while still paying proper respect to its roots. Steve looked at me and said: "Just cook."

Things began to click. I got out of my own head, and I began to create dishes that reflected my Israeli-American identity but were designed to connect with our guests right here in Philadelphia. Crispy Haloumi (page 129), previously a simple plate of fried cheese, got dressed up with dates, apples, and walnuts, making an addictive sweet-and-salty dish that became an instant hit. An Ashkenazi staple of smoked fish became the basis for our Smoked Sable Egg-in-the-Hole (page 136), a soulful version of

an American classic. The Mexican influence on Philadelphia's restaurant scene led to a dish of Baked Kashkaval with Sweet Tomato Relish and Egg Yolks (page 130), utilizing Israeli staples in a cross-cultural mash-up. Our growing customer base responded to these changes with genuine enthusiasm. So did our staff, and so did Steve and I.

Zahav was finally becoming the restaurant that we'd dreamed about on the back steps of Marigold almost three years before. Not a monument to a static notion of Israeli cuisine, but a dynamic restaurant that celebrated everything that was great about Israel *and* Philadelphia. In May 2009, *Philadelphia* magazine ranked us number one on their list of the city's top fifty restaurants, and we haven't looked back since.

You would have a hard time finding many of the recipes in this chapter at a restaurant in Israel. But I've come to understand that the success of my cooking at Zahav is not a result of a slavish devotion to a canon of traditional dishes. It comes from a deeper well of Israeli hospitality. It comes from the intimacy created when friends and family gather together to share food. It comes from the variety of small plates that, taken together, create a satisfying and delightful meal. And it comes from the way that time slows down at the table when you have everything you need. The dishes I've chosen are not all traditional mezze, and each could be a perfect first course to any meal. To me, mezze is just a state of mind.

MEDITATION
At sunrise in 2008, contemplating the world before Zahav after hiking up the steep cliffs to Masada, the ancient historic site overlooking the Dead Sea.

FRIED POTATOES AND OKRA WITH KASHKAVAL-ANCHOVY DRESSING

WATERMELON AND FETA SALAD

BAKED KASHKAVAL WITH SWEET TOMATO RELISH AND EGG YOLKS

FRIED CAULIFLOWER WITH HERBED LABNEH

CRISPY HALOUMI
CHEESE WITH DATES,
WALNUTS, AND APPLES

STUFFED GRAPE LEAVES
WITH BARLEY, KALE,
AND POMEGRANATE

WATERMELON AND FETA SALAD

Serves 4

THIS COMBINATION SEEMS straight out of modernist cuisine, but it's actually an old-school Bulgarian favorite. To me, it feels like summertime in Tel Aviv: a baby watermelon (seedless watermelons were invented in Israel!), cut into wedges, a slab of Bulgarit (Bulgarian feta), and oil-cured black olives. Once you taste it, you understand why the combination is such a classic: The briny and funky cheese is perfectly balanced with the sweet, juicy watermelon. I like to jazz it up with a bit of grassy za'atar, but this is a New World application; the Bulgarians never would have touched the stuff.

This formula loves improvisation. Any kind of persimmon or another ripe melon would be great as a substitute for the watermelon. When the local peaches from Lancaster County or South Jersey are just ripe, there's nothing better. In the fall, I like to use fragrant figs. The cheese is interchangeable, too. French chefs serve watermelon with goat cheese. In Bulgaria, where the feta is often made from cow's milk, they will sometimes substitute an aged sheep's milk kashkaval cheese for a nuttier effect.

½ small watermelon, rind removed and cut into 1-inch wedges (4 cups)
    Kosher salt
⅓ cup pitted oil-cured black olives
¼ cup olive oil, plus more for drizzling
½ cup crumbled feta
¼ cup toasted pistachios, chopped
2 tablespoons chopped fresh mint

● Arrange the watermelon on a platter and season well with salt.

● Combine the olives and oil in a food processor and puree until smooth. Spoon the puree on the watermelon, then the feta, pistachios, and mint. Drizzle on a bit more oil.

STUFFED GRAPE LEAVES WITH BARLEY, KALE, AND POMEGRANATE

Makes 36 grape leaves

4   garlic cloves, minced

½   cup chopped fresh cilantro

¼   cup canola oil

1   teaspoon ground turmeric

1   teaspoon ground fenugreek (see page 172)

1   teaspoon ground cumin

1   teaspoon kosher salt

½   teaspoon black pepper

36   grape leaves

½   cup pomegranate molasses (see page 304)

MANY PEOPLE THINK that stuffed grape leaves come out of a giant can, packed in fluorescent oil and citric acid juice, cold and mushy, with no redeeming qualities. On the contrary: The genuine article is a simple delicacy with nowhere to hide any flaws. The best stuffed leaves I know are made with grape leaves picked from someone's backyard—a far cry from the canned variety. If I can't pick (and quickly blanch) fresh grape leaves, I'll use jarred grape leaves. But our filling is always fresh, and we roll and cook the stuffed leaves from scratch. Grape leaves are incredibly versatile and can be stuffed with any number of grain, meat, or other kinds of filling. They are served slightly warm, and the filling, often rice, retains its integrity. I particularly like stuffing them with Egyptian rice, a creamy short-grain variety, mixed with feta, dill, and walnuts. This toothsome barley version is a bit untraditional, but I enjoy the way it soaks up the pomegranate-juice braising liquid. Plus, you get bonus points for utilizing two of the Seven Species (barley and pomegranate) mentioned in the Bible as special products of Israel.

1   cup barley

1   tablespoon olive oil

1   small bunch kale, shredded (about 3 cups)

● Put the barley in a large bowl and cover with at least 3 inches of water. Let soak overnight. Drain.

● Warm the olive oil in a skillet over medium-high heat. Add the kale and half the garlic and cook until the kale has wilted and is tender, about 5 minutes. Set aside.

● Combine the remaining garlic, cilantro, canola oil, turmeric, fenugreek, cumin, salt, and pepper in a food processor and puree until a smooth paste forms. Transfer the mixture to a large bowl and stir in the drained barley and kale.

● Preheat the oven to 350°F. Spread the grape leaves out on a large cutting board and trim the thick stem from the base of each leaf. Fill one leaf with a heaping teaspoon of the barley mixture and roll the leaf around the mixture, burrito style, into a long cigar. Repeat filling the rest of the leaves, and tightly pack the rolled leaves in a small baking dish.

● Combine the pomegranate molasses with 1½ cups hot water and whisk to blend. Pour over the stuffed grape leaves. (They should be just barely covered—add more water if needed.) Cover the baking dish tightly with foil and bake for 50 to 60 minutes, until the barley filling and grape leaves are very tender. Serve hot or at room temperature.

FRIED CAULIFLOWER WITH HERBED LABNEH
Serves 4

HERBED LABNEH
¼ cup chopped fresh parsley
¼ cup chopped fresh dill
¼ cup chopped fresh chives
¼ cup chopped fresh mint
½ garlic clove, grated on a Microplane
1 cup labneh
Kosher salt

FRIED CAULIFLOWER
Canola oil, for frying
1 head cauliflower, broken into florets
Kosher salt

THIS IS BY FAR the best-selling mezze of all time at Zahav, which is kind of a big deal because, come on, we're talking about cauliflower. Fried cauliflower is a staple of falafel-shop salad bars, but it's often undercooked, underseasoned, and limp from being fried too far ahead of time. Cauliflower is an amazing vegetable—you can eat the florets, the hearts, and even the leaves! I wanted to showcase it on its own. This is such a simple dish, but I always get asked about my secret. Here it is: Treat the cauliflower like French fries! Cook it long enough to develop a crispy, golden-brown exterior. And make sure you salt the hell out of it. Labneh is drained yogurt, but you can use Greek yogurt or yogurt cheese.

● **FOR THE LABNEH:** Combine the herbs, garlic, and labneh in a food processor and puree until bright green and smooth. Season well with salt.

● **FOR THE CAULIFLOWER:** Heat about 2 inches oil in a heavy-bottomed pot over medium-high heat. (You can tell when the oil is hot enough to fry by sticking the handle of a wooden spoon into the oil; if bubbles form around it, it's ready. Or heat until the oil reaches 375°F on a candy thermometer.) Fry the cauliflower until the exterior is dark golden brown and crisp, 5 to 8 minutes, then drain briefly on paper towels. Salt well and serve with the herbed labneh.

• INGREDIENT •

LABNEH

LABNEH (OR LABANEH OR LABNÉ) IS YOGURT that has been salted and drained to remove excess water. The result is a thick, tart, and creamy spread that's similar in texture to Greek-style yogurt, but richer in flavor. The tradition of drained yogurt comes from the Levant, but Israelis adopted it wholeheartedly and use labneh in sauces, eat it instead of yogurt, and just smear it on bread with a drizzle of olive oil and a sprinkling of za'atar. Although kosher laws mean that labneh seldom appears on the Israeli dinner table (where meat is typically served), I use it often at Zahav. Pureed with tons of soft herbs and garlic, labneh is the base of the striking jade-green sauce for Zahav's famous fried cauliflower (above). Labneh also works beautifully as a sauce for fish (amazing when mixed with amba, mango pickle). I

CRISPY HALOUMI CHEESE WITH DATES, WALNUTS, AND APPLES

Serves 4

WHEN I TRIED TO TAKE this dish starring Cypriot sheep's milk cheese off the menu at Zahav, our guests turned into a pack of angry villagers. I can't blame them—there's something so primal and delicious about the pairing of crispy and salty warm cheese with sweet and tangy date paste.

More than 50,000 European Jewish refugees were detained on Cyprus following World War II, after the British turned away their ships from Palestine. Most of them, including my great-grandparents, moved to Israel after independence in 1948, bringing haloumi with them. Haloumi has a high melting point, which makes it great for frying, searing, or grilling. Just make sure to serve the fried cheese right after you cook it. It gets really firm as it cools and your guests will be making squeaking noises as they eat it.

There's really no good substitute for haloumi and its ability to take heat. Haloumi is increasingly available in markets.

1 cup roughly chopped dried dates

½ cup walnuts, toasted and chopped

⅓ cup olive oil

1 tablespoon sherry vinegar

Kosher salt

Canola oil

8 ounces haloumi cheese, cut into 1-inch cubes

1 apple, peeled and cut into matchsticks

Chopped fresh dill

½ teaspoon ground Urfa pepper (see page 48)

● Combine the dates, walnuts, olive oil, vinegar, a couple pinches of salt, and ½ cup hot water in a food processor and puree until smooth. Set the date paste aside.

● Film a skillet with canola oil and heat over medium-high heat until the oil is shimmering but not smoking. Arrange the cheese cubes in a single layer in the skillet and cook, turning, until the exteriors are golden and crisp, about 2 minutes per side.

● Spread the date paste over the bottom of a serving plate and add the fried haloumi. Top with the apple, dill, and Urfa pepper, and serve immediately.

love to use labneh in desserts (like White Chocolate Cake with Rhubarb, Labneh, and Sorbet, page 346) because it mellows the sweetness.

Prepared labneh is available in Middle Eastern markets. Making it is simple: Add salt to taste to plain (not nonfat) yogurt, scoop it into a cheesecloth-lined colander, and set that over a bowl. Place the whole contraption in your refrigerator to drain overnight, and you'll have labneh for breakfast.

BAKED KASHKAVAL WITH SWEET TOMATO RELISH AND EGG YOLKS

Serves 4

PHILADELPHIA HAS THE BEST Mexican food I've eaten outside of Mexico (yes, including California). Without the Mexican immigrants who work in our restaurant industry here, we'd likely have nowhere to eat. Not only do Mexicans keep our restaurants running, but we also now have a great number of taquerias and other joints that have popped up to cater to this community and the rest of us lucky Philadelphians. This dish was inspired by queso fundido, a Mexican dish of melted cheese scooped up with flour tortillas and sprinkled with chorizo or roasted poblano peppers. In my Israeli version, I replace the mild cow's milk cheese with kashkaval, the nutty and piquant sheep's milk cheese from Bulgaria. A Moroccan sweet tomato relish called matbucha balances the saltiness of the cheese and is there to make sure everyone has a good time. The finished dish, served in a skillet, is like a flamboyant cousin of Shakshouka (page 299), the Israeli poached-egg casserole. I like to make individual servings in tiny pans, too. With crusty bread, it can satisfy most cravings. Kashkaval is known as the cheddar of the Balkans, so a good pale English cheddar will work too.

1 tablespoon canola oil

½ onion, diced

½ red bell pepper, diced

2 garlic cloves, minced

1 teaspoon kosher salt

1 teaspoon ground coriander

4 small tomatoes, diced; or 1 (14-ounce) can diced tomatoes

2 cups (8 ounces) shredded kashkaval cheese

4 large egg yolks

Crusty bread, for serving

● Preheat the oven to 425°F. Warm the oil in a skillet over medium-high heat and add the onion, red pepper, and garlic. Cook, stirring occasionally, until the vegetables begin to soften but not brown, about 5 minutes. Add the salt, coriander, and tomatoes. Cook until slightly reduced, about 8 minutes. Set the relish aside.

● Spread the cheese in an even layer on the bottom of a 12-inch ovenproof skillet. Spoon the relish into 4 circles placed evenly around the pan and make an indentation at the center of each with a spoon to hold the egg yolks. Bake until the cheese is melted and browning, about 15 minutes. Add the egg yolks to the relish circles and bake for another minute. Serve immediately with crusty bread.

FRIED POTATOES AND OKRA WITH KASHKAVAL–ANCHOVY DRESSING

Serves 4 to 6

CRISPY POTATOES TRUMP ALL THINGS. These potatoes are boiled, smashed, then fried. I start them in cold oil, which takes longer than hot but gives me more control over the finished product. A riff on a classic Caesar dressing—one of my guilty pleasures—brings together the crispy potatoes and fried okra. This dish is a great introduction to okra, that often-maligned vegetable, as fried okra tastes sweet and grassy, not gooey and weird. Marinated white anchovies (boquerones) from Spain are great for the dressing if you can find them. If not, use good salt- or oil-packed anchovies.

¼	cup finely grated kashkaval cheese
4	anchovy fillets, minced
	Generous ¼ cup olive oil
2	tablespoons red wine vinegar
1½	pounds small Yukon Gold potatoes (about 22)
	Kosher salt
	Canola oil, for frying
12	small okra pods (about 6 ounces)

• Combine the kashkaval, anchovies, olive oil, and vinegar in a small bowl. Whisk well to blend. Set the dressing aside.

• Cover the potatoes with water (about 2 quarts) in a saucepan and season liberally with salt (about 2 tablespoons). Bring to a boil and cook until the potatoes are fork-tender, about 12 minutes. Drain and let cool slightly. Gently press each potato with the palm of your hand to flatten it, being careful to keep it intact.

• Pour about 2 inches canola oil into a heavy-bottomed pot. Add the potatoes to the cold oil and place over medium-low heat. Fry until the exteriors are golden and crisp, 30 to 45 minutes. Drain briefly on paper towels and salt well.

• Fry the okra in the same pot of hot oil until golden and crisp, about 3 minutes. Drain briefly on paper towels and salt well.

• Combine the hot potatoes, okra, and dressing in a large bowl. Mix to evenly coat the potatoes and okra with the dressing, and serve immediately.

A SPICY CHAT WITH LIOR

LIOR LEV SERCARZ is a friend, and the owner of La Boîte, the spice shop in New York City that makes Zahav's spice blends. Lior was born in Israel, studied at Institut Paul Bocuse in France, and was a sous chef at Daniel in Manhattan before leaving in 2002 to start La Boîte. To get your hands on his spices, see Resources, page 359.

MIKE: We met right after we opened Zahav in 2008, or no?

LIOR: That was my basement era. The first three years, La Boîte was in my basement apartment. Didn't talk about that much, but today it sounds awesome: Every cool business started in a basement.

MIKE: Go back even further. You were born in Israel.

LIOR: I started cooking in Israel. I had hair down to here, three earrings. But I needed to learn more. So I went to Bocuse. They required a six-month *stage,* and I ended up in Cancale in Brittany, working for a chef named Olivier Roellinger. For me, Cancale was an eye-opener: a Michelin three-star restaurant that uses tons of spices. We became friends, and he pushed me into this, in a way. It just took me twelve years to get there.

MIKE
"Well, to me this is super Persian smelling, right? There's dried lime in here, or no?"

MIKE: We began collaborating when you came down, and we did a dinner with our favorite spices. Your background is so relevant to what we're doing here. So when I say: "Hey, I want to do something that's inspired by Yemenite soup," your relationship to spices and to flavors is so visceral that you know immediately what I mean.

LIOR: My thought process is trying to capture an essence of a place, a person, an experience, in a spice blend. The blend has to be dry. I don't use fresh ingredients.

So, if you had to pick five ingredients to go into a Zahav blend, what would they be?

LIOR

"And sumac. And rose. And coarse ground Urfa peppers. That always does it for me."

MIKE: The quality of your Urfa and Aleppo peppers and hawaij is amazing. We've got your baharat and we've got Shabazi. But we're not in Israel, and I'm not an Israeli grandmother. And we're not cooking for an Israeli audience. But because we cook everything over charcoal, I'd start with what you get from this restaurant: smoke.

LIOR: Good. I like that.

MIKE: So smoked cinnamon would have to be in it. And we use a lot of lemon, so dried lemon or dried lime would be really important, too.

LIOR: I'll get right on it.

MIKE: Your process comes not just from growing up in Israel and knowing the flavors I have in my mind,

but it goes through all these layers of refinement—spice blending in France, working at Daniel, and 20-plus years of hard work. Tell the story of Shabazi.

LIOR: A chef named Dan Silverman is a friend and a client. Every time we met, he'd say, "So tell me, what's the story with schug?" "Schug is the Yemenite hot sauce." "But why do you have to make it every day?" "Because it's made with fresh ingredients and doesn't last." "So what if we made a schug powder?" I thought, sure, let's do it. And that was the birth of Shabazi.

MIKE: And you named it after the poet?

LIOR: The seventeenth-century Yemenite poet Shalom Shabazi, and the Yemenite quarter in Tel Aviv.

MIKE: And that's what we use on our fried chicken Shabazi at Federal Donuts.

LIOR: So listen to this: One Saturday morning, I was sitting with my wife at Federal Donuts, and these two really big guys walked in. One says, "Dude, the Shabazi chicken is off the hook." And I looked at Lisa, and I said, "I think I can retire. My mission on this planet is done."

SAVORY KONAFI WITH
APPLE–OLIVE SALAD

SMOKED SABLE EGG-IN-THE-HOLE

FLUKE CRUDO WITH OLIVES,
GRAPEFRUIT, AND FENNEL

BAKED MOZZARELLA "KIBBE"
WITH FREEKAH AND GREEN PEAS

LATKE WITH GRAVLAX

SMOKED SABLE EGG-IN-THE-HOLE

Serves 4

4 thick slices Challah
   (page 208 or store-bought)

   Canola oil

4 large eggs

4 ounces smoked sable

½ teaspoon lemon juice

1 teaspoon minced red onion

   Pinch poppy seeds

   Pinch grated lemon zest
   (grated on a Microplane)

   Chopped fresh chives

EVERYONE LOVES EGG-IN-THE-HOLE. It can be the first thing you eat in the morning or the last thing late at night. In my version, oily, smoky sable, rich egg yolk, and buttery challah come together to create decadently satisfying mouthfuls. You can't help but get excited as your fork pierces the crunchy bread and the vivid yellow yolk oozes out. This is the original gangster of liquid-yolk preparations; our Jewish version of bacon and eggs.

● Cut a 2-inch circle from the center of each slice of challah.

● Film a nonstick skillet with oil and place over medium heat. Put the challah slices in the skillet and toast until the bread just begins to color, about 2 minutes. Crack an egg into each hole. Cook until the bread is toasted and the egg begins to set, about 2 minutes more. Flip and continue cooking just until the second side is toasted, about another minute.

● Put each slice of bread on a serving plate and top with sable. Drizzle the sable with the lemon juice and sprinkle with red onion, poppy seeds, and lemon zest. Sprinkle with chives and serve.

LATKE WITH GRAVLAX

Serves 6 to 8

IT SEEMS WEIRD TO ADMIT that I had to work at a northern Italian restaurant to learn how to make great latkes (sorry, Mom). The trick is to use pure potato. There is more than enough starch in the potatoes to bind the latkes without using egg or flour (which make them less crispy and more dense). Potatoes can handle much more salt than seems reasonable, so make sure to taste your mixture (or fry off a small test latke) before you cook up a bland batch. Starchy things like to stick to the pan, so let the latkes cook undisturbed for a few minutes and the crust will set up and release on its own. A cast iron pan is ideal; but if you're scared, a nonstick skillet is foolproof. I make one big latke here, but you can make many small ones, too.

Pairing cured salmon with latkes is almost a cliché, but for good reason. Gravlax is elegant and super simple to make. The hardest part is actually slicing it into thin ribbons. I've found that freezing it for just 15 minutes makes the slicing much easier. Use a long sharp knife held at a very shallow angle to the surface of the gravlax and draw the knife through it from heel to tip. Placing the flat open palm of your other hand on the surface of the fish will ensure a thin, even slice.

GRAVLAX

¼ cup kosher salt

2 tablespoons brown sugar

1 cup chopped fresh dill

1 pound center-cut salmon fillet, skin and pin bones removed

LATKE

2 russet potatoes, peeled and shredded (about 3½ cups)

1½ teaspoons kosher salt

Canola oil, for frying

Sour cream, for serving

Minced fresh chives, for serving

● **FOR THE GRAVLAX:** Combine the salt, sugar, and dill in a small bowl. Lay a large sheet of plastic wrap in a baking dish and sprinkle half the salt-sugar mixture down the center. Put the salmon on top of the salt-sugar mixture and cover with the rest of the salt-sugar mixture. Wrap the salmon tightly in the plastic wrap and refrigerate for 48 hours to cure, turning the fish over a few times. Rinse the excess salt-sugar mixture off the salmon and thinly slice to serve. Refrigerated, gravlax will keep for a week.

● **FOR THE LATKE:** Toss the potatoes with the salt and wring them out in a clean towel to remove excess water. Put ¼ inch oil in a large skillet. Spoon the potatoes into the cold oil in the pan in a single layer and flatten with the back of a spatula. Turn the heat to medium and cook the latke undisturbed until a deep golden crust forms on the bottom, about 15 minutes, pressing occasionally with the spatula. Flip the latke onto a plate and add more oil to the skillet. Slide the latke back into the hot skillet, uncooked side down. Cook on the second side until deep golden brown, about 8 more minutes.

● Slice the latke into wedges, top with gravlax slices, sour cream, and chives, and serve.

FLUKE CRUDO WITH OLIVES, GRAPEFRUIT, AND FENNEL

Serves 4

THIS DISH MAKES ME THINK of an Israeli still life, with a landscape covered in citrus trees, olive groves, and wild herbs growing everywhere. Fluke is quite mild and requires a delicate touch to not overpower it. The grapefruit and green olives have a slight bitterness that's balanced by the sweetness of the caramelized fennel and mint. We get amazing fluke out of Cape May, New Jersey but you can use any firm fish that's fresh enough to eat raw. If you can't find sushi-grade fish, smoked salmon or gravlax is terrific with these ingredients.

1 *pound sushi-grade fluke fillet, sliced as thinly as possible*

Kosher salt

Olive oil

½ *bulb fennel, cut into cubes (about ½ cup)*

¼ *cup minced pitted green olives*

1 *grapefruit, segments peeled of their white membrane*

Fresh mint or cilantro, for serving

• Arrange the fluke slices on a plate and salt well. Set aside.

• Film a skillet with oil and set over medium-high heat. Arrange the fennel cubes in a single layer and cook, undisturbed, until seared well on one side, about 5 minutes.

• Toss the fennel with the olives and ½ cup oil in a bowl and spoon over the fluke slices. Top with the grapefruit segments and mint or cilantro and serve immediately.

BAKED MOZZARELLA "KIBBE" WITH FREEKAH AND GREEN PEAS

Serves 4

1 cup green peas
2 cups shredded mozzarella cheese
Pine nuts, for serving

● Bring 6 cups water to a boil. Adjust the heat to maintain a low simmer.

● Heat 2 tablespoons oil in a large skillet over medium heat. Add the onion, carrot, and garlic and cook, stirring occasionally, until the vegetables have begun to soften but not brown, about 10 minutes. Salt well. Add the freekah and cook, stirring, until lightly toasted, about 3 minutes. Add the simmering water in ½ cup increments, stirring until the water is absorbed each time, until the freekah is tender, about 40 minutes. Add the flour and stir well to blend. Set aside.

● Bring a pot of water to a simmer and add the peas. Cook for 1 minute, drain, and transfer to a bowl of ice water to cool. Drain well. Combine the cheese and peas in a mixing bowl and salt well.

● Preheat the oven to 400°F. Brush a 12-inch cast iron skillet or baking dish with olive oil. Press half of the freekah mixture into the bottom and up the sides of the skillet. Spoon the cheese filling evenly over the bottom, then top with the remaining freekah mixture.

● Brush the top with olive oil and bake until the crust is golden brown, about 40 minutes. Let stand for 5 minutes before unmolding onto a serving platter. Top with pine nuts and serve.

BAKED KIBBE IS SIMILAR TO the fried version (page 153), except that the filling is sandwiched between two layers of crust and baked. Traditionalists will boo me for using freekah (toasted green wheat) instead of bulgur in this recipe, but the texture is so fun and snappy. This version is also missing any meat (strike two on traditional kibbe), but that's fine, as I love the contrast between the crunchy freekah crust and the gooey mozzarella filling. You could easily substitute ground beef or lamb for the cheese. And if you want to go big, a little grated truffle in there would be awesome. I like to make kibbe in one big skillet, but sometimes bake up individual servings, as pictured. (For more on kibbe, see page 152.)

Olive oil
1 onion, diced
1 carrot, peeled and diced
3 garlic cloves, sliced
Kosher salt
1½ cups freekah (see page 277)
1½ cups all-purpose flour

SAVORY KONAFI WITH APPLE–OLIVE SALAD

Serves 8

KONAFI IS A CLASSIC Middle Eastern pastry made by wrapping kataifi (a store-bought shredded wheat dough similar to phyllo) around a sweet filling, often fresh cheese like ricotta. The konafi are placed on a baking sheet, syrup is poured over, and then they're baked so the top layer becomes crispy and brown while the inside remains soft and creamy. You'll see konafi piled high in Middle Eastern markets, sometimes dyed bright orange. My konafi dessert recipes are on pages 336 and 339.

Years ago, the great French chef Joël Robuchon dropped a shrimp wrapped in kataifi into the deep fryer and—voila!—konafi became a savory dish. I make savory konafi by pressing a mixture of kataifi, eggs, feta, cream, and vegetables—in this case grated and pureed winter squash—into a shallow casserole and baking it gently. Once it cools, I cut it into squares and sear it on both sides, creating a caramelized, crispy exterior with a molten interior. I serve this version with a bright salad of apples and olives and finish it with grated bottarga (cured and dried mullet roe) for a briny punch. This recipe is extremely versatile—you can mix the kataifi with any number of vegetables to create a flavorful and satisfying vegetarian dish.

KONAFI

2 tablespoons butter, plus more for the baking dish

2 cups grated peeled winter squash (red kuri, acorn, or butternut)

3 garlic cloves, sliced

1 teaspoon onion powder

1 teaspoon mustard powder

1 teaspoon garlic powder

3 cups cubed peeled winter squash

1 tablespoon olive oil

2 cups (8 ounces) crumbled feta

½ cup heavy cream

1 large egg

1 (1-pound) box kataifi (see Resources, page 359), cut into 1-inch sections

SALAD

2 apples, diced

¼ cup sliced pitted green olives

3 tablespoons olive oil

1 tablespoon lemon juice

Kosher salt

Canola oil

Grated bottarga, for serving (optional)

● Preheat the oven to 350°F. Rub a 9-by-11-inch baking dish with butter and set aside.

● **FOR THE KONAFI:** Melt the butter in a large skillet over medium heat. Add the grated squash, garlic, onion powder, mustard powder, and garlic powder. Cook until the squash is tender, about 8 minutes.

● Toss the cubed squash with the olive oil and arrange on a baking sheet. Bake until the squash is tender, about 15 minutes. Let cool for a few minutes. Combine the roasted squash, feta, cream, and egg in a food processor and puree until smooth.

"The restaurant Machneyuda in the old Jerusalem Market is high-energy hospitality."

● Place the kataifi in a large bowl, pulling apart the threads with your fingers. Add the cooked grated squash and the pureed squash mixture and mix well. Spoon the mixture into the prepared baking dish and smooth the top with the back of a spatula to make an even surface. Bake for 30 minutes, until firm. Refrigerate for at least 1 hour.

● **FOR THE SALAD:** Combine the apples, olives, olive oil, lemon juice, and salt in a bowl and toss to combine. Set aside.

● When ready to serve, cut the chilled konafi into squares. Film the bottom of a skillet with canola oil and heat until shimmering but not smoking. Arrange the squares in the skillet and let cook undisturbed until they turn dark golden brown on the bottom, about 4 minutes. Flip and continue cooking until equally browned on the second side.

● Serve the fried konafi with the apple-olive salad and bottarga, if you like.

CRISPY SWEETBREADS WITH CHICKPEAS, GREEN CHILES, AND LEMON

CHICKEN PASTILLA WITH CINNAMON AND ALMONDS

LAMB BASTURMA

CHOPPED LIVER
WITH GRIBENES

MINA WITH GROUND BEEF,
CARDAMOM, AND COFFEE

CRISPY LAMB'S TONGUE
WITH GRAPES AND
SUGAR SNAP PEAS

CHICKEN PASTILLA WITH CINNAMON AND ALMONDS

Makes 12 pastilla "cigars"

PASTILLA IS A TRADITIONAL Moroccan meat pie with Spanish origins. It is usually made as one large dish, but I like to make pastilla "cigars" for perfect individually portioned, handheld mezze. They are ridiculously easy to make and inexpensive, too. I try to time everything just right so that the cigars are coming out of the oven just as my guests arrive; the fragrance of cinnamon, almonds, and orange blossom is an excellent welcome. Dusting the chicken cigars with confectioners' sugar may sound wrong, but millions of Moroccans know how right it is.

2 tablespoons olive oil, plus plenty more
   for brushing the phyllo

½ onion, thinly sliced

½ bulb fennel, thinly sliced

1 pound ground chicken
   Kosher salt

½ teaspoon ground cinnamon

½ teaspoon orange blossom water
   (see page 330)

6 sheets phyllo dough, thawed

1 large egg, beaten

½ cup sliced almonds
   Confectioners' sugar, for serving

● Warm the oil in a skillet over medium heat. Add the onion and fennel and cook, stirring occasionally, until the vegetables have softened but not browned, about 8 minutes. Add the chicken and continue cooking, stirring to break up the meat, until it begins to brown, about 8 minutes. Add several big pinches of salt, the cinnamon, and orange blossom water. Stir to combine.

● Brush one sheet of phyllo generously with oil and layer 2 more sheets on top, brushing each generously with oil. (Keep the rest of the phyllo under a damp towel to prevent it from drying out.) Cut the 3 stacked sheets in half lengthwise, putting one half aside. With a short side facing you, top the stacked phyllo with half of the chicken mixture, leaving a small margin all around all the sides. Roll into a cigar shape, cutting the phyllo once it's overlapped a bit (you should get 3 cigars from each half of the phyllo stack). Repeat with the other half of the phyllo stack, then repeat the process with the remaining 3 sheets phyllo to make the rest of the cigars. (This is the same process as for Cashew Baklava Cigars; see photographs, page 332.)

● Preheat the oven to 350°F. Arrange the cigars on a baking sheet and brush them with the beaten egg. Top with the sliced almonds. Bake until golden brown, about 10 minutes. Dust the cigars with confectioners' sugar and serve immediately.

CRISPY SWEETBREADS WITH CHICKPEAS, GREEN CHILES, AND LEMON

Serves 4

I POACH SWEETBREADS and then press them overnight so that when seared in a pan, the exterior becomes crispy and the interior remains creamy. The sweetbreads are then dredged in a coating of chickpea flour and sesame seeds—a mixture reminiscent of hummus (and also gluten-free). The fried and salted chickpeas are addictive on their own, so try not to eat them all while you're cooking. Finishing the dish with chiles and lemon makes it really pop.

    Kosher salt
1 *pound sweetbreads*
1 *cup dried chickpeas*
    Canola oil
    Olive oil
1 *garlic clove, crushed*
1 *cup chickpea flour*
1 *large egg*
2 *tablespoons sesame seeds*
    Serrano chiles, thinly sliced, for serving
    Lemon wedges, for serving

● Dissolve ½ cup plus 2 tablespoons salt in 1 quart cold water and add the sweetbreads. Refrigerate in the brine overnight. Soak the chickpeas overnight with water to cover in a large bowl.

● Drain the chickpeas, transfer to a large pot, and cover with water by several inches. Bring to a boil, lower the heat to a bare simmer, and cook until they are creamy and tender, about 2 hours. Drain and refrigerate until you're ready to fry them.

● Heat about 1 inch canola oil in a heavy-bottomed pot over medium-high heat. (You can tell when the oil is hot enough to fry by sticking the handle of a wooden spoon into the oil; if bubbles form around it, it's ready. Or heat until the oil reaches 375°F on a candy thermometer.) Fry the chickpeas until golden brown, about 5 minutes. Drain on paper towels and salt well.

● Drain the sweetbreads, season with 1 teaspoon salt, and transfer to a heavy pot. Cover with olive oil and add the garlic. Poach over medium-low heat until the sweetbreads are tender, about 1 hour. (A thermometer pushed into a sweetbread should read 160°F.) Drain, then put the sweetbreads between two plates and weight with a large can. Refrigerate overnight.

● Remove any visible membrane from the sweetbreads and slice into slabs ¾ inch thick. (Once cut, the pieces will break along their membranes.)

● Set up your breading station with three wide, shallow bowls: Put ½ cup of the chickpea flour in the first bowl, beat the egg in the second, and mix the remaining ½ cup chickpea flour with the sesame seeds in the third. Dredge each sweetbread piece first in the chickpea flour, then in the beaten egg, and finally into the chickpea flour–sesame seed mixture.

● Heat about ¼ inch canola oil in a large skillet until shimmering but not smoking. Arrange the sweetbread pieces in the skillet and let cook undisturbed until golden brown on the bottom, 2 to 4 minutes. Flip and cook until golden brown on the second side, 2 minutes more. Serve with the fried chickpeas, sliced chiles, and lemon wedges.

LAMB BASTURMA

Makes about ¾ pound

HOUSE-MADE CHARCUTERIE is common on restaurant menus these days. Basturma is a cured meat that can actually be made quite easily in *your* house. It originated in Turkey and is a distant cousin of pastrami, although it is more similar to bresaola (air-cured beef) or, as we say in South Philly, *bra-JHOL*. Essentially, a lean cut of meat is salted, and then rubbed with spices and allowed to air-dry in the refrigerator for at least 2 weeks. Basturma is made with a wide variety of meats depending on where it's made—think beef, camel, or goat. Since we don't have easy access to camel, I like to use lamb loin, which is often overlooked in the world of charcuterie. Because it's a small cut of meat, the loin cures and dries relatively quickly, which means you won't have to wait too long to eat it.

Chemen, the spice paste that is rubbed on basturma, typically contains paprika, cumin, fenugreek, and a touch of fresh garlic. You can customize the blend however you like. Black pepper and coriander make a pastrami-like cure. Fennel seed and crushed red pepper will taste Italian. Lior Lev Sercarz (see page 132) makes a great basturma spice called Ararat, named after the mountain range in Turkey where Noah's Ark is said to have come to rest.

Whichever spices you choose, I recommend including the garlic; its moisture helps the dried spices form a paste that will coat the meat, and garlic's antibacterial properties are helpful in the curing process.

My favorite way to appreciate the texture and subtle flavors of basturma is on its own, in thin slices. I serve it with olives, crackers, and spiced nuts. But you can slice it finely and toss it with bitter greens, or even use it as a pizza topping. I love basturma warmed in a pan with scrambled eggs on challah.

> 1 *lamb loin (about 1 pound)*
> 2 *teaspoons kosher salt*
> 2 *teaspoons pink salt (see Resources, page 359)*
> 1 *garlic clove, mashed to a paste*
> 1 *teaspoon fenugreek seeds (see page 172)*
> 1 *teaspoon sweet paprika*
> 1 *teaspoon ground cumin*
> 1 *teaspoon black pepper*

● Trim any visible fat from the exterior of the lamb loin with a sharp knife. Make a paste with the kosher salt, pink salt, and garlic and rub all over the loin. Put the lamb loin on a rack set inside a tray and refrigerate, uncovered, for 7 days, turning daily.

● Mix the fenugreek, paprika, cumin, and black pepper together on a plate. Wipe any remaining salt mixture off the lamb and roll it in the spice mixture. Return the lamb loin to the rack set in the tray and refrigerate for at least another 7 days, turning daily.

● For basturma with a softer texture, you can thinly slice after a week or two, but the basturma will continue to age well for a month or more.

MINA WITH GROUND BEEF, CARDAMOM, AND COFFEE

Serves 6

MINA IS THE LADINO WORD FOR PIE. This Passover dish, common throughout the Sephardic world, is almost too good to be true. Once the matzo is soaked and baked, it magically transforms into something more like traditional pastry than unleavened bread. Mina has great vegetarian potential and can be filled with anything from eggplant to spinach and cheese to potatoes. But I like the way the matzo soaks up the fat and juices from ground beef in this version. The mina is topped with the fruit-and-nut condiment so crucial to the Passover table: charoset. Cardamom is used to flavor coffee and in sweets throughout the Middle East, but the cardamom-coffee combination works perfectly in savory recipes like this one. The cardamom is super piney and fragrant, with a sweetness that balances the roasty, bitter coffee and the rich, salty meat.

CHAROSET

4	carrots, peeled and grated
½	apple, peeled and grated
½	cup chopped walnuts
1	cup chopped fresh cilantro
2	tablespoons fresh horseradish
2	tablespoons raisins
1	tablespoon white vinegar
	Kosher salt

MINA

1	tablespoon canola oil, plus more for brushing
1	pound ground beef
½	onion, diced
5	garlic cloves, minced
1½	teaspoons kosher salt
1	teaspoon finely ground coffee
½	teaspoon ground cardamom
4–6	sheets matzo
1	large egg, beaten

● **FOR THE CHAROSET:** Combine the carrots, apple, walnuts, cilantro, horseradish, raisins, vinegar, and salt in a medium bowl. Toss to combine. Set aside.

● **FOR THE MINA:** Preheat the oven to 400°F. Brush the bottom of a 10-inch cast iron skillet or a baking dish with oil.

● Heat the 1 tablespoon oil in another large skillet over medium-high heat. Add the ground beef and cook, stirring to break up the meat, until it begins to brown, about 5 minutes. Add the onion, garlic, and salt and continue cooking until the vegetables have softened but not browned, 5 to 8 minutes more. Add the coffee and cardamom and stir to combine.

● Soak the matzo in warm water until pliable, about 1 minute. Line the bottom of the oiled cast iron skillet with the matzo, breaking up the pieces as needed to completely cover the bottom and sides of the skillet. Spoon the beef mixture over the bottom and cover the top with more matzo, pressing at the edges to seal. Brush with the beaten egg and bake until the mina is golden brown and crisp, about 30 minutes. Let stand for 5 minutes.

● Invert the mina onto a serving platter. Slice into wedges and serve topped with the charoset.

CRISPY LAMB'S TONGUE WITH GRAPES AND SUGAR SNAP PEAS

Serves 4 to 6

TONGUE FREAKS PEOPLE OUT for understandable reasons, but it has more flavor than almost any other cut of meat I know. It's one of the most utilized muscles in the animal's body and that blood flow produces a meat that tastes like the uber version of the animal, whether it's cow or lamb. If you avoid telling your guests what they are eating until they're finished, you might win over a few converts. The process of taking an inexpensive cut like tongue and transforming it into something delicious requires a bit of patience (I ask you to brine the tongues for 5 days) and you may have to order them in advance from your butcher, but I assure you the result is well worth it. Seared in a pan, the thinly sliced tongue remains unctuous as it gets crispy. Fresh grapes and snap peas, peaches, and mint are lively contrasts.

TONGUE

1½	*cups kosher salt*
1⅓	*cups sugar*
1	*tablespoon black pepper*
1	*tablespoon fennel seeds*
1	*tablespoon allspice berries*
1	*head garlic, halved*
4	*lamb tongues*
¼	*onion*
	Canola oil

SNAP PEAS

2	*teaspoons olive oil*
¼	*cup sliced sugar snap peas*
1	*tablespoon minced red onion*
	Squeeze of lemon juice
1	*peach, thinly sliced*
½	*cup red or green grapes, halved*
2	*tablespoons pistachios*
	Fresh mint, for serving

● **FOR THE TONGUES:** Combine the brine salt, sugar, black pepper, fennel seeds, allspice berries, garlic, and 2 quarts water in a large pot and bring to boil. Let cool completely and then add the lamb's tongues. Refrigerate the tongues in the brine for 5 days.

● Drain the tongues and put in a clean pot with enough fresh water to cover. Add the onion quarter and bring to a boil. Reduce the heat to maintain a bare simmer and cook until the tongues are tender, 1 to 1½ hours. Drain, and when the tongues are cool enough to handle, peel away the outer layer and refrigerate for at least 1 hour.

● Slice the chilled tongue into ¼-inch-thick slices. Heat ¼ inch canola oil in a skillet until shimmering but not smoking. Cook the tongue slices in the skillet until they crisp, about 4 minutes per side.

● **FOR THE SNAP PEAS:** Heat the olive oil in a small skillet over medium heat and add the sugar snaps and minced red onion. Cook until the peas just begin to soften, about 5 minutes. Toss with a squeeze of lemon juice.

● **TO SERVE:** Arrange the tongue slices on a serving plate with the snap pea–red onion mixture, peach slices, grapes, pistachios, and mint.

CHOPPED LIVER WITH GRIBENES

Serves 6 to 8

THIS IS NOT YOUR GRANDMOTHER'S chopped liver—I could never handle that kind of competition. But it is a very simple recipe, and with a little finesse, you can have the smoothest "chopped" liver in the land, a pâté that's a great introduction to liver for people who find it too, well, liver-y. By baking the mixture in a water bath, you prevent the metallic, organ-y flavors that come from overcooked liver. Caramelized onions lend their savory sweetness to the livers. I use schmaltz in this recipe, but you can easily substitute melted butter. One benefit of rendering your own schmaltz is the gribenes (chicken cracklings) that are left over. I like them here to provide a nice crunchy contrast to the super-creamy chopped liver.

CHOPPED LIVER

- 1 *pound chicken livers*
- 2 *large eggs*
- 2 *tablespoons Caramelized Onions (see page 287)*
- ½ *pound schmaltz (see page 167 or store-bought) or melted butter*
- 1½ *teaspoons kosher salt*
  Simple Sumac Onions (page 97), for serving

GRIBENES

Skins from 2 chicken breasts

Kosher salt

Ground sumac (see page 97)

Challah (page 208 or store-bought), toasted, for serving

● **FOR THE CHOPPED LIVER:** Preheat the oven to 275°F. Line a loaf pan with plastic wrap and set aside.

● Combine the chicken livers, eggs, and caramelized onions in a blender and puree until perfectly smooth. Force the mixture through a mesh strainer into a bowl. (You'll have about 2 tablespoons of undesirable bits left over in the strainer. Discard them.) Return the mixture to the blender, add the schmaltz or butter and salt, and puree until perfectly smooth.

● Pour the mixture into the prepared loaf pan, press a rectangle of parchment paper onto the surface, and cover with aluminum foil. Set the loaf pan on a rack inside a roasting pan. Fill the roasting pan with just-boiled water so that it comes halfway up the sides of the loaf pan. Bake until the pâté is just set but still wiggles slightly at the center when shaken, 45 minutes to 1 hour. Refrigerate until chilled, about 2 hours.

● **FOR THE GRIBENES:** Put the chicken skins in a small skillet over medium heat with enough water to just cover. Bring to a boil to render the fat and continue cooking until the water has evaporated and the chicken skin is crisp, about 10 minutes. Drain off the fat (schmaltz) and reserve for another use. Season the skin well with salt and sumac and then crumble.

● **TO SERVE:** Slice the pâté and serve on challah toast topped with sumac onions and gribenes.

KIBBE NAYA WITH
APPLES AND WALNUTS

FRIED KIBBE

FRIED KIBBE

A FEW MONTHS BEFORE WE OPENED ZAHAV, we took a few key managers to Israel to eat the food they had been hearing me talk about for so long and show them what hospitality means in the Middle East. One day toward the end of our trip, we stopped for lunch at an Arabic restaurant in Nazareth. Start to finish, it was perhaps the best meal of the trip, from the hummus and salads to the kebabs grilled over charcoal. But what stood out the most were the fried kibbe—perfect little football-shaped shells of bulgur wheat and lamb, stuffed with ground lamb and pine nuts—the ancient version of "lamb, two ways." The kibbe were golden brown and crispy on the outside and hot and moist inside. Crack one open and inhale a cloud of allspice-scented steam.

"Kibbe is the ancient version of 'lamb, two ways.'"

The owner of the restaurant was very proud, and he took us to the kitchen. One of the cooks was sitting on a stool at a table fitted with a hand-operated meat grinder. To his left was a bowl of kibbe-shell mixture and to his right was a tray of impossibly thin kibbe shells. Looking hard, we saw the blade and die had been removed from the meat grinder and it had been retrofitted with a thick metal dowel attached to the crankshaft, so that it extruded a "casing" of 3-inch-long kibbe shells. Stuffed with the filling and pinched closed, they made beautiful kibbe. I knew we had to have this setup for Zahav, so as soon as we got back to Philadelphia, I took a meat grinder to a local machine shop to have him convert it. The machinist looked at me funny, but he did it.

Kibbe is a hugely important dish throughout the Middle East—considered the national dish of Lebanon—but it is labor-intensive. In less enlightened times, a woman's prowess at making the torpedo-shaped kibbe was considered a sign of her value as a wife. Serving these great fried kibbe at Zahav without employing an army of Lebanese grandmothers was totally cool. But eventually, our modified meat grinder had to be retired. Now we serve fried kibbe—made entirely by hand—only on special occasions. Don't be afraid to make these at home. In small quantities, making them is manageable and even therapeutic. Form a ball of the shell mixture around your thumb to create a pocket. Add the filling, pinch the open end shut, and then massage the ends into the classic football shape. Fried (or pan-fried) and served with tehina sauce and a blast of lemon, this is one of my favorite bites ever.

FRIED KIBBE
Makes 15 kibbe

FILLING

- 1 tablespoon canola oil
- ½ onion, chopped
- 2 garlic cloves, minced
- ½ pound ground lamb
- ½ cup pine nuts
- ½ teaspoon ground allspice
- 1 teaspoon kosher salt

SHELLS

- 1½ cups bulgur wheat
- 1 pound ground lamb
- Kosher salt

Canola oil, for frying
Basic Tehina Sauce (page 32),
lemon wedges, for serving

● **FOR THE FILLING:** Warm the oil in a large skillet over medium-high heat and add the onion and garlic. Cook, stirring, until the onion has begun to soften but not brown, about 8 minutes. Add the lamb and continue cooking, stirring to break up the meat, until it begins to brown, about 8 more minutes. Add the pine nuts, allspice, and salt and continue to cook, stirring, until the meat is well browned and the nuts begin to toast, about 3 more minutes. Transfer the mixture to a plate and refrigerate until cool.

● **FOR THE SHELLS:** Soak the bulgur in cold water for 1 hour. Drain, squeeze out the excess water, and refrigerate until chilled, about 1 hour. Combine the soaked bulgur and lamb in a large bowl, season well with salt, and stir until well blended.

● **TO FORM THE KIBBE:** Shape about ¼ cup of the shell mixture around your thumb. Fill the cavity with about 2 teaspoons of the filling, press the open end closed, and shape into a little football. Repeat until all the kibbe are formed. Refrigerate until ready to cook.

● **TO COOK THE KIBBE:** Heat about 2 inches oil in a heavy-bottomed pot over medium-high heat. (You can tell when the oil is hot enough to fry by sticking the handle of a wooden spoon into the oil; if bubbles form around it, it's ready. Or heat until the oil reaches 375°F on a candy thermometer.) Fry the kibbe, working in batches if needed to avoid crowding the pot, until deep golden brown, about 5 minutes. Remove with a slotted spoon and drain on paper towels. Serve with the tehina sauce and lemon wedges.

ARAK is a clear distillation of wine that has been flavored with aniseed, similar to Greek ouzo or Turkish raki. Arak is the classic accompaniment to mezze throughout the Eastern Mediterranean. Lebanon is particularly renowned for the quality of its arak. Serve it mixed with water over ice and watch it turn from clear to milky in the glass. Or mix it with fresh grapefruit juice for a classic Israeli cocktail.

KIBBE NAYA WITH APPLES AND WALNUTS

Serves 4 to 6

THERE ARE MANY VARIATIONS of kibbe beyond the fried version, and this plated version may be the simplest. Kibbe naya (*naya* means "raw") is simply raw lamb mixed with bulgur wheat and onion and seasoned with warm spices like cumin and allspice. In southern Lebanon they sometimes use goat instead of lamb. Traditionally, a mallet is used to mash the mixture into a smooth paste, but I like the meat to retain some integrity, so I either chop it by hand or run it through the coarsest blade of a meat grinder.

Kibbe naya can be flavored in a million different ways. I love to include a bit of raw horseradish or harissa for an earthy kick. Here, I add sweet and bitter elements with apples and walnuts. (You can substitute ground walnuts for the bulgur for a gluten-free version.) Kibbe naya is fun to eat scooped up with slices of crisp cucumber or wrapped in baby romaine lettuce leaves.

⅔ cup bulgur wheat

1 pound lamb loin, minced, or ground on
   the coarsest setting of a meat grinder

½ cup minced onion

¼ cup peeled and diced apples

1 teaspoon ground cumin

½ teaspoon ground allspice

Kosher salt

Chopped toasted walnuts

Chopped fresh mint

Ground Urfa pepper (see page 48)

Romaine lettuce leaves, for serving

● Put the bulgur in a bowl, cover with cold water by at least 2 inches, and let stand for 1 hour. Squeeze out the excess liquid and transfer to a large bowl. Refrigerate for 30 minutes.

● Add the lamb, onion, apples, cumin, allspice, and 1½ teaspoons salt to the bulgur and mix to combine. Top with walnuts, mint, Urfa pepper, and more salt. Serve immediately with the lettuce leaves for wrapping.

KIBBE
Hussam Abbas, the first
Palestinian chef to elevate
home cooking, supervises
lamb chopping at El Babour in
Umm al-Fahm, north of Tel Aviv.

4

BEYOND CHICKEN SOUP

• The World in a Bowl •

IF I HAD KNOWN that I was face to face with a bowl of Yemenite curry soup, I might never have taken that first spoonful. But there was something intoxicating about the steaming broth that lowered my defenses and drew me in. I can still taste it. The warmth of the black pepper. The way the potatoes soaked up the beef fat and turned a neon orange from the turmeric, which made them taste

> ## "There was a tension in that bowl that held everything together in perfect balance."

somehow even more like potatoes. The tender chew of braised beef. The savor of cumin and the rich, clean broth that was both cleansing and satisfying. There was a tension in that soup that held everything together in perfect balance. And there was a moment sitting at the table with my father, neither of us speaking, when the soup cut through everything.

It was 1995, and my family had moved back to Israel from Pittsburgh. I was sixteen years old and wanted nothing to do with the country where I was born. I didn't want much to do with my parents, either. I was an American teenager and I was angry. So they shipped me off for a one-year stint at a boarding school in rural Pardes Hanna, an hour north of Tel Aviv. For the Israeli and American students there, it was the end of the line—their parents didn't know what to do with them either. I fit right in.

It was not a rigorous academic institution. The school had a farm attached to it, and whenever the teachers couldn't think of anything else for us to do, they sent us into the orchard to pick pomelos, grapefruit, and oranges. Mainly we threw them at each other. I thought I was pretty tough until I met some of the Russians. We were sent out to wrestle on a wooden plank stretched across a pit of mud and animal shit until only one of us was left standing. It wasn't me. Yet we were allowed a degree of freedom that was unheard of back home. Every other Friday afternoon, they released us into the wild—free to roam a country the size of New Jersey, unsupervised. We had to be back for class on Sunday morning, but the buses didn't start running again until sundown on Saturday, so we lived every second of that time off.

We challenged ourselves to get as far away as possible or as fucked up as possible or into the weirdest situation possible. If we wanted to go to the old Jewish neighborhood of Mea Shearim in Jerusalem and get ourselves invited to lunch at the home of an important Hasidic rabbi, then that's what we did. If we ended up on a beach somewhere with no money, we would sleep on the beach. Only later would I realize that I was in the middle of one of the best years of my life. And that some of my classmates would become lifelong friends whose defining relationships with Israel were being formed alongside my own.

FATHER / SON
Intense conversation at a party at my dad's house in 2008; Mom is at left. Schug, the fiery Yemenite condiment, *above*.

Previous spread:
Steve and I do our best thinking over Vietnamese soup at Pho 75.

The food at the *chedar ochel* (dining hall) was disgusting, and we lived off government-subsidized bread and chocolate milk from the local convenience store. Sometimes my father would come to visit and take me out to lunch. We didn't have much to do with each other at the time, but I was grateful for a real meal. He was a pretty scary dude. Sometimes it seemed like he glared at me more than he spoke to me. But I'm pretty sure that I got my love of food from him. Later, I would learn my first lessons in food service from working in the Subway franchises he owned in Pittsburgh: how to control employee theft by counting the rolls and how mise en place in preparing food allowed speed and consistency. But at the time we settled in at Opera, a Yemenite restaurant in Hadera, a drab city near school, I was still a picky eater.

YEMENITE SOUP
At Ronen Shlomo's house in Hadera, I lose myself in a soulful meal of Yemenite chicken soup. He's our contractor, Ofer's, brother.

At the end of that year, I took my parents up on their halfhearted offer to let me return to America to finish high school (they offered to buy me a moped to stay!). I bounced around a few friends' couches in Pittsburgh, getting into trouble, barely finishing high school, and reluctantly applying to college. I felt disconnected from my American friends. I wondered why they didn't know about Israel or anything real. In the fall of 1995, when I learned that Yitzhak Rabin had been killed, I felt Israeli for perhaps the first time.

My next encounter with Yemenite soup came almost a decade later, in the spring of 2004. My brother, Dave, had been killed the previous fall, and I was struggling. I was the sous chef at Vetri and living in the office above the restaurant. I slept badly. Some nights as I lay awake on the pullout couch, I could hear the sounds of transvestites beating each other up in the parking lot. That Passover, Marc Vetri decided to host a family seder in the restaurant. I don't know if he or anyone realized how far down the rabbit hole I had gone—I was good at hiding things. But we were all looking for something meaningful to do.

One of the guests at the seder was Ofer Shlomo, a successful Philadelphia contractor who did a lot of work for Marc. When Ofer's wife, Michelle, came in carrying a big pot

of chicken soup, I assumed it was full of matzo balls. But as soon as I got close, I caught a whiff of hawaij, the curry-spice blend that is the hallmark of Yemenite soup. The chicken version of Yemenite soup is a whole different animal (literally) than what I had eaten at Opera nine years earlier. It's not quite as rich, but it has more clarity, and the incomparable, soul-warming, and bottomless depth that only chicken broth can reach. This was the Jewish chicken soup I had grown up eating in Pittsburgh, only it wasn't. The two soups clearly shared some DNA, but were as distinct as could be. This was chicken soup separated at birth.

Ofer is a first-generation Israeli who grew up in Hadera with his Yemenite immigrant parents, seven brothers and sisters, and countless aunts, uncles, and cousins. His mother cleaned the yeshiva where he went to school. As a second grader, Ofer badgered his classmates to put their chairs on top of their desks so that his mother would have an easier time with the floors. After school, little Ofer would wait for his mother to finish her work and then the two of them would walk home together. To Ofer, the term Yemenite soup is redundant—it's just soup. "We ate soup every day, all day, all year long," he says. "Shabbat dinner was challah and soup and that's it. We weren't Moroccan. We didn't have twelve salads on the table."

In 1979, Ofer met Michelle, an Ashkenazi Jew from Pennsylvania, on a soccer field in Jerusalem. They were soon married and living in Jerusalem. Whenever Ofer was called

HOT SOUP
Some like it hotter.
Photographer Mike
Persico always adds
Sriracha to his pho.

"Whenever things seem overwhelming, Steve and I head over to Pho 75 for beef noodle soup."

up for reserve duty, Michelle would go and stay with Ofer's mother in Hadera. It wasn't long before she was making Yemenite soup that rivaled her mother-in-law's. In 1986, Ofer and Michelle and their two young boys moved to the States to be closer to Michelle's family. The economic opportunities were also hard to deny. "My mother and brothers couldn't live the way they do now without me being here," says Ofer.

To see Ofer and his family today makes it difficult to imagine what life was like for the Shlomo family only a generation earlier. In the fall of 1949, fourteen-year-old bride Malkah Shlomo, Ofer's mother, left her home in the Yemenite capital of Sana'a with her husband and his family. Israeli independence had made life difficult for Jews living in Muslim countries, and the Israeli government was in the middle of an operation that would airlift fifty thousand Jews to Israel in a span of a little more than a year. There is no telling how long Ofer's forebears had lived in Sana'a. One legend dates the isolated Jewish community in Yemen back nearly three thousand years.

But that November, the Shlomos left everything behind and walked 250 miles to the port city of Aden. Hundreds of Yemenite Jews died during this journey, either en route over an unforgiving terrain or at a desert transit camp while they waited for crowded transport planes to carry them to the promised land. Even more died upon their arrival in Israel, where they found a country unprepared to care for them. But the Shlomo family stuck together and made it to Israel intact, at first living in makeshift shacks of corrugated metal called *pachonim*. The family was very religious and the patriarch, Yefet Shlomo, was a *shochet*, trained in the ritual slaughter of kosher animals. This made him employable, and the family moved first to Afula, and later to the slightly more affluent Hadera. As a side benefit, there were always plenty of chickens for soup.

Our seder tradition with Ofer continued for several more years, and when it came time to build Zahav, we knew right away who the contractor would be. The first meal we ever served at the restaurant was a Passover seder—with Yemenite soup, of course—about a month before we opened. The dining room was still a construction site, and I remember Ofer, broom in hand, rallying the troops to get things in order before the guests arrived.

Only a month earlier, we had been in Ofer's mother's tiny apartment in Hadera, learning to make the soup from Malkah Shlomo herself. My sous chefs and I crowded around her tiny range, peeking into the pot as she used her hands to measure ingredients and communicate in a language that all cooks understand. Afterward, we squeezed in around a table filled with Ofer's siblings and cousins and children and nieces and nephews. I think I ate six servings of soup that night, with all of Ofer's relatives laughing at me and egging me on.

Whenever my business partner, Steve, and I need to clear our minds and step away from the day-to-day headaches of running the restaurants, we go get coffee. But when things are really stressful and overwhelming, we go get soup. This usually means a trip over to Pho 75 for a bowl of Vietnamese beef noodle soup. The restaurant serves nothing but soup, and with its utilitarian, dining-hall vibe and immigrant-run ethos, it isn't entirely unlike Opera in Hadera, where, twenty years ago, I ate Yemenite soup for the first time. All of our restaurants, and almost all of our important or difficult decisions, in fact, have been worked out over soup. There's almost no problem that doesn't feel insignificant or more manageable after slurping down a bowl of steaming, crystal-clear broth.

Soup is transformative. It is cheap and warming. Eating too much of it makes you feel better, not worse. It is said to have healing properties. But what I love most about soup is the social aspect, the ritual of it. You can't eat soup driving in your car. It forces you to sit down and think about something other than your problems.

Make soup. Eat soup. Everything will be OK.

MATZO BALLS
Cinnamon brings out the iconic deliciousness of chicken in soup. A touch of baking powder makes the matzo balls puff up just a bit.

SCHUG

LACHUCH

HILBEH

YEMENITE CHICKEN SOUP

YEMENITE CHICKEN SOUP
Serves 4

KOSHER CHICKENS MAKE the best soup. Don't get me wrong, some of my best friends are gentile birds. But the salt content of kosher chickens contributes to a round, rich broth that just tastes more chicken-y. If you are using a conventional bird, consider adding a teaspoon of salt at the beginning of the cooking process.

You can buy a chicken in parts, but I highly recommend cutting up your own. For one thing, it's much easier than it looks and you get the carcass for free, which will make your soup better. Second, mastering this simple task will give you immeasurable confidence in the kitchen, which, as any skilled cook will tell you, is at least half the battle. This is a perfect recipe to start with; by the time you're finished with the soup, your knife work won't be recognizable. Serve with schug (see page 169) and hilbeh (see page 170) on the side.

> 1 whole chicken (about 4 pounds)
>   Kosher salt
> 1 tablespoon plus 2 teaspoons hawaij (see page 168), plus more for serving
> 2 tablespoons schmaltz (see opposite) or olive oil
> 1 onion, sliced
> 4 garlic cloves, sliced
> 2 quarts My Chicken Stock (opposite)
> 12 baby Yukon Gold potatoes, peeled
> 1 bunch ramps or scallions, sliced

● Slice the chicken breasts from the bone and discard the skin; reserve the bones. Season the breast meat generously on both sides with salt and 1 teaspoon of the hawaij, put on a plate, and refrigerate. Remove the drumsticks, thighs, and wings from the carcass.

● Warm the schmaltz or oil in a large pot over medium heat. Add the onion, garlic, and a pinch of salt and cook, stirring frequently, until the onion begins to soften, about 10 minutes. Add the chicken stock and the chicken pieces (except for the reserved breast meat), breast bones, and carcass. Raise the heat to medium-high and bring to a boil, skimming off any foam that rises to the surface. Lower the heat to a simmer and add 1 tablespoon of the hawaij. Simmer for about 45 minutes, until the chicken is cooked through. Transfer the thighs and drumsticks to a plate, cover, and refrigerate. Simmer the soup for another 2 hours. Pour the soup through a fine-mesh strainer into a clean soup pot; discard the solids.

● Place the pot over medium heat and add the reserved chicken thighs and drumsticks, along with the potatoes and remaining 1 teaspoon hawaij. Bring to a simmer and cook until the potatoes are tender, about 20 minutes. Add the reserved chicken breasts and ramps or scallions and simmer until the chicken is just cooked through, about 10 minutes more. Remove the chicken breasts from the soup and gently pull the meat apart using two forks. Season the broth with salt and more hawaij if you like.

● To serve, transfer the chicken thighs and drumsticks and potatoes to a platter. Divide the shredded chicken and ramps among four soup bowls, ladle in the broth, and serve with the platter of chicken and potatoes.

MY CHICKEN STOCK

Makes 4 quarts

> 1 whole chicken (3–4 pounds) or
>   2 chicken carcasses
> 2 medium onions, unpeeled, quartered
> 3 carrots, roughly chopped
> 2 heads garlic, cut in half horizontally
> ½ teaspoon black peppercorns
> 2 parsley sprigs
> 1 teaspoon kosher salt

● Put the chicken, onions, carrots, garlic, peppercorns, parsley, and salt in a large stockpot. Add just enough cold water to cover the chicken (about 4 quarts) and bring to a simmer over high heat. Lower the heat to maintain a gentle simmer and cook, uncovered, until the liquid is pale golden and flavorful, 3 to 4 hours. Strain and store for up to 1 week in the refrigerator or up to 6 months in the freezer. Remember to save the schmaltz that rises to the top when the stock is chilled.

• INGREDIENT •

SCHMALTZ

SCHMALTZ IS THE YIDDISH WORD for rendered chicken (or sometimes goose) fat, derived from the German word for melting. Because of kosher laws, Eastern European Jews couldn't cook with lard or butter, the typical cooking fats of the region. Nor did they have access to the olive oil and other vegetable oils used in more southern climates. So they turned to chicken fat, an economical and available option that converts a by-product into a golden elixir. Chicken fat adds depth and richness to dishes while remaining somewhat neutral and not over-the-top meaty. It's great for frying potatoes and for searing meat for stews. Perhaps the best application is the simplest: slathered on good bread with salt.

Schmaltz is often sold in little tubs in the grocery store, but it appears for free in your kitchen in the form of the solidified fat that rises to the top of your chicken soup. Just scrape it off and store it in the refrigerator or freezer to use whenever.

Schmaltz is very easy to make with raw chicken skins, which many butchers will sell, or even give, to you. The fattier the skin, the better, so thighs work particularly well here. Finely chop the skins and place them in a saucepan with a splash of water and some chopped onion if you like. Cook over low heat until the fat is completely rendered and the skin and onion turn deep golden brown, an hour or so. Strain the schmaltz and refrigerate. The crispy bits of skin and fried onion that are left behind are called gribenes. Seasoned with salt, they are a delicacy in their own right, best when sprinkled over a salad or on top of a piece of buttered (or schmaltzed) bread.

YEMENITE INFLUENCE

YEMENITE CUISINE IS FAMOUSLY POOR. Legend has it that the Jewish community in Yemen once survived a great famine on tomatoes, fenugreek, and chiles alone. Yet it is out of this necessity that an astonishingly sophisticated cuisine emerged. Hawaij (ha-WAJ), a simple but complex blend of three common spices, is the guts of Yemenite soup. The soup is always served with hilbeh (HIL-bay), a fenugreek-based condiment, schug (CHug), the peppery green chile paste, and the pancake-bread called lachuch (la-CHUCH). It's interesting to think that each of these iconic and elemental preparations may well not have developed under more prosperous circumstances. Each enhances Yemenite soup in its own way. Using them depends on your preference and taste buds. Experiment and see what you like.

• INGREDIENT •

HAWAIJ

HAWAIJ IS A YEMENITE SPICE BLEND composed of turmeric, black pepper, and cumin. Sometimes cardamom, coriander, or ginger finds its way into the mix as well. The spices reflect Yemen's position along the spice trade routes to Africa, India, and the Orient. Cumin is what gives Yemenite soup its trademark curried flavor; black pepper provides extra warmth; turmeric lends earthiness. Fresh turmeric, above, which you sometimes see in health-food stores, is a rhizome in the same family as ginger, with a papery skin and bright orange flesh. Turmeric is almost always sold in powdered form, and its primary contribution to the world is the beautiful golden color it lends to everything it comes into contact with (i.e., chicken broth or your hands). It is earthy and slightly pungent and full of beta-carotene. To me, it makes root vegetables taste more like themselves. Turmeric is famous, too, for its anti-inflammatory and other health benefits.

> ¼ cup plus 2 tablespoons ground turmeric
> ¼ cup ground cumin
> 2 tablespoons black pepper

Combine the turmeric, cumin, and black pepper in a 1- or 2-cup container and seal with a tight-fitting lid. Shake to combine. Store in the pantry for up to 3 months. Makes ¾ cup.

SCHUG

SCHUG (SOMETIMES SPELLED ZHOUG, s'chug, shoug, and many other ways) is a fiery condiment made from fresh green chiles. One of the cool things about it is that although it is Yemenite in origin, it's now used throughout Israel, where cuisine and culture develop in real time. Now, not only must you have harif (the generic term for hot sauce), which is typically based on Moroccan harissa (see page 61), on the table, but you must make room for schug, too. I love the bright quality that comes from using fresh chiles instead of dried, indicative of its Indian influence. Schug can be as simple as chiles, vinegar, and oil. I like to make it even fresher by using lemon juice instead of vinegar and adding tons of cilantro and parsley. I add cardamom and coriander, too, and you can play around with other spices like fenugreek and cumin.

Schug can be seriously hot, depending, of course, on the type of chiles you choose. The serranos called for here are fiery, but not so scorching as to obliterate the other flavors. Jalapeños also work well. We used to serve schug on every table at Zahav as a condiment for our hummus, but we had to stop because we were burning too many mouths! Now we use it a little more judiciously to season specific dishes, like fried potatoes or Spicy Fennel Salad (page 113). Schug is a classic accompaniment to malauch, a flaky Yemenite flatbread traditionally eaten with hard-boiled egg and grated tomato. At our donut and fried chicken shops, Federal Donuts, we serve chicken dusted with Shabazi, which is Lior's name for the dried schug blend he makes for us. It numbs your lips just the perfect amount.

20 serrano chiles, stems removed
1 cup parsley leaves
1 cup cilantro leaves
4 garlic cloves
1 tablespoon kosher salt
1 tablespoon ground cardamom
1 tablespoon ground coriander
2 tablespoons lemon juice
1 cup canola oil

Combine the serrano chiles, parsley, cilantro, garlic, salt, cardamom, coriander, and lemon juice in a food processor and pulse until a coarse paste forms. Transfer the mixture to a large bowl and stir in the oil—the sauce should be streaky and broken, not smooth and emulsified. Store in a sealed jar in the refrigerator for up to 1 month. Makes 1½ to 2 cups.

YEMENITE BEEF SOUP

Serves 4

THIS IS MY VERSION OF THE FIRST Yemenite soup I ever tasted at Opera in Hadera over twenty years ago (and it's what I crave whenever I visit Israel). Other than the obvious, the main difference between the chicken and beef versions is the addition of crushed tomatoes, which combine with the short ribs to produce a serious punch of umami and just enough acidity to keep you coming back for more.

1 pound boneless beef short ribs, cut into 2-inch chunks

4 tablespoons schmaltz (see page 167) or olive oil

4 tablespoons hawaij (see page 168)

Kosher salt

1 onion, thinly sliced

4 garlic cloves, slivered

1 cup crushed tomatoes

2 quarts My Chicken Stock (page 167)

2 cilantro sprigs, plus more leaves for serving

2 parsley sprigs, plus more leaves for serving

12 baby Yukon Gold potatoes, peeled

● Combine the short ribs, 2 tablespoons of the schmaltz or oil, 2 tablespoons of the hawaij, and 1 tablespoon salt in a large bowl. Mix well to evenly coat the meat and transfer to a plate. Cover loosely with parchment paper and refrigerate for at least 1 hour or up to overnight.

● Heat the remaining 2 tablespoons schmaltz or oil in a large pot over medium-high heat until shimmering but not smoking. Cook the short ribs, turning occasionally, until browned on all sides, about 5 minutes. Remove the meat to a plate and set aside.

● Lower the heat to medium-low and add the onion, garlic, and remaining 2 tablespoons hawaij. Cook, stirring frequently, until the onion has softened but not browned, about 10 minutes. Add the crushed tomatoes and cook for about 5 minutes more. Add the reserved short ribs, chicken stock, cilantro, and parsley and bring to a simmer. Cook, covered, for 2 hours. Add the potatoes and continue cooking until tender, about 20 more minutes. Serve the soup in bowls topped with cilantro and parsley leaves.

• INGREDIENT •

HILBEH

HILBEH IS A FENUGREEK-BASED thickener that's traditionally stirred into Yemenite soup. Fenugreek is a unique spice whose aromatic properties can perhaps be best described as similar to pungent maple syrup. (I can sniff out whether the person sitting next to me on the flight back from Israel has eaten Yemenite soup within the last 24 hours.)

Of all its remarkable qualities, I prize hilbeh's ability to incorporate air when dispersed in liquid and whipped. This makes it a valuable thickener, especially in a kosher kitchen. Essentially, it allows you to make a cream soup without mixing milk and meat, a big no-no in kosher cooking.

2 tablespoons ground fenugreek (see page 172)

¼ cup chopped fresh dill

¼ cup chopped scallions

1 teaspoon kosher salt

Soak the fenugreek in 1 cup water overnight. Whisk until fluffy in a small bowl. Add the dill, scallions, and salt and stir to combine. Stir it by spoonfuls according to taste into Yemenite soup. Makes 1½ cups.

KID SOUP
Our children
Sally Cook, David
Solomonov, and
Leo Cook dig into
Yemenite soup.

• INGREDIENT •

FENUGREEK

FENUGREEK IS AN AMAZINGLY versatile spice that is available whole or ground in some supermarkets. Its notes of celery and sweetness bring to mind carrots, onions, and garlic. Like those aromatics, it gives backbone to other flavors in a dish. Fenugreek seeds resemble tiny corn kernels. You'll often find this spice listed on the labels of powdered soup mixes because it amplifies meaty flavors, particularly chicken, more cheaply than using actual meat. Occasionally you may find fresh fenugreek leaves, as delicate as pea shoots, in the market. Use them as you would bay leaves to reinforce the fenugreek seed in a dish. (See Resources, page 359.)

LACHUCH

YEMENITE SOUP IS COMMONLY SERVED with lachuch, a spongy, pancake-like bread with nooks and crannies just perfect for soaking up the broth. It is similar to Ethiopian injera, which is not surprising considering that the two countries are separated by just a small sliver of Red Sea. Lachuch is a yeasted bread whose batter is mixed and allowed to rest while the yeast activates. Sometimes fenugreek is added to the batter to aid the fermentation and help give the bread its characteristic tangy edge. Then lachuch is cooked in a skillet on one side only, and the trick is to get just the right amount of batter in the hot pan and spread it quickly enough to achieve the proper thickness. The bottom of the pancake turns golden brown, while the trademark bubbles form on the top. Lachuch is great with any soup or stew, as well as with eggs and schug (see page 169), or even on its own with butter, jam, or honey.

> 1 teaspoon active dry yeast
> 2 cups all-purpose flour
> 1½ teaspoons sugar
> 1½ teaspoons kosher salt
> ½ teaspoon baking soda
> 1 tablespoon ground fenugreek (see opposite)
>   About 1 tablespoon canola oil

Mix the yeast with 2½ cups warm water in a large bowl and let stand until slightly bubbly, about 5 minutes. Add the flour, sugar, salt, baking soda, and fenugreek and stir to combine—the mixture should look like pancake batter. Cover with plastic wrap and let stand in a warm spot in the kitchen until the surface of the mixture is dotted with bubbles, about 1 hour. (In a cold kitchen, it will take longer. Wait for the bubbles!)

Brush an omelet pan with oil just to coat. Set over medium heat and pour about ½ cup of the batter into the pan. Cook until brown on the bottom and set on top, 4 to 8 minutes. Repeat, brushing the pan with more oil between cooking each bread.

MATZO BALL SOUP WITH BLACK GARLIC
Serves 4

JUST BECAUSE I'M A JEWISH CHEF doesn't mean I was born with a natural talent for matzo balls. Early in my career, I was hired to cater an upscale Passover meal, and I put foie gras matzo balls on the menu. I cooked hundreds of dollars' worth of foie gras, using the rendered fat in the matzo ball mix and then stuffing each ball with a little nugget of the liver. The matzo balls fell apart and ended up in the garbage can.

There are a lot of theories on how to produce fluffy matzo balls, from folding in whipped egg whites to lightening the mix with seltzer. For my money, a little bit of baking powder does the trick nicely. Matzo balls are comfort food, and there is also something warm and comforting about black garlic. Like soy sauce, its fermented taste both elevates and deepens the broth. Like tamarind, it has a rich sweetness balanced by enough acidity to keep it in the savory realm. Fortified with the black garlic, this soup is how I always imagine Passover in Southeast Asia would taste.

MATZO BALLS

- 2 large eggs, beaten
- 2 tablespoons schmaltz (see page 167), at room temperature
- ½ cup matzo meal
- ½ teaspoon baking powder
- Pinch ground cinnamon

BROTH

- 2 quarts My Chicken Stock (page 167)
- 2 carrots, sliced
- 2 stalks celery, sliced
- 4 black garlic cloves (see page 56)
- 1 teaspoon kosher salt

Chopped fresh dill, for serving

● **FOR THE MATZO BALLS:** Combine the eggs and schmaltz in a medium bowl and stir until blended. Add the matzo meal, baking powder, and cinnamon and mix well. Using wet hands, tear off golf ball–size pieces of the dough and shape into rounds.

● Bring a lightly salted pot of water to a boil and cook the matzo balls for 30 minutes, or until cooked through (cut one open to be sure).

● **FOR THE BROTH:** Combine the stock, carrots, celery, black garlic, and salt in a large pot. Bring to a simmer and cook for 30 minutes. Remove and discard the black garlic.

● Ladle the broth into soup bowls and add 2 matzo balls to each bowl. Top with dill and serve.

CHICKEN SOUP WITH GHONDI
Serves 4

GHONDI ARE THE WEALTHY, EXOTIC (and gluten-free) Persian cousins of the matzo ball—dumplings made from chickpea flour and ground chicken that are poached and served in broth. Like matzo balls, ghondi are a staple at many Friday night tables. In fact, I first ate them at a Shabbat meal at my half-brother-in-law Avi's house. Avi's family immigrated to Israel after the Iranian revolution in 1979 and brought with them a distinctive Persian cuisine. Avi has taught me much: His Persian Rice (page 270), in particular, is legendary in my family.

Ghondi can be plagued with the same affliction as matzo balls: a tendency toward leadenness. Part of this is because they are usually enormous—bigger than tennis balls. That's an awful lot of dumpling to get through. I like to make mine smaller and daintier, so they cook faster and lighter. The whipped egg whites help make them lighter, too. This recipe calls for chicken legs for the broth, which is a basic chicken soup amped up with the traditional Persian flavorings of saffron, turmeric, and lemon zest.

BROTH

2 *boneless, skinless chicken breasts*
  Kosher salt
2 *teaspoons ground turmeric*
  Pinches grated dried lime (see page 92)
2 *whole chicken legs (drumsticks and thighs)*
  Pinch saffron threads
1 *teaspoon finely grated lemon zest*
  About 2 quarts My Chicken Stock (page 167)

GHONDI

½ *pound ground turkey or chicken*
½ *cup chickpea flour*
1 *teaspoon kosher salt*
  Pinch ground turmeric
2 *large egg whites*

2 *cups cooked or canned chickpeas*

● **FOR THE BROTH:** Season the chicken breasts aggressively with salt, 1 teaspoon of the turmeric, and a pinch of the dried lime. Put on a plate, cover with plastic wrap, and refrigerate.

● Combine the chicken legs, saffron, remaining 1 teaspoon turmeric, lemon zest, and a couple more pinches of dried lime in a large pot. Add enough chicken stock to cover. Bring to a simmer and cook, skimming the foam, for about 2 hours.

● **FOR THE GHONDI:** Combine the ground turkey or chicken, chickpea flour, turmeric, and salt in a large bowl. Whisk the egg whites (or beat with a hand mixer) to soft peaks in a medium bowl. Fold the whites gently into the ghondi mixture until combined. Cover with plastic wrap, pressing the plastic onto the surface of the mixture, and refrigerate for 1 hour.

● When the broth is finished, strain, discarding the chicken legs, and return the broth to the clean pot. Add the reserved chicken breasts, bring to a simmer, and cook until the chicken is cooked through, about 20 minutes. Shred the chicken with two forks; reserve in a bowl. Keep the broth simmering over low heat.

● **TO FORM AND COOK THE GHONDI:** With damp hands, shape the turkey mixture into small football-shaped pieces about the size of walnuts. Drop the ghondi into the broth and simmer until cooked completely through, 30 to 40 minutes.

● To serve, add the chickpeas to the broth to heat through. Add the shredded chicken and cook just long enough to warm it, about 2 minutes. Ladle into bowls and serve.

KUBBE SOUP WITH VEAL, CORN, AND ZUCCHINI
Serves 4

KUBBE ARE SEMOLINA DUMPLINGS stuffed with ground meat, then boiled and served in broth. I first had them when my brother, Dave, took me to a little Iraqi soup stall just outside of the Machane Yehuda Market in Jerusalem. Like all dumplings, kubbe are pure comfort food and deeply nourishing. And there is something irresistible about the way the dumplings interact with the broth.

It seems there are as many versions of kubbe as there are Iraqi grandmothers, and disagreements over the authentic recipe have been known to lead to fistfights between their grandsons. To stay out of this debate, I like to make my kubbe as nontraditional as possible. Kubbe are amazingly adaptable to the seasons. In winter, I infuse the broth with red beets and stuff the dumplings with beef (think hot borscht). But in summer, when the local corn tastes like candy, we stuff the kubbe with veal and load the corn cob–fortified broth with corn kernels and tons of zucchini. You could even make French-onion kubbe, with Gruyère-stuffed dumplings floating in caramelized onion broth. The variations are endless. This is a great recipe for the whole family to play around with; kids love to get their hands into the semolina dough.

BROTH

- 2 quarts My Chicken Stock (page 167)
- 2 ears corn, kernels removed and reserved

DOUGH

- 1 cup plus 3 tablespoons finely ground semolina flour
- 1½ teaspoons kosher salt
- ½ teaspoon onion powder
- ½ teaspoon garlic powder
- ½ teaspoon mustard powder

FILLING

- 1 tablespoon olive oil
- 1 small onion, chopped
- 4 garlic cloves, thinly sliced
- ½ pound ground veal
- ¼ cup pine nuts
- 1½ teaspoons kosher salt
- ½ teaspoon sweet paprika
  Pinch ground turmeric
  Pinch grated dried lime (see page 92), optional

SERVING

- 1 small zucchini, halved and sliced into half-moons
  Chopped fresh dill

● **FOR THE CORN-INFUSED BROTH:** Combine the chicken stock and corncobs in a large pot over high heat and bring to a boil. Lower to a simmer and continue simmering until the broth tastes of corn, about 1 hour. Remove and discard the corncobs. Refrigerate until you are ready to serve the soup.

● **FOR THE DOUGH:** Combine the semolina flour with ½ cup hot water, the salt, onion powder, garlic powder, and mustard powder in the bowl of a stand mixer. Mix on medium speed until the mixture forms a ball that pulls away from the side of the bowl, about 2 minutes. Finish kneading the dough on a floured work surface. Wrap tightly with plastic wrap. Let the dough rest in the refrigerator for 30 minutes.

● **FOR THE FILLING:** Heat the oil in a skillet over medium heat and add the onion and garlic. Cook, stirring occasionally, until they have softened but not begun to brown, about 10 minutes. Add the veal and pine nuts and continue cooking, breaking up the meat as you stir, until the veal begins to brown, about 8 minutes more. Add the salt, paprika, turmeric, and dried lime, if you like, and stir to combine.

● **FOR THE KUBBE:** Take a golf ball–size piece of dough and flatten it gently with damp hands into a round about ⅛ inch thick. Place a heaping tablespoon of the filling in the center and gently wrap the dough around the filling, pressing at the seams to seal well. Repeat with the remaining dough and filling. Transfer the kubbe to a plate, cover with plastic wrap, and refrigerate for 30 minutes.

● **TO COOK THE KUBBE:** Bring a large pot of lightly salted water to a boil. Cook the kubbe in the boiling water for 40 minutes. (The kubbe can be cooked up to 3 days in advance—refrigerate in their cooking liquid.)

● To serve, bring the corn broth to a simmer in a large pot. Add the reserved corn kernels, zucchini, and kubbe and cook until the vegetables are tender and the kubbe are warmed through, 10 minutes. Scatter the dill on top.

PINK LENTIL SOUP WITH LAMB KOFTE

Serves 4

ONE AFTERNOON IN THE FALL OF 2005, my business partner, Steve, walked into the kitchen at Marigold, and said, "I think I might have just made a reservation for Craig LaBan." As restaurant critic for the *Philadelphia Inquirer*, Craig was (and still is) the most authoritative voice judging the city's restaurants. And then Steve added, "By the way, the lobster soup on the menu isn't going over very well with our customers." As a first-time executive chef, I was in love with this dish of hot lobster broth poured over chilled coconut panna cotta. To me, it was an ingenious technique that brought these two delicious preparations together tableside. But to our guests, apparently, it was just lukewarm soup.

With my first opportunity to have my cooking professionally reviewed, I scrambled to find a new soup. Searching for inspiration at a local market, I spied a container of pink lentils. Pink lentils have great flavor but lose their shape after cooking—perfect for a pureed soup. They cook quickly and color the soup a beautiful golden orange. I had a whole lamb in the walk-in, so I smoked the neck and added it to the pot to give the soup some depth. Then I ground the shoulder to make lamb-stuffed cabbage dumplings.

As I mixed together the ingredients for the stuffing—ground lamb, grated onion, parsley, and cinnamon—the soup surprised me: It took on an Israeli profile. Following my instincts, I charred the ground lamb kofte in a pan and then wrapped them in cabbage leaves to finish cooking in a low oven. To me, the soup tasted just like an Israeli kebab shop, or as Craig LaBan was to write a few weeks later, "Jerusalem in a bowl."

SOUP

1 tablespoon canola oil
2 cups pink or red lentils, rinsed
1 large carrot, sliced
2 garlic cloves, sliced
1 tablespoon cumin seeds
¾ teaspoon kosher salt
1 cup Caramelized Onions (page 287)
6 cups My Chicken Stock (page 167)
2 smoked turkey wings (optional)

KOFTE

1 pound ground lamb
1 onion, grated
1 cup chopped fresh parsley
1 tablespoon kosher salt
2 teaspoons sugar
2 teaspoons black pepper
½ teaspoon ground cinnamon
2 garlic cloves, minced
⅓ cup club soda

Canola oil, for cooking the kofte
8 large Napa cabbage leaves

● **FOR THE SOUP:** Warm the oil in a large pot over medium heat. Add the lentils, carrot, garlic, cumin seeds, salt, and caramelized onions. Cook, stirring occasionally, until the carrot begins to soften, about 10 minutes. Add the chicken stock and turkey wings, if you like, raise the heat to high, and bring to a simmer. Reduce the heat to low and simmer, covered, until the lentils have fallen apart and the flavors have thoroughly blended, about 1½ hours. Discard the turkey wings if using. Puree the soup in a blender until smooth, adding up to 1 cup water to thin the soup to the desired consistency.

● **FOR THE LAMB KOFTE:** Combine the lamb, onion, parsley, salt, sugar, black pepper, cinnamon, garlic, and club soda in a large bowl. Mix gently by hand until well blended. Cover with plastic wrap, pressing the plastic onto the surface of the mixture, and refrigerate for at least 1 hour or up to overnight.

● Working with damp hands, form the mixture into logs about 1 inch in diameter and 3 inches long. Arrange on a plate, cover with plastic wrap, and refrigerate for 1 hour.

● **TO COOK THE KOFTE:** Heat ¼ inch oil in a large skillet until shimmering but not smoking. Add the kofte and sauté until nicely brown on all sides but still rare in the middle, about 3 minutes total.

● **TO WRAP AND BAKE THE KOFTE:** Preheat the oven to 275°F. Bring a large pot of salted water to a boil. Add the cabbage leaves and cook for 2 minutes,

until softened. Transfer to a large bowl of ice water to chill, remove, and pat dry. Cut away and discard the tough vein at the bottom of each leaf. Wrap each kofte in a cabbage leaf, burrito style, and arrange in a small baking dish.

● Lightly brush the wrapped kofte with oil and bake until the lamb is just cooked through, about 20 minutes.

● To serve, reheat the soup, ladle it into wide, shallow bowls, then slide in the lamb kofte.

FISH KOFTE IN BROTH

Serves 4

KOFTE GENERALLY REFERS TO a highly seasoned ground-meat mixture that is formed on a stick and grilled like a kebab. Most commonly made with lamb or beef, kofte in various forms are a staple throughout the Middle Eastern world, from Turkey to Iran to Southeast Asia and, of course, Israel. In this version, the kofte are made with ground fish mixed with bulgur wheat, which acts as a binder and helps them retain moisture. Poaching the delicate fish balls in a rich, aromatic broth also keeps the fish succulent, and the exchange of flavor between the fish and the broth elevates each component.

I love grouper or striped bass here, but you can use any fish with firm flesh so that the kofte have some texture and the right density. Because the fish is ground, this recipe is great for the thinner fillets near the tail that are difficult to cook without drying out. As with many of the soups in this chapter, the basic elements of this recipe can be easily adapted to whatever is in your refrigerator or in season. In springtime, I like to load up the broth with ramps, fresh favas, and English peas, plus a ton of herbs.

KOFTE

½ cup bulgur wheat

1 tablespoon olive oil

½ cup minced shallots

1 pound raw firm white fish, such as grouper, striped bass, or branzino, coarsely pulsed in a food processor

¼ cup chopped fresh parsley

1 garlic clove, minced

1½ teaspoons kosher salt

1 teaspoon baharat (see page 54)

BROTH

2 quarts Fish Fumet (page 48)

1 cup sliced asparagus (tips left whole)

½ cup shelled fresh fava beans, boiled for 1 minute and peeled

½ cup trimmed and halved green beans
Chopped fresh mint and parsley, for serving
Lemon juice, for serving

● **FOR THE KOFTE:** Put the bulgur in a large bowl and cover with cold water by several inches. Let the bulgur soak until it doubles in size, about 1 hour. Drain well and set aside.

● Warm the oil in a skillet over medium-low heat and add the shallots. Cook, stirring frequently, until they have softened but not browned, about 10 minutes. Transfer the shallots to a large bowl and let cool to room temperature.

● Add the bulgur, ground fish, parsley, garlic, salt, and baharat to the shallots and mix gently by hand until well combined. Cover with plastic wrap, pressing the plastic onto the surface of the mixture, and refrigerate for 1 hour.

● **FOR THE BROTH:** Bring the fumet to a gentle simmer over medium heat in a stockpot. Using two spoons or by hand, form the fish mixture into small football-shaped balls about 2 inches long and drop them into the simmering broth. Add the asparagus, fava beans, and green beans. Cook until the fish is cooked through and the vegetables are just tender, about 8 minutes. Ladle into serving bowls, top with mint, parsley, and a squeeze of lemon juice, and serve.

CHRAIME

Serves 4

CHRAIME IS A NORTH AFRICAN DISH in which fish fillets or steaks are braised in a tomato-and-pepper-based sauce. More soup than stew, it is typically served at the Friday night Shabbat meal, which means the fish needs to be sturdy enough to be cooked in advance and served at room temperature. I like to use whole black grouper because its dense flesh makes it very forgiving if you happen to cook it for a minute or two longer than you intended. Red snapper or any other firm white fish works well, too.

Being Moroccan, this dish is spicy and full flavored, with a big personality. Using both dried and fresh peppers gives the stew a deep flavor that's smoky, fresh, and fruity all at once. It's also a great way to make an impact with a relatively small amount of fish. Just make sure to have plenty of bread around to sop up every last delicious drop of sauce.

> 2 tablespoons olive oil
>
> 1 onion, *diced*
>
> 2 red bell peppers, *diced*
>
> 2 Italian long hot peppers, *diced*
> *(remove the seeds for a less spicy dish)*
>
> ¼ cup ground *Aleppo pepper*
>
> 3 garlic cloves, *sliced*
>
> 1 cup crushed tomatoes

Kosher salt

1   (2-pound) whole red snapper or black grouper

3   parsley sprigs

3   cilantro sprigs plus ¼ cup chopped fresh
    cilantro

● Preheat the oven to 350°F. Warm the oil in a large ovenproof skillet over medium-high heat. Add the onion, red bell peppers, long hot peppers, Aleppo pepper, and garlic. Cook, stirring frequently, until the vegetables have softened and the garlic has become fragrant, about 5 minutes. Add the crushed tomatoes, 1 teaspoon salt, and 2 cups water and bring the mixture to a simmer.

● Season the fish aggressively inside and out with salt and stuff the cavity with the parsley and cilantro sprigs. Put the fish in the skillet, cover tightly with foil, and bake until the fish is cooked through, about 30 minutes.

● Transfer the fish to a large cutting board and pull it into bite-size chunks, discarding the skin and bones. Fold the fish into the sauce, top with the chopped cilantro, and serve.

BELUGA LENTIL SOUP WITH MARROW BONES

Serves 4

LENTILS ARE A STAPLE in the Middle East and one of the healthiest foods you can eat. They take on a deep, earthy flavor that is satisfying in a meaty way. On a cold day, I could eat a gallon of this soup. The rich fragrance of onions cooking with baharat in a pan instantly transports me to Israel. Though it's not traditional, I use beluga lentils because they retain their shape after cooking, which gives the soup texture and a slightly more elegant presentation.

Bone marrow is mild and buttery, and a by-product of this recipe, so I urge you to give it a try. The bones are briefly roasted so that you can easily remove the marrow. Then the bones are returned to the soup to add richness to the broth. The marrow can be spread on toast with a bit of salt or pureed with some of the cooked lentils to give the soup an extra creamy texture.

    4   marrow bones, about 4 inches long
        Kosher salt
    1   tablespoon olive oil
    1   onion, diced
    4   garlic cloves, slivered
    1   carrot, peeled and diced
    1   celery rib, diced
    1   cup tomato puree
    2   tablespoons baharat (see page 54)
    1   tablespoon black pepper
    2   cups dry white wine
    1   cup beluga lentils, rinsed
    1   quart My Chicken Stock (page 167)
    ½   cup chopped fresh cilantro
    ½   cup chopped fresh parsley, plus
        more for serving
    1   rosemary or sage sprig
        Finely grated zest of ½ lemon

● Put the marrow bones in a large pot and cover with cold water. Add several pinches of salt and let soak for 2 hours to remove impurities.

● Preheat the oven to 450°F. Drain the marrow bones, pat dry with paper towels, and set in a rimmed baking pan. Roast until lightly browned, about 20 minutes. Let cool to room temperature and then refrigerate until chilled, at least 4 hours or overnight. Extract the marrow from the bones with the handle of a wooden spoon and store in the refrigerator. Reserve the bones.

● Warm the oil in a large pot over medium-low heat and add the onion, garlic, carrot, celery, and 1 tablespoon salt. Cook, stirring frequently, until the vegetables have softened but not begun to brown, about 15 minutes. Add the tomato puree and cook for 5 more minutes. Add the baharat, black pepper, and wine. Raise the heat to medium-high and cook until the wine has evaporated, about 10 minutes.

● Add the lentils and chicken stock, raise the heat, and bring to a simmer. Use a wooden spoon to scrape up the business on the bottom of the pan. Add the reserved marrow bones, cilantro, parsley, rosemary or sage, and lemon zest. Cover, lower the heat to maintain a gentle simmer, and cook until the lentils are tender, about 45 minutes. Return the marrow to the soup and heat through. Ladle the soup into bowls, scatter chopped parsley on top, and serve.

PUMPKIN BROTH WITH FIDEOS
Serves 4

AFTER LIVING THROUGH DECADES of Northeastern winters, I sometimes feel as though there is nothing but pumpkins at the market. One year I challenged myself to do something different with them and came up with this vegan soup that uses the pumpkin skins as the basis for the broth. Sure, you can use chicken stock instead of water, but it will be cooler if you don't.

The broth gets help from warm spices like cinnamon, ginger, and cloves that give the soup depth, and tomatoes for acidity and richness. I like to add a brûléed onion to the broth. Brûléeing is a French technique that involves searing the cut side of an onion in a smoking-hot skillet until it is nearly black. You would think this would give the soup a burnt flavor, but fortunately it only sets off the smoke alarm in your house—and lends the broth a golden color and a deep, oniony savor.

Fideos are short vermicelli noodles that are popular in Sephardic kitchens and can be traced to the Moorish influence on Spain beginning in the eighth century. I toast the noodles first to add a nutty quality to the broth, and the pasta's starch gives the soup a bit of body. (For Fideos Kugel, see page 288.)

1 onion, halved

2 tablespoons plus 1 teaspoon olive oil

1 red kuri or acorn squash, peeled and cut into 2-inch pieces, skin and seeds reserved

1 cup crushed tomatoes

1 cinnamon stick

1 (2-inch) piece ginger, sliced

4 cloves

2 teaspoons kosher salt

1 cup fideos

2 *cups shredded kale*

½ *cup pearl onions*

● Heat a cast iron pan over high heat until smoking, about 3 minutes. Add the onion halves, cut side down, to the pan and cook undisturbed until the onion has a black layer of char across it, about 5 minutes. Reserve.

● For the broth, warm 1 tablespoon of the oil in a large pot over medium heat. Add the squash skin and seeds and cook, stirring occasionally, until the color darkens and some squash residue begins sticking to the bottom of the pot, about 5 minutes. Add 2 quarts water, the reserved onion, tomatoes, cinnamon, ginger, cloves, and salt. Bring to a simmer and cook for 1 hour. Strain, pressing on the solids to extract as much liquid as possible, and return the broth to the pot.

● Preheat the oven to 400°F. Toss the fideos with 1 teaspoon of the oil and arrange on a baking sheet. Toast in the oven until the fideos have darkened in color and smell a bit nutty, about 4 minutes. (Watch them closely; they go from perfectly toasted to burned quickly.) Set aside.

● Toss the squash with the remaining 1 tablespoon oil, arrange on a baking sheet, and roast until dark brown but not fully cooked, about 15 minutes.

● Return the broth to a simmer and add the kale and pearl onions. Simmer until the vegetables just begin to soften, about 5 minutes. Add the roasted squash and toasted fideos and cook, stirring, until the soup has thickened and the fideos are tender, about 4 more minutes. Serve immediately in bowls.

CELERY ROOT SOUP WITH APPLES AND HAWAIJ

Serves 4

THIS COMBINATION TASTES LIKE FALL, when local apples flood the market and the first frost produces celery root that is super-earthy and mildly sweet. The apples add brightness and acidity, while the hawaij keeps their sweetness in check. When it's pureed, this great vegan soup turns silky and luxurious, stained golden by the turmeric in the hawaij. (Sometimes I serve it with our lamb bacon, as shown, but happily you don't have to!) The soup is best if refrigerated overnight; the flavors will improve.

½ cup olive oil

1 onion, thinly sliced

2 celery ribs, thinly sliced

2 tablespoons hawaij (see page 168)

1 tablespoon kosher salt

2 celery roots, peeled and sliced (about 8 cups)

2 apples, peeled, cored, and sliced

● Warm the oil in a large pot over medium heat. Add the onion, celery, 1 tablespoon of the hawaij, and the salt. Cook, stirring frequently, until the vegetables have softened but not browned, 5 to 8 minutes. Add the celery root, reduce the heat to low, cover, and continue cooking until the celery root is falling apart, about 45 minutes. Add the apples and the remaining 1 tablespoon hawaij and stir to combine. Add 2 quarts water and bring to a simmer. Cook until the apples are tender, about 10 minutes.

● Using an immersion blender or working in batches in a regular blender, puree the soup. Strain. Reheat the soup if necessary, and serve.

GRANDMOTHER'S
BOREKAS

· *Tradition Was My Teacher* ·

MY BULGARIAN grandmother, Savta Mati, didn't speak English and I didn't speak Hebrew or Bulgarian, so borekas formed the bond between us. Before I ever had the slightest interest in food (as an eater, let alone as a cook), these flaky filled pastries occupied a special place in my heart. As a child, I would watch Savta Mati patiently roll out the dough by hand, spreading each layer with margarine

"That bakery was not full of French chefs in starched whites; it was a band of misfits working their asses off for insane hours."

(which is all they used then) before folding and rolling it out again and then repeating. After the dough was rolled out for the third time, she cut it into squares and carefully filled each parcel with potato or cheese. I never had the patience to wait for the borekas to cool once they were out of the oven, so I always burned my mouth.

I was eighteen when I returned to Israel. I had barely finished my freshman year at the University of Vermont, "majoring" in photography while spending most of my time snowboarding or engaged in independent botanical studies. As a sophomore, I had the brilliant idea of going to school part-time so that I would be eligible to move off campus with friends. With no pretense of being a full-time student, things went from bad to worse, and I ended up in the hospital. I was broken. When my parents suggested I move back to Israel, I said yes. I had no other option. When I arrived, things were very different from the good memories I had of my year at boarding school. There were no American teenagers, freed from their parents' grip and ready to party. I was living with my mother in Kfar Saba, a small city north of Tel Aviv. I didn't speak a word of Hebrew. I was an immigrant.

To get out of the apartment, I trudged up and down Weizmann Street every morning, looking for a job that I knew I wouldn't be qualified for. One morning, as I walked past a bakery with display cases piled high with borekas, my footsteps slowed. A year earlier, as the possibility of a college diploma faded away, I had suggested to my father that we open a boreka shop together. "I don't care if you want to be a photographer or open a falafel shop," he told me. "Just stop talking so much shit and do something." I heard my father's voice in my head as I walked into that bakery on Weizmann Street and asked for a job in broken Hebrew. I fully expected to be sent away, but instead, I was told to show up the next day. I don't know what I was expecting when I returned, but if I had known that I would be scrubbing sheet pans for eight hours, I probably wouldn't have gone back. That bakery was not full of French chefs in starched whites making croissants while listening to classical music. It was a band of misfits—Jews and Arabs alike—in torn T-shirts who chased rats around with pizza slicers and worked their asses off in a hot bakery for insanely long hours.

We made borekas in batches so large that it took four of us to lift the block of dough. One baker would run the dough through a series of mechanical rollers, producing sheets that covered a huge prep table. Another baker would follow with a giant

CHALLAH
From late Thursday until sundown on Friday, fresh challah shows up at the Machane Yehuda market in Jerusalem, in time for the Sabbath table.

"Working in that bakery, I thought about my grandmother often. I loved that I was making borekas for a living."

accordion slicer to portion the dough into individual pieces; a third baker followed with a piping bag of whatever filling we were using for that batch. My job was to trail behind the third baker, fold the finished borekas, then load them onto sheet trays and roll rack after rack into giant ovens.

I was the low man on the totem pole. The other bakers called me Shithead or, on good days, Johnny Borekas. *Magashim,* "sheet pan," was one of the first Hebrew words I learned. There was always an endless supply of dirty ones to clean. When the bakery was slow, the owner drove me to his house to do yard work. He spoke in Hebrew about the *mafiya,* bakery, but I heard the Italian word and was convinced he was asking me to do something illegal.

Early on, the other bakers discovered my father was Bulgarian. To them, this meant I had a strong work ethic. For some reason, I didn't want to disappoint them with the truth: my history of quitting when things got too difficult. Maybe I sensed that this was a chance to remake myself into someone I could be proud of. I felt cleansed by the hard, physical work, and I enjoyed the camaraderie among men who shared this secret. On our breaks, we'd sit around eating pastries, drinking sweet coffee, and smoking. This was my first taste of the bond that is formed among cooks. It is the exact feeling I still get after a busy Saturday night service at Zahav—a sense of pride in myself and in the cooks who stand with me shoulder to shoulder. When I look back at my time at the bakery, it's hard not to think about the dishwashers who work in my kitchens today. Most of them have made incredible sacrifices to come to this country and do the jobs that no one else wants to do, all to make a better life for their children. It is the story of America, and it is the story of Israel and of my grandparents, too.

Before World War II, my grandparents were upper-middle-class Bulgarian citizens. Grandmother Mati was a pharmacist, and Grandfather Moni taught music and was first violinist with the Varna Philharmonic. In early 1943, the Bulgarian government agreed to authorize the deportation of Bulgaria's Jews to concentration camps in German-occupied Poland. Through the heroic efforts of Bulgarian politicians and the Bulgarian church, the orders were halted on the eve of the deportation. The trains, which were literally waiting in the station, left Bulgaria empty, sparing the lives of more than 48,000 Jews, including my grandparents.

In order to pacify the Germans, the Bulgarians removed their Jewish male citizens to labor camps to wait out the war. Women and children were sent from the cities to stay out of sight. My grandfather was too young for the camps, but he went anyway. Often, he would escape to the countryside to visit his girlfriend (my grandmother) and then sneak back into the camp. Looking at pictures, it's difficult to tell which were the laborers and which were the guards. After the war, nearly all of Bulgaria's Jews were swept up in a wave of Zionism and emigrated to Israel. In Varna, the departing Jews were escorted to the harbor by their fellow citizens. Together they sang the Bulgarian national anthem and cried their farewells.

BOREKAS
Before my grandparents and other Eastern Europeans arrived in the mid-1940s, borekas were not known in Israel. Now they're sold everywhere.

My father was two years old in 1948, when his parents made the journey from Bulgaria to Israel. Small and fragile as a baby, as their ship arrived in the Jaffa harbor, he was fighting such a dangerously high fever that my grandparents feared he wouldn't make it. As soon as the boat reached port, he was whisked away for medical treatment. All my grandparents knew was that he was in a hospital in Haifa, 100 miles away. They spoke no Hebrew and no English. They had no money; no idea what to do. My grandfather borrowed the equivalent of two dollars for bus fare and went to Haifa, walking from hospital to hospital looking for his son. He was leaving the children's ward at one hospital when he heard the faint word *tatka*, "father" in Bulgarian, from across the room. My two-year-old dad had recognized his father.

My grandparents settled in an agricultural community, a moshav, called Tzur Moshe, near Netanya. The moshav was founded in 1937 by twenty Greek immigrants and was now home to several hundred Greeks, Turks, and Bulgarians. My grandmother was a licensed pharmacist, but since she didn't speak Hebrew, she couldn't practice yet. Until she got her license, she earned a living raising chickens and picking tomatoes. My grandfather was an accomplished musician, but a Bulgarian immigrant didn't stand a chance with the Israel Philharmonic. He found work as a carpenter in an orange-packing plant and pulled overnight shifts as a security guard at the moshav. Life was difficult for my grandparents during their early years in Israel, especially for my grandfather, who had been used to a European way of life. His hands would swell up so severely from building orange crates that he could barely make a fist, let alone play the violin. My dad says it drove my grandfather crazy, and he died when I was six. The only real memory I have is a picture: He's playing the violin; I'm eating French toast.

After a few years on the moshav, my grandparents, my father, and my aunt moved into a two-room house in Lod, near Tel Aviv, with my great-grandparents and great-great-grandmother. Israel was poor in those days, and food rationing was a fact

SWEETEST SOUND
The only real memory I have of my Bulgarian grandfather, Moni, is this picture. He's playing the violin, I'm eating French toast.

of life in the years between 1949 and 1959. As a boy, my father thought a sandwich was bread dipped in oil and seasoned with salt and paprika. There were no ovens. Cooking was done on paraffin burners or over wood fires. My great-grandmother made her own pasta, spreading huge sheets of dough on the bed, then cutting it into noodles that would dry all over the house. My great-grandfather made homemade pickles and wine from his own vines, brining and stuffing the grape leaves. Meat was scarce. My great-great-aunt's husband worked at the local kosher slaughterhouse. Every Friday, the workers would get a package of meat to take home for Shabbat. Often it was beef liver, which my great-grandmother would use to make red soup. My great-grandparents raised their own chickens, but the family only ate those that died, since they couldn't be sold. The same was true for broken eggs.

Fruit was rare. A bucket of guavas could be sold on the streets of Tel Aviv for more than a week's wages. My father remembers Friday afternoons at his grandparents' house in Lod as the family (and the whole country) put down their tools and welcomed Shabbat. My great-grandmother would serve him black coffee and watered-down arak, the anise-flavored alcoholic drink, with mezze like hard-boiled eggs, Bulgarian cheese, pickles, and homemade caviar—Tarama (page 216).

Around the time of my father's bar mitzvah, his parents moved to their own home in Lod. Some of my most vivid childhood memories include visits to their tiny apartment where, in the late afternoons, you could smell kitchens coming alive all over the crowded building. The perfume of tomatoes, garlic, and paprika cooking together poured from every window; this smell will forever remind me of my Savta Mati.

Years later, when I was working in that bakery, I thought about my grandmother often. I loved that I was making borekas for a living, proud to be part of a tradition that she had brought with her from Bulgaria. And I loved working in a place that was so much a part of daily life in Israel. On Friday mornings, we would arrive at 2 a.m. to start baking, mixing giant batches of challah dough that we'd braid into loaves that would soon grace Shabbat tables in every home in the village. When I came back to Israel, I had nothing. But when I left the bakery a year later, I felt that I had a home.

BOREKAS

"Back when real ovens were too expensive for most Israeli homes, my grandmother would bake her borekas in a toaster oven."

BOREKAS ARE EVERYWHERE IN ISRAEL, from coffee shops to gas stations, which is cool because they didn't even exist before the major Bulgarian immigration in the late 1940s—another example of cuisine developing in real time. Borekas make a great portable meal, and if you want to be really Israeli, try eating one while driving, smoking a cigarette, and talking on the phone.

Borekas can be filled with almost anything you can think of, although cheese and potatoes are probably the most popular fillings. You can almost always tell what's inside a boreka by the shape and the garnish on the top—triangles with sesame seeds for potatoes; rectangles with poppy and sesame seeds for Bulgarian cheese; half circles with poppy seeds for mushrooms. Borekas are best still warm from the oven. For a ridiculous sandwich, they can be cut in half and stuffed with sliced hard-boiled egg, tomatoes, and schug,

the spicy Yemenite condiment. When we served them at Zahav, I always had to make extra since I can't not eat a boreka whenever I see one. I took them off the menu when my Savta Mati died in 2006. Somehow it felt sacrilegious to me to see sheet trays of borekas loaded into commercial ovens. Back when real ovens were too expensive for most Israeli households, my grandmother used to bake hers in a toaster oven.

Borekas are made with a laminated dough, similar to puff pastry, which does take a little time to make. My grandmother actually referred to this as Spanish dough, which is interesting in that it traces her roots from pre-Inquisition Spain to Bulgaria and finally to Israel. Softened butter (or, more traditionally for those times, margarine) is spread on rolled-out sheets of dough, which are then folded, rolled out again, and spread with more butter. The dough is folded and rolled out one last time and cut into squares or circles to be filled and baked. When the butter hits the heat of the oven, steam expands to create the layers that give the dough its trademark flakiness. It's a dough that takes a little practice and some confidence to get right. My Aunt Erna (my grandmother's sister) says that before you start adding the butter, the dough should feel like a woman's breast. I recommend you try making boreka dough at least once, but you can certainly substitute store-bought puff pastry if you're short on time.

BOREKA DOUGH

Makes 3 pastry sheets (roughly 10 by 15 inches each); 1 sheet makes about 8 borekas

> 6½ cups all-purpose flour
> 2 tablespoons kosher salt
> ¼ cup white vinegar
> 2⅓ cups seltzer water
> 3¾ sticks (15 ounces) butter, softened

● Combine the flour, salt, and vinegar in the bowl of a stand mixer fitted with the paddle attachment. Mix on low while adding the seltzer in a slow, steady stream. Continue mixing until the dough begins to pull away from the sides and bottom of the mixer, about 2 minutes.

● Flour a work surface and knead the dough by hand just until it feels smooth and homogenous, about a minute. Cover with a clean cotton cloth and let rest for 30 minutes.

● Working with a floured rolling pin, roll the dough out to a rough ¼-inch-thick rectangle with a long side facing you. (It should be at least 20 by 15 inches.) Spread half the butter evenly across the middle third of the dough rectangle. Fold the left third of the dough over the butter, then fold the right third over the left third (they'll overlap). Fold the top and bottom edges toward the center the same way, forming a square. Wrap tightly with plastic wrap and refrigerate overnight.

● Flour a work surface. Orient the dough square so that it's turned 90 degrees from the first time you folded it (that is, with the folded ends on the sides). Roll the chilled dough out to a ¼-inch-thick rectangle (again, about 20 by 15 inches). Spread the rest of the butter evenly across the middle third of the rectangle. Fold the sides over the butter, and fold the top and bottom toward the center, forming a square. Wrap tightly with plastic wrap and refrigerate overnight.

● Flour a work surface. Orient the dough square so that it's turned 90 degrees from the last fold and roll the chilled dough out to a ¼-inch-thick rectangle. Repeat the folding process, folding the sides into the center and then folding the top and bottom toward the center to make a square. (This time, don't add more butter.) Wrap tightly with plastic wrap and refrigerate overnight.

● The next day, divide the dough into 3 pieces and freeze for later use; or, roll each piece into a 10-by-15-inch sheet to use in recipes. Make sure to keep the dough cold at all times (except when you're working with it).

● Filled borekas can be frozen before baking. In that case, put them directly in a preheated 425°F oven; don't thaw them first.

● Don't refrigerate baked borekas. They'll keep at room temperature for 2 days. Reheat in a 325°F oven for 5 minutes.

MUSHROOM BOREKAS

Makes 8 borekas

> 1 tablespoon olive oil
> ½ pound mushrooms, chopped (about 2 cups)
> ¼ cup chopped onion
> 2 garlic cloves, minced
> ½ teaspoon kosher salt
> 2 large eggs
> 1 sheet Boreka Dough (page 201) or store-bought puff pastry
> 2 tablespoons poppy seeds

● Warm the oil in a large skillet over medium heat and add the mushrooms, onion, garlic, and salt. Cook, stirring, until the mushrooms and onion are tender and beginning to brown. Transfer to a large mixing bowl and cool. Beat one of the eggs and stir into the mushrooms. Refrigerate until cold.

● Place the cold sheet of dough on a floured work surface. Cut out 8 circles, 4 inches in diameter. (If the dough shrinks after you've cut out the circles, roll them out again briefly before filling.)

● Spoon about 2 tablespoons of the mushroom filling on one half of a circle, leaving a ¼-inch border at the edge. Fold the dough over into a half-moon shape and press at the edges to seal. Repeat until all the borekas are formed. Arrange on a parchment-lined baking sheet and refrigerate for an hour, until very well chilled; they should be cold and firm to the touch.

● Preheat the oven to 425°F, with a rack in the upper third. Beat the remaining egg and brush the tops of the borekas, then sprinkle with the poppy seeds. Bake until the dough is golden brown, about 15 minutes.

● Covered, at room temperature, borekas will keep for 2 days. Don't refrigerate them. They'll reheat quickly and well in a 325°F oven for 5 minutes.

● Filled borekas can be frozen before baking. In that case, put them directly in a preheated 425°F oven; don't thaw them first.

POTATO AND KALE BOREKAS
Makes 8 borekas

2 Yukon Gold potatoes, peeled and diced
  Kosher salt
1 tablespoon olive oil
½ bunch kale, shredded (about 2 cups)
2 large eggs
1 sheet Boreka Dough (page 201) or
  store-bought puff pastry
2 tablespoons sesame seeds

● Put the potatoes in a pot with 1 teaspoon salt and cover with cold water. Bring to a boil over high heat and cook until the potatoes are fork-tender, about 10 minutes. Drain and mash.

● Warm the oil in a large skillet over medium heat. Add the kale and cook, stirring, until wilted and tender, about 5 minutes. Combine the mashed potatoes and the kale in a mixing bowl and stir to combine. Add salt. Refrigerate until cold. Beat one of the eggs and mix into the potato-kale mixture.

● Spread the cold sheet of boreka dough on a floured work surface. Cut the dough into 8 (4-inch) squares. Spoon about 2 heaping tablespoons of the potato-kale filling onto one half of a square, leaving about a ½-inch border at the edge. Fold the dough over into a triangle and press at the edges to seal. Repeat until all the borekas are formed. Arrange on a parchment-lined baking sheet and refrigerate for an hour; they should be cold and firm to the touch.

● Preheat the oven to 425°F, with a rack in the upper third. Beat the remaining egg and brush the tops of the borekas, then sprinkle with the sesame seeds. Bake until the dough is golden brown, about 15 minutes.

● Covered, at room temperature, borekas will keep for 2 days. Don't refrigerate them. They'll reheat quickly and well in a 325°F oven for 5 minutes.

● Filled borekas can be frozen before baking. In that case, put them directly in a preheated 425°F oven; don't thaw them first.

FETA BOREKAS

Makes 8 borekas

>   2   large eggs
> 2 ½   cups crumbled feta
>   1   sheet Boreka Dough (page 201) or
>   store-bought puff pastry
>   2   tablespoons poppy seeds
>   2   tablespoons sesame seeds

● In a mixing bowl, beat one of the eggs and add the feta. Stir well to combine.

● Place the cold sheet of boreka dough on a floured work surface. Cut the dough into 8 (4-inch) squares. Spoon about 2 heaping tablespoons of the feta filling onto one half of a square, leaving about an ½-inch border at the edge. Fold the dough over into a rectangle and press at the edges to seal. Repeat until all the borekas are formed. Arrange on a parchment-lined baking sheet and refrigerate for an hour; they should be cold and firm to the touch.

● Preheat the oven to 425°F, with a rack in the upper third. Beat the remaining egg and brush the tops of the borekas, then sprinkle with the poppy and sesame seeds. Bake until the dough is golden brown, about 15 minutes.

● Covered, at room temperature, borekas will keep for 2 days. Don't refrigerate them. They'll reheat quickly and well in a 325°F oven for 5 minutes.

● Filled borekas can be frozen before baking. In that case, put them directly in a preheated 425°F oven; don't thaw them first.

BOREKA SHAPES
You can almost always tell what's inside a boreka by its shape: triangles with sesame seeds for potatoes, rectangles with poppy and sesame seeds for Bulgarian cheese, half moons with poppy seeds for mushrooms.

FETA BOREKAS

POTATO AND KALE BOREKAS   MUSHROOM BOREKAS

CHALLAH

Makes 1 loaf

IN THE WORLD OF BREAD BAKING, this traditional braided Sabbath bread is extraordinary in its ratio of satisfaction to the amount of effort required to make it. This recipe is so fast and easy and the results are so delicious that it should be a sin *not* to make it. Challah makes a beautiful braided loaf that's fun to rip apart at the table; baked in a loaf pan and sliced, it becomes the backbone of our Smoked Sable Egg-in-the-Hole (page 136). Enriched with eggs and oil, challah stays fresh for a long time. There is nothing better the next day than challah slathered with butter and salt. Except, perhaps, a leftover brisket sandwich on challah with fresh horseradish. When it eventually does go stale, challah makes insane French toast and fantastic bread crumbs.

  1 tablespoon active dry yeast

  4 cups bread flour

  7 large egg yolks

  ¼ cup sugar

  1 teaspoon kosher salt

  6 tablespoons canola oil

  1 large egg, beaten

  2 tablespoons sesame seeds

  1 tablespoon poppy seeds

● Mix the yeast with 1 cup warm water in a small bowl and let stand for 5 minutes, until foamy.

● Combine the bread flour, egg yolks, sugar, salt, and oil in the bowl of a stand mixer. Add the yeast mixture and knead with the hook attachment until the dough comes together and pulls away from the sides of the bowl, about 2 minutes. Cover with a towel and let rise until doubled in volume, 1 to 1½ hours, depending on the warmth of the kitchen.

● Punch the dough down and then divide it into 3 equal pieces. On a lightly floured surface, roll each piece into a rope about 18 inches long. Braid the ropes to form a loaf, place on a parchment-lined baking sheet, and cover with a towel. Let rise again until doubled in volume, about 30 minutes.

● Meanwhile, preheat the oven 350°F. Brush the loaf with the beaten egg and sprinkle with the sesame seeds. Bake until golden brown, 20 to 25 minutes. Let cool completely before slicing and serving. Keep at room temperature in a zip-top bag.

"Shabbat is the most important holiday in Judaism, yet it happens every week. So does challah. And it's surprisingly easy to master."

LAFFA AND PITA IN THE HOME OVEN
Makes 8 breads

LAFFA IS AN IRAQI-STYLE flatbread—a little bigger than pita (and minus the pocket) and crispier too, but still with a great chew. Laffa is traditionally cooked in a taboon, a clay oven with an opening at the top and a fire in the bottom, very similar to a tandoor. Flattened rounds of dough are loaded onto a pillow with a handle on one side. The baker presses the dough against the inside wall of the taboon. If he has any hair left on his arms, he's doing it wrong. The bread is done just before it releases from the wall of the taboon and incinerates in the 800-degree fire below.

I knew it would be tough to incorporate an authentic taboon into a commercial restaurant in Philadelphia, but when I discovered the hand-built brick pizza oven in a vacant Italian restaurant, I knew I was standing in the future Zahav. Traditional taboons are sometimes fueled with dried animal dung, but at Zahav we use recycled, compressed hardwood—it burns super-hot and clean, and it's environmentally friendly to boot.

By now, you're probably saying to yourself, "This is all lovely, Mike, but what I really want to know is, can I do this at home, without a taboon or a wood-burning oven?" Yes! Yes, you can. Both laffa and pita are remarkably easy to make from the same dough and bake in your own oven. A pizza stone works well, but even a baking sheet turned upside down and preheated in a hot oven will produce beautiful laffa and pita that forms its own pocket.

2½	teaspoons active dry yeast
2	teaspoons sugar
2	cups all-purpose flour
2	cups bread flour
1½	teaspoons kosher salt
2	tablespoons olive oil

● Mix together ½ cup water, the yeast, and sugar in a small bowl and let stand until foamy, about 5 minutes.

● Combine the all-purpose flour, bread flour, and salt in the bowl of a stand mixer fitted with the dough hook. Mix on low speed until blended. Add the yeast mixture, another ½ cup water, and the oil and mix on low until the dough forms a ball that pulls clear of the sides and bottom of the bowl. (If after a minute the mixture doesn't form a ball, add a tablespoon of water.) The moment the dough starts to pull clear of the bottom of the bowl, add ½ cup water and continue mixing until incorporated. The dough should feel tacky when slapped with a clean hand, but it should not stick. (If it sticks, add more flour, a tablespoon at a time.)

● Cover the dough with plastic wrap and let rise at room temperature until doubled in size, about an hour. Alternatively, let it rise in the refrigerator overnight.

● Preheat the oven to 500°F, with a rack in the upper third. Place a baking stone or an inverted baking sheet in the oven to preheat as well.

● Roll the dough into 8 balls the size of baseballs. Cover with a cloth and let rise until they are about the size of softballs.

● **FOR LAFFA:** Roll each dough ball as thin as possible (less than ⅛ inch is ideal—the laffa should be the size of a Frisbee) with a floured rolling pin on a floured work surface. Drape one laffa over your outstretched hand and quickly invert it onto the baking stone or baking sheet, quickly pulling any wrinkles flat. Bake the laffa until puffy and cooked through, about 1 minute. Serve immediately.

● **FOR PITA:** Roll each dough ball to about a ¼-inch thickness (about the size of a hockey puck) with a floured rolling pin on a floured work surface. Place one or two at a time on the baking stone or baking sheet and bake until puffed and cooked through, about 3 minutes. Serve immediately, or let cool.

RISE
Wait for the dough to double in volume.

PULL
Moisten hands and always keep a bowl of water nearby.

PINCH
After first rise, pinch at bottom so dough will rise again in a ball.

FLATTEN
Use your hands to gently flatten the dough into a soft, even shape.

LAFFA AND PITA
Both breads are made from the same dough and are baked on the back of a baking sheet in the home oven, *left*. Laffa, *far left*, puffs nicely, then gets a pour of olive oil and a sprinkling of za'atar. Disks of pita dough inflate beautifully, *above*.

SALT COD "TARAMA"
Serves 4

MY GRANDFATHER CURED his own tarama, the roe of cod, carp, or mullet, turning what was a cheap by-product into a delicacy. The dish has Ottoman origins, and is most common in Greek cuisine (taramasalata), although it is popular, too, in Romania and Bulgaria. Nowadays, you can find it in supermarkets throughout Israel (mostly labeled with the Romanian word *ikra*). The last time I visited, I was served tarama as one of the salatim at a Bulgarian restaurant in Jaffa. I find the briny fish eggs are delicious, but they're not for everyone, so I use salt cod to create this version. Salt cod is an excellent product, but it must be soaked overnight to leach out the excess salt. So plan ahead.

4	*ounces dried salt cod*
1½	*cups whole milk*
½	*teaspoon black peppercorns*
¼	*cup sour cream*
2	*tablespoons lemon juice*
¼	*small red onion, sliced into thin rings*
2	*tablespoons minced fresh chives*
1	*tablespoon olive oil*

● Place the dried cod in a large bowl filled with cold water. Soak in the refrigerator for 8 hours, changing the water twice. Drain.

● Preheat the oven to 300°F. Combine the soaked cod, milk, and peppercorns in a small ovenproof pot (the cod should be submerged). Bake until the cod is falling apart, 2 to 3 hours. Drain. Break the cod into shreds.

● Combine the cod, sour cream, and lemon juice in a bowl and stir. Spoon onto a platter, top with the red onion, chives, and oil, and serve.

TARATOR (CUCUMBER-YOGURT SOUP)

Serves 2 to 4

I'M NOT REALLY A YOGURT GUY, but I've grown to appreciate this incredibly refreshing soup, wonderful in summer because it's served cold and requires no cooking. You can throw it together in a couple of minutes: cucumber and onions mixed with thick yogurt, walnuts, lemon juice, and tons of olive oil and herbs. Traditionally, tarator is served in Turkey and across the Balkans, but with a minor tweak to its consistency (less yogurt and lemon juice), it's a great spread for breads or a dip for anything crispy, like fried potatoes. A little dollop on a raw oyster would be out of control and on fish, well, see Walnut Tarator (page 48).

- 2 cups Greek yogurt
- 2 tablespoons lemon juice
- 4 Persian or Kirby cucumbers, chopped (about 2 cups)
- ½ cup chopped toasted walnuts, plus more for serving
- ¼ red onion, minced
- 2 tablespoons chopped fresh mint
- 2 tablespoons chopped fresh parsley
- 2 tablespoons chopped fresh dill, plus more for serving
- ½ teaspoon kosher salt
  Pinch black pepper
  Pinch mace
  Olive oil, for serving

● Combine the yogurt, lemon juice, 1 cup of the cucumbers, the walnuts, onion, mint, parsley, dill, salt, pepper, and mace in a large bowl and stir well to blend. Ladle into serving bowls and top with the remaining 1 cup cucumbers, plus additional dill and toasted walnuts. Drizzle with oil and serve.

PASTEL

Makes one 9-by-11-inch casserole, serves 12

THIS MEAT PIE WAS MY BROTHER DAVE'S favorite
thing to eat, and my grandmother stopped making it
entirely after he died. When we took the Zahav staff
to Israel in 2008, just before Zahav opened, she made
pastel for the first time in five years for us to try. If
you're investing time in making boreka dough, be
sure to save some for this simple but super-satisfying
meat pie. Because I can't bring myself to make boreka
dough with margarine (as my grandmother did)
instead of butter, this is the only explicitly nonkosher
dish in the book. I don't think Savta Mati would mind.

3 *large eggs*
   Seasoned Ground Beef (recipe follows)
1 *sheet Boreka Dough (page 201) or*
   2 sheets store-bought puff pastry
2 *tablespoons chopped fresh parsley*

2 *tablespoons chopped fresh dill*
2 *tablespoons sesame seeds*

● Beat 2 of the eggs in a large bowl, add the seasoned
beef, and mix to blend. Set aside.

● Divide the boreka dough into 2 pieces. With a
floured rolling pin, roll each piece into a sheet roughly
larger than 9 by 11 inches.

● Press one of the dough sheets onto the bottom and
up the sides of a 9-by-11-inch baking dish. Spoon the
beef-egg mixture into the dish and sprinkle with the
parsley and dill. Lay the remaining sheet of dough on
top, pressing lightly to seal the edges. Transfer the
pie to the refrigerator for an hour or the freezer for
15 minutes to chill well before baking; the dough
should be firm and cold to the touch.

SEASONED GROUND BEEF

Makes 5 cups

THIS DELICIOUS BEEF MIXTURE is used in Pastel (opposite), Moussaka (page 222), and Stuffed Peppers (page 220).

> 2 tablespoons olive oil
> 2 onions, chopped (about 2 cups)
> 2 carrots, peeled and chopped
> 2 pounds ground beef
> 1½ teaspoons ground cinnamon
> 1 tablespoon kosher salt
> ½ teaspoon black pepper

● Warm the oil in a large skillet over medium heat. Add the onions and carrots and cook, stirring occasionally, until the vegetables have softened but not begun to brown, about 10 minutes. Add the beef, cinnamon, salt, and pepper, stirring to incorporate the beef, and continue cooking until the beef is cooked through and begins to brown, another 15 minutes.

● Preheat the oven to 400°F. Beat the remaining egg and brush the top of the dough, then sprinkle with the sesame seeds. Bake until the top is golden brown, about 40 minutes. Let cool for 15 to 20 minutes, then cut into pieces and serve.

David with our Savta Mati, in 2002.

STUFFED PEPPERS
Serves 6

THIS IS THE FIRST MEAL I CRAVE when I get off the plane in Israel. Thankfully, my mother usually indulges me. I begin salivating just thinking about it on the short ride from the airport to her apartment in Kfar Saba. Bell peppers are an underrated vegetable—they're sweet but with a unique vegetal quality that makes them super-savory—especially the green ones. And I love the way that the rice soaks up all the juices from the meat. This recipe couldn't be simpler. Like Moussaka (page 222), it relies on Seasoned Ground Beef and Basic Tomato Sauce coming together quickly for a delicious one-dish meal. Bulgarians haven't met a vegetable they didn't try to stuff, so this basic approach works with many other vegetables, from eggplants to tomatoes to zucchini. And you can vary the fillings depending upon what's in your refrigerator. Cubed or grated cheese makes a great addition to, or substitution for, the ground beef.

> 1½ cups jasmine rice
>
> 2 cups Seasoned Ground Beef (page 219)
>
> 1 large egg
>
> 1½ cups Basic Tomato Sauce (page 222)
>
> 6 red or green bell peppers, top third, ribs, and seeds removed
>
> 2 tablespoons olive oil
>
> ¼ cup chopped fresh parsley

● Cover the rice with water by several inches and let stand for at least 1 hour or up to overnight. Drain.

● Preheat the oven to 375°F. Bring a large pot of salted water to a boil and add the rice. Boil until the rice is about three-quarters cooked, just until it is no longer crunchy but still sticks to your tooth when you bite a grain. (Start checking after 1 minute, but it could take up to 10.) Drain and transfer to a large bowl. Let cool. Add the seasoned ground beef and egg and mix well.

● Oil a medium baking dish and spread ½ cup of the tomato sauce evenly over the bottom. Divide the meat and rice mixture evenly among the peppers, leaving about ½ inch of room at the top. Set the prepared bell peppers in the dish. Top each pepper with a spoonful of the remaining tomato sauce and drizzle with the oil. Add ½ cup water to the baking dish and cover tightly with foil. Bake until the peppers are tender, about 1 hour and 15 minutes. Sprinkle with the parsley and serve.

TOMATOES STUFFED WITH DIRTY RICE

Serves 4

YOU MIGHT WONDER HOW A DISH of Cajun rice found its way into my grandmother's Israeli kitchen. Truth is, she would stuff a tomato with almost anything, and I just know she would have loved this "dirty rice" with chicken livers.

> 1 *cup jasmine rice*
> *Kosher salt*
> 4 *tablespoons schmaltz (see page 167) or olive oil*
> ¼ *onion, chopped*
> 1 *garlic clove, sliced*
> 1 *large chicken liver, minced*
> ½ *teaspoon sesame seeds*
> *Pinch ground cinnamon*
> *Pinch cayenne*
> *Pinch crushed dried rose petals (see Resources, page 359), optional*
> 1 *cup My Chicken Stock (page 167)*
> 1 *large egg, beaten*
> 4 *firm beefsteak tomatoes*

● Cover the rice with water by several inches and add a pinch of salt. Let soak for at least 60 minutes or up to overnight. Drain well.

● Preheat the oven to 350°F. Warm 2 tablespoons of the schmaltz or oil in a large ovenproof pot with a tight-fitting lid over medium heat. Add the onion, garlic, and chicken liver. Season with ¾ teaspoon salt and cook, stirring constantly with a wooden spoon to mash the liver into mere specks, until the vegetables begin to soften but not brown, about 8 minutes. Add the rice and cook, stirring, until it is evenly coated and begins to lightly toast, about 3 more minutes. Add the sesame seeds, cinnamon, cayenne, and dried rose petals, if you like. Stir to combine.

● Add the chicken stock, raise the heat to high, and bring to a simmer. Stir with a fork once or twice, cover, and transfer to the oven. Bake until the rice is cooked through, about 20 minutes. Let stand, covered, off the heat for 10 minutes before fluffing with a fork. Let cool completely, and then fold in the egg.

● Increase the oven temperature to 375°F. Meanwhile, oil a small baking dish. Cut the tops off the tomatoes and remove the seeds and flesh with a small spoon. Coat the tomatoes, inside and out, with the remaining 2 tablespoons schmaltz or oil. Salt the tomato cavities well. Spoon one quarter of the dirty rice into each tomato. Transfer to the prepared baking dish and cover tightly with foil. Bake until the tomatoes are a bit wrinkly and the stuffing feels firm, about 45 minutes. Serve hot or at room temperature.

MOUSSAKA

Makes 1 medium casserole, serves 8

COMPARED TO OTHER European Jewish communities, Bulgarians were relatively integrated into secular society. As a result, my grandparents had a pretty loose relationship with kosher laws. Mati's moussaka was a delicious casserole of eggplant, beef, and potato, bound together with a creamy béchamel sauce. I simplify it here (to avoid cooking milk and meat together), making eggplant the star. It's a kind of eggplant pie with a filling of seasoned ground beef and tomato sauce. But by all means, feel free to improvise with cheese, béchamel, or anything else that sounds good.

1　medium eggplant (about 1¼ pounds), sliced ¼ inch thick on a mandoline or with a sharp knife

¼　cup olive oil, plus more for the baking dish
　　Kosher salt

2　cups Seasoned Ground Beef (page 219)

¼　cup chopped fresh parsley

1　cup Basic Tomato Sauce (recipe follows)

● Preheat the oven to 400°F. Line a baking sheet with parchment paper. Brush each side of the eggplant slices with the oil, arrange on the prepared baking sheet, and season with ¾ teaspoon salt. Bake until the eggplant softens, about 5 minutes. Lower the oven temperature to 350°F.

● Brush the bottom of a baking dish with olive oil and line it with the eggplant slices, leaving plenty to overhang the sides. Mix the parsley with the ground beef, spoon over the eggplant. Top with the tomato sauce. Fold the overhanging eggplant over the filling; top with additional eggplant slices to cover completely. Drizzle the top with more oil. Bake until the top begins to brown in spots, about 30 minutes. Let the moussaka rest at room temperature for 30 minutes before serving. Or cool completely and reheat to serve.

BASIC TOMATO SAUCE

Makes 4 cups

5　tablespoons olive oil

1　cup diced onion

2　garlic cloves, minced

3　cups tomato puree

2　tablespoons ground coriander

1½　teaspoons kosher salt

● Warm 2 tablespoons of the oil in a pot over medium heat. Add the onion and garlic and cook until the vegetables have softened but not browned, about 8 minutes. Add the tomatoes, coriander, salt, and 1 cup water and cook until the sauce has thickened and concentrated, 15 to 20 minutes. Off the heat, whisk in the remaining 3 tablespoons oil. The sauce will keep for a week in the refrigerator; 3 months frozen.

CHICKEN ALBONDIGAS

Makes about 24 meatballs

YOU'LL FIND VERSIONS OF THIS DISH on many Spanish tapas menus, but these little meatballs traveled all the way to Bulgaria from Spain many generations ago with my grandmother's family. Chicken makes great meatballs—it's lighter than beef, and its high protein content gives the albondigas a slightly dense texture. The addition of almonds, cinnamon, and smoked paprika helps turn the meatballs from something relatively mundane into something exotic. My grandmother sometimes added the little chicken balls to her soup. Here I stew them in Basic Tomato Sauce. They are perfect over rice.

¼   *cup olive oil, plus more for frying*

2   *onions, chopped*

2   *celery ribs, finely chopped*

5   *garlic cloves, minced*

2   *pounds ground chicken*

1   *cup sliced almonds, plus more for serving*

2   *tablespoons smoked paprika*

1   *teaspoon ground cinnamon*

1   *tablespoon kosher salt*

1½ *cups Basic Tomato Sauce (page 222)*
    Cooked rice, for serving

● Warm the oil in a large skillet over medium heat and add the onions, celery, and garlic. Cook, stirring, until the vegetables have softened but not browned, about 8 minutes. Let cool.

● In a large bowl, combine the cooled onion mixture with the chicken, almonds, paprika, cinnamon, and salt. Mix well with clean hands and shape into golf ball–size balls.

● Film the bottom of a large skillet with oil and heat over medium-high heat until shimmering but not smoking. Working in batches to avoid crowding, add the meatballs in a single layer and let cook undisturbed until they've browned on the bottom and can be easily turned, 3 to 5 minutes. Continue cooking until they are browned on all sides, about 8 minutes total.

● Return all the albondigas to the pot, add the tomato sauce, and stir gently to coat. Continue cooking just until the tomato sauce is hot and the meatballs are cooked through, about 5 more minutes. Serve over rice, topped with additional sliced almonds.

AGRISTADA (EGG-LEMON SAUCE)
Makes 1¾ cups

THE FIRST TIME MY MOTHER met her future in-laws was at a dinner in Savta Mati's apartment in Lod, near Tel Aviv. Everyone was terrifically nervous (except for my grandfather—he thought the whole thing was hysterical). My mother, who spoke very little Hebrew at the time, could not figure out what the breaded piece of meat on her plate was. "*Moach*," whispered my father under his breath, as my grandfather tried to contain his laughter. "What's moach?" asked my mother through her teeth as she chewed on this surprisingly soft and tender mystery meat. "Brains," said my father. My mother turned white. When she went to work the next day, one of her coworkers (who also happened to be married to a Bulgarian) asked her how the brains were.

PHARMACIST
It took fifteen years, but by the 1960s, my Savta Mati learned enough Hebrew to secure her pharmacist's credentials and practice once again. My grandfather earned a teaching certificate.

It turns out that being served brains in a Bulgarian home is quite an honor, albeit a dubious one. We serve some weird stuff at Zahav, but not brains. Although delicious, they are extremely perishable and there's no euphemistic name for them, like sweetbreads. However, the sauce, agristada, that was traditionally served with brains is absolutely delicious and worth repurposing for less, um, cerebral dishes.

Related to, and possibly the origin of, the famous Greek sauce and soup avgolemono, agristada is a sauce of eggs and lemon that is thickened with flour. Agristada provides another interesting look at the influence of kosher laws on the Jewish kitchen. Sephardic Jews used this sauce in place of dairy-based sauces to accompany meat dishes. I serve it as a sauce for three other Sephardic-influenced dishes: Fried Artichokes (page 229), Fried Leek Patties (page 228), and Fried Kashkaval Cheese (opposite).

> 2 large eggs
> 2 tablespoons all-purpose flour
> 1 tablespoon finely grated lemon zest
> 2 tablespoons lemon juice
> ¼ cup olive oil
> 2 tablespoons chopped fresh parsley
>   Kosher salt and black pepper

● Bring a couple inches of water to a simmer in a medium saucepan over medium-low heat.

● Combine the eggs, flour, lemon zest, and lemon juice in a heat-resistant bowl that will fit on top of the saucepan and whisk well until smooth. Set the bowl over the simmering water and add 1 cup water in a slow, steady stream, whisking constantly. Cook, whisking constantly, until the sauce thickens enough to coat the back of a spoon, 10 to 15 minutes. Off the heat, whisk in the oil, parsley, several big pinches of salt, and a pinch of black pepper. Serve immediately.

FRIED KASHKAVAL CHEESE

Serves 4

KASHKAVAL IS THE ORIGINAL super-salty cheese that was combined with watermelon long before feta. Its density holds up perfectly in frying.

½ cup challah (or other) bread crumbs

½ cup sesame seeds

½ cup all-purpose flour

1 large egg, beaten

8 ounces kashkaval cheese, cut into ⅜-inch-thick slices

Canola oil, for frying

Agristada (opposite)

• Combine the bread crumbs and sesame seeds in a wide, shallow bowl. Put the flour in another wide, shallow bowl and the egg in a third.

• To bread the kashkaval, first dredge it in the flour, shaking to remove excess, and then dip in the egg. Finally, dredge it in the bread crumb mixture, and set aside until all the cheese is breaded. Freeze for 30 minutes or until the cheese feels very firm.

• Heat about ¼ inch oil in a large skillet over medium heat until shimmering but not smoking. Working in batches if necessary, arrange the cheese in a single layer and cook until golden brown, about 2 minutes per side. Serve immediately with the agristada sauce.

FRITAS DE PRASA (FRIED LEEK PATTIES)
Makes 10 patties

THESE PATTIES ARE GOOD with agristada sauce or
on their own alongside meat dishes.

1 tablespoon olive oil

2 leeks, white and light green parts only,
   halved and sliced (about 3 cups)

2 garlic cloves, sliced

1 large egg, beaten

½ cup challah (or other) bread crumbs

½ cup mashed potato

   Kosher salt

   Canola oil, for frying

   Agristada (page 226)

● Warm the olive oil in a large skillet over medium-
high heat and add the leeks and garlic. Cook, stirring
occasionally, until the leeks have softened but not
begun to brown, about 5 minutes. Transfer to a large
bowl and refrigerate until chilled.

● When the leeks are cold, add the egg, bread crumbs,
mashed potato, and a couple of big pinches of salt.
Stir to blend well, and then form into small patties
with damp hands.

● Film the bottom of a large skillet with canola oil
and heat until the oil is shimmering but not smoking.
Arrange the leek patties in a single layer and cook
until golden brown, about 2 minutes per side. Serve
hot, with the agristada.

FRIED ARTICHOKES
Serves 4

FRIED ARTICHOKES ARE ALWAYS A TREAT for dinner; they're best with the Agristada sauce.

> 4   *medium artichokes*
>   *Canola oil, for frying*
>   *Kosher salt*
>   *Agristada (page 226)*

● Trim the tough bottom from each artichoke stem and peel the remaining stem. Chop away the top third of the artichoke and discard. Peel off all the tough, green outer leaves with a sharp paring knife, removing the leaves around the base of the artichoke. Cut the whole artichoke in half lengthwise and remove the fuzzy choke and inner leaves with a small spoon.

● Add about ¼ inch oil to a large skillet. Arrange the artichoke halves in a single layer, cut side down. Place the skillet over medium heat and cook until the artichokes are golden brown on the bottom, about 10 minutes. Flip and cook on the other side, about 3 minutes more. While hot, salt well. Serve with the agristada sauce.

MARZIPAN
Makes about 24 candies

MY GRANDFATHER MONI made marzipan all the time—it was his thing. My great-aunt Erna still makes it, and I love to visit with her and eat marzipan over a cup of tea. This is a super-simple candy to make at home. All you need are almonds, confectioners' sugar, corn syrup, and a food processor. Most almond-flavored confections feature the assertive flavor of bitter almond extract, but I love the way that this recipe showcases the clean, subtle flavor of raw almonds.

Marzipan is extremely versatile. Here I flavor it with orange blossom water, which Moni would never do. But you can add anything from sea salt to cinnamon to vanilla. Little cubes of marzipan dipped in melted chocolate make absolutely delicious petits fours that will impress your friends with your sophistication.

1½   cups sliced almonds

1½   cups confectioners' sugar

  6   tablespoons light corn syrup

  ½   teaspoon orange blossom water
       (see page 330)

       Pinch of kosher salt

 24   pistachios

● Pulse the almonds in a food processor until they form a fine meal but before they become pasty, about 2 minutes. Add the confectioners' sugar, corn syrup, orange blossom water, and salt and continue to process until the mixture is sandy and holds together when you pinch it between your fingers, about 2 minutes longer.

● Shape the mixture into 1-inch balls or cubes and press a pistachio into each piece. Marzipan will keep, well wrapped, in the refrigerator for several months.

• INGREDIENT •

PISTACHIOS

I LOVE THE TEXTURE of pistachios—somewhere between crunchy and tender. They are a great addition to ground meat in a kebab mix or sprinkled over marinated vegetables for a heady crunch. We normally use California pistachios, but sometimes we splurge on the Iranian or Sicilian varieties. The difference is immediately visible in the vivid, beautiful green color of the superior specimens. All pistachios taste like spring to me, but the fancy ones taste almost like cooked English peas—super-sweet. A perfect complement to the nutty marzipan. (See Resources, page 359.)

6

LIVE FIRE

• As Close to Magic as I'll Come •

THERE'S A SAD BUT TRUE saying that Israelis are always prepared for two things: war and barbecue. In a country as small as Israel, you can be anywhere in a matter of hours—the desert, the beach, the mountains. Weekend trips, or tiyulim, are a popular diversion. People get in their cars and go. And when they're hungry, they pull over on the side of the road and have a barbecue.

"Fire has a powerful hold over us. There's something spiritual about cooking this way."

Israeli barbecue doesn't even require a grill—just a metal box that can hold burning charcoal. You can buy one, along with charcoal, at every gas station in the country. This low-tech setup is incredibly functional.

The image of American backyard barbecue is a father in an apron that says "Kiss the Cook," wielding oversized tools over a tricked-out Weber or propane-burning rig the size of a small car. In Israel, it's a macho dude in a tank top hovering over a small metal box on the roadside, gingerly fanning the coals with a scrap of cardboard. On a traditional American grill, you're essentially searing the meat on the grill grates—most of the browning and crust comes from the heat of the grates. Since gas doesn't burn nearly as hot as charcoal (and imparts no flavor), you're not doing anything that couldn't happen on a stovetop. Even with real charcoal, there's lots of space between the coals and the meat.

GLOWING COALS
At one of my favorite Arabic grill restaurants in Nazareth, *left.* **In the Southern desert, I made this roadside barbecue,** *above.*

Previous spread: **Inside our wood-burning taboon at Zahav.**

On an Israeli grill, in contrast, the meat is suspended directly over, and very close to, the charcoal. All of the browning and crust comes from the intense heat of the coals. The lack of airflow means that the coals burn slower and hotter. And they smolder without flaring up, so that when the fat from the meat drips on the charcoal below, it doesn't set everything on fire. Instead, it produces a fragrant smoke that bathes the meat as it rises.

Part of the reason we chose the location for Zahav was that the place already had a kitchen with a working exhaust hood—20 feet of expensive steel and welded ductwork we wouldn't have to pay for when we installed our grill. It was March 2008, and the restaurant was six weeks from opening. Construction delays brought us close to the edge of disaster; each day an unexpected development pushed the finish line further away and our budget further underwater. One day Jay Rosenthal, our equipment vendor and friend, came to the site. The heavy stuff had already been delivered. We were just going over the small things—pots and pans, mixing bowls. But Jay took one look at our shiny new charcoal grill sitting next to the gas range, all under the same exhaust hood, and said, "You can't do that—it'll never pass inspection." As I quickly learned, gas vapors and creosote buildup produced by burning charcoal don't mix. For

235

GRILL MASTER
My dad, Solo, at home in Tzur Yigal, near Tel Aviv, making Bulgarian ground meat kebabs.

"Each day at the grill I try to be a little bit better, more in control, honing my ability to manipulate fire."

a few thousand dollars, we could have simply installed a gas charbroiler and moved on. But a Zahav without live fire was unthinkable. So we borrowed another $30,000 to replace the existing hood with two separate ones and held our breaths.

In culinary school and in my first few restaurant jobs, I thought the grill was there to just make food look good. Most restaurants were equipped with gas charbroilers—essentially a grill grate suspended over gas burners. You'd take a piece of meat or fish, grill it for a minute or two, and then rotate it 45 degrees. This produced beautiful diamond-shaped grill marks on the surface of the meat, which would finish cooking in the oven. Flavor was an afterthought.

Later in my career, I came face to face with the rise of modernist cuisine. It seemed like every line cook I knew was turning solids into foams and liquids into caviar. Chefs were gluing meat together and cooking it at a precise temperature inside a bag. Now I have nothing against modernist cuisine. In the right hands, its techniques can help us cook more consistently, efficiently, and with the element of theater so important in restaurants these days. You may even find a recipe or two in this book that borrow from its bag of tricks. But the more I cook, the more I find meaning in the old way of doing things, and the more I find virtue in simplicity. You don't need a chemistry book to understand this kind of cooking: meat on sticks grilled over charcoal.

Every immigrant group that has contributed to the canon of Israeli cuisine has something to say about grilled meat on sticks. Romanian kebabs are little garlic torpedoes. Their Balkan cousins from Bulgaria are sweeter and less pungent, but contain baking soda, so the kebabs puff a bit over the grill and are springy but not dense. They're served medium-rare, unlike Arab-style kebabs, which are cooked through and more highly spiced, likely with cumin, cinnamon, and black pepper. Turkish kebabs often have pistachios; North African kebabs can be fiery with harissa.

In the melting pot of Israel, everything goes, as long as it goes on the grill. At a place like Busi, the amazing Yemenite-owned grill in Tel Aviv, the menu transcends its owners' ethnic background, offering excellent examples of kebabs and shishlik from a dozen different traditions. (In this book, when I refer to kebabs, I mean seasoned ground meat formed around skewers; shishlik refers to chunks of marinated meat or vegetables threaded on skewers.) Every Israeli supermarket sells preformed kebabs and marinated shishlik. Because you never know when a barbecue is going to break out.

Even recent immigrant groups have made lasting contributions to the ever-evolving Israeli barbecue tradition. The summer before my brother, Dave, died, we'd go to the beach together almost every weekend. At the end of the day, we would take the coastal road home to Kfar Saba from Netanya. We'd get off the highway at a nondescript exit and follow a small dirt road into the middle of an orange grove. In a clearing stood an old concrete block building that had been converted into a makeshift kitchen. At one end, a low fire was smoldering on the ground, above which were suspended huge chunks of meat—beef shoulders and lamb legs—on hooks. Their sizzling fat dripped on the coals below, sending up clouds of smoke to perfume the meat. This was an asado, organized by Argentinean immigrants and patronized by Israelis of all stripes. It was a barbecue, after all.

MAKING SMOKE
At Percy Street, our barbecue restaurant in Philadelphia, we use red oak to produce the pungent smoke that flavors our lamb shoulders and other meats.

Wearing flip-flops and with our towels wrapped around our waists, we shuffled in line on the cracked, clay-tile floors, pointing to the meat we wanted and watching as it was carved off in thick, juicy slabs. Of course, since this was Israel, there was hummus and pita and salatim; the air thick with the scent of oranges, fertilizer, and smoke. We sat at wooden picnic tables and ate, experiencing a satisfaction nearly as old as humanity.

There's something spiritual about cooking the same way it has been done for millennia. Before there were gas or electricity, before there were microwaves or induction cooktops, there was wood, and there was fire. Fire has a powerful hold over us. It can sustain life and it can take it away. When I look at a fire, I stare at the glowing coals, trying to learn their secrets. I like to imagine the smoke traveling through time and space, connecting us to our past and future. And each day at the grill, I try to be a little bit better, a little more in control, honing my ability to manipulate the fire to coax out flavor and texture. It's as close to magic and alchemy as I have ever been.

For me, the flavor of charcoal-grilled meat has always represented the flavor of Israel, and so I knew that it needed to be the flavor of Zahav. That is why we truly had no choice but to spend the $30,000 to keep the grill. Of course, you can make any of the recipes in this chapter over a gas grill, or even under a broiler, and they will taste great. But I encourage you to give hardwood charcoal a try. It may take a bit more time and advance planning, but the joy of eating food can't be separated from the effort that goes into cooking it (unless, of course, you're our guest at Zahav).

BRUSSELS
SPROUTS

LAMB SHISHLIK

DUCK HEARTS

BRANZINO

EGGPLANT

JAPANESE EGGPLANT

PARGIYOT THREE WAYS

TRUMPET MUSHROOMS

BULGARIAN KEBABS

PARGIYOT THREE WAYS

BULGARIAN KEBABS
Serves 8

GROUND KEBABS ARE MY FAVORITES. They let you control the fat content of the meat—super-important when you're cooking over the extreme heat of live charcoal. A proper ratio of fat to meat (somewhere in the 20- to 30-percent range) results in a juicy and unctuous kebab. Ground kebabs also provide an opportunity to flavor the meat from the inside. Onion and parsley are pretty standard, and Arabic kebabs often turn green from so many herbs. The flavor profile of Bulgarian kebabs is pretty basic: Made with beef or a mix of lamb and beef, they're all about the meat. A spicy version made with hot paprika is always formed in patties, to distinguish it from the mild, rounder version.

Unlike hamburgers, where you want to keep the patties as loose as possible so that the meat remains tender, kebabs need to be packed fairly tightly so they'll stay on the skewer during cooking. Our skewers are long, flat, and wide, excellent for keeping the meat off the coals. Working with very cold meat and letting it rest in the refrigerator before cooking helps solidify the fat, making a juicy kebab that won't drop onto the charcoal below. Savta Mati, my Bulgarian grandmother, always added club soda to lighten her kebab mix. I use a bit of baking soda, which causes the kebabs to puff a little over the heat, resulting in a springy but still tender kebab.

> 1 *pound ground beef*
> 1 *pound ground lamb*
> ¼ *cup grated onion*
> ¼ *cup chopped fresh parsley*
> 2 *tablespoons ground Aleppo pepper*
> 1 *tablespoon ground cumin*
> 1 *teaspoon black pepper*
> 1 *teaspoon kosher salt*
> 1 *teaspoon sugar*
>   *Pinch smoked paprika*
>   *Pinch baking soda*

● Combine the beef, lamb, onion, parsley, Aleppo pepper, cumin, black pepper, salt, sugar, smoked paprika, and baking soda in a large bowl. Mix with your hands until well blended. Form into meatballs about 2 inches in diameter and thread onto skewers. Refrigerate for 1 hour.

● Grill directly over hot coals until the exterior is lightly charred and the middle is cooked through, 3 to 7 minutes per side. Serve hot off the grill.

ROMANIAN KEBABS
Serves 4

MY FATHER CALLS these kebabs garlic torpedoes because of their traditional shape and pungency. Growing up with a Bulgarian father, I was taught that a key difference between the food of Bulgaria and its Balkan neighbor, Romania, is a ton of garlic (due, obviously, to all those vampires in Romania). These kebabs are typically beef and, like the Bulgarian kebabs, contain a touch of sugar. The sugar does two things: It helps to evenly caramelize the exterior and it also helps tame all that garlic.

We serve these kebabs with the Romanian Charred Eggplant Salad (page 109) flavored with garlic. Romanians take their eggplant very seriously, traditionally prepping the eggplant with a wooden knife to keep it white (steel knives can cause discoloration). In its purest form, the salad is made with raw garlic, roasted or grilled eggplant, and salt. When serving the salad with kebabs, we lighten it a bit with lemon and olive oil.

1	*pound ground beef*
¼	*cup chopped fresh parsley*
3	*garlic cloves, minced*
2	*tablespoons chopped fresh chives*
2	*tablespoons grated onion*
1½	*teaspoons kosher salt*
½	*teaspoon sugar*
3	*tablespoons club soda*

• Combine the ground beef, parsley, garlic, chives, onion, salt, sugar, and club soda in a large bowl. Mix with your hands until well blended. Form into balls about 2 inches in diameter and thread onto skewers. Flatten each ball into a torpedo shape that hugs the skewer. Refrigerate for 1 hour.

• Grill directly over hot coals until the exterior is lightly charred and the middle is cooked through, 2 to 5 minutes per side. Serve immediately.

LAMB SHISHLIK WITH PISTACHIO TEHINA

Serves 4 to 6

LAMB LOIN IS AN EXPENSIVE CUT of meat, and I can't think of a better way to honor it than to cook it quickly over super-hot charcoal. The regular shape of the loin allows for cutting it into uniform chunks to ensure even cooking. You could easily substitute cubes of lamb leg here—they won't be quite as tender but will still be delicious. Lamb chops would work well, too. This recipe helps dispel the myth that all red meat is best cooked to medium-rare. I prefer the lamb to be a still rosy and juicy medium for two reasons: One, I think it makes the lamb much more tender; and two, the longer cooking time gives the meat a chance to express the flavor of the charcoal. Sweet, nutty pistachios add another dimension to tehina sauce, and I love the way that the rich, bitter tehina pairs with the slight gaminess of the lamb.

Serve with the tabbouleh of your choice, but I love it with the Quinoa, Pea, and Mint Tabbouleh (page 99) shown here.

MARINADE AND LAMB

1½ *cups roughly chopped onions*

1 *cup roughly chopped fresh parsley*

½ *cup roughly chopped fresh cilantro*

¼ *cup roughly chopped fresh mint*

¼ *cup canola oil*

1 *tablespoon finely grated lemon zest*

1 *garlic clove*

1 *tablespoon kosher salt*

½ *teaspoon black pepper*

  Pinch ground cinnamon

1 *lamb loin (about 1½ pounds), cut into 1½-inch pieces*

PISTACHIO TEHINA

2 *cups shelled raw pistachios*

1 *cup Basic Tehina Sauce (page 32)*

● **TO MARINATE THE LAMB:** Combine the onions, parsley, cilantro, mint, oil, lemon zest, garlic, salt, black pepper, and cinnamon in a blender and puree until the mixture is smooth and about as thick as a milkshake. You may need to add a couple of tablespoons of water to thin the mixture. Toss the lamb pieces with the marinade in a zip-top bag, seal, and marinate in the refrigerator for at least 4 hours or up to 2 days.

● **FOR THE PISTACHIO TEHINA:** Put the pistachios in a saucepan and add just enough water to cover. Bring to a simmer over medium heat and cook until the water has evaporated and the pistachios have softened, about 20 minutes. Combine the pistachios with the tehina sauce in a blender and puree until smooth, adding water a tablespoon at a time if necessary to loosen the puree.

● **TO GRILL THE LAMB:** Wipe excess marinade from the lamb and thread the pieces onto skewers. Grill directly over hot coals, turning every few minutes, until the lamb has lightly charred on the exterior and is cooked through, about 8 minutes total.

● Spread a serving platter with the pistachio tehina and top with the lamb skewers.

PARGIYOT THREE WAYS

Serves 4

PARGIYOT TRANSLATES as "baby chicken." I saw this at a restaurant with my mother in Kfar Saba, where she lives, and she laughed when I asked her if they were using poussin (real baby chicken). "Pargiyot is chicken thighs," she said. I guess the marketing people took over! Chicken has a mild reputation, but the flavor of chicken cooked over charcoal is ridiculously good. The dark meat of chicken thighs is ideal for the grill—it's far easier to keep succulent than white. Chicken takes a marinade incredibly well. For our staple marinade at Zahav, I puree onions in the blender with lemon juice, garlic, oil, salt, and tons of parsley. The interaction of the onion juice with the coals infuses the chicken with the pure essence of the grill. The sugars in the onions caramelize into smoky sweetness, and the lemon and parsley turn the flavor bright and fresh.

At Marigold Kitchen, I kept a hibachi just outside the back door and when an order came in, I'd run outside with a marinated chicken thigh and throw it on the grill. If I left it on the fire a minute or two too long, the customers never knew. A basic marinade (for any meat) can be adapted in so many ways. Three favorites: The first, based on Zahav's, is greenish—onion, lemons, and parsley; the second relies on harissa for its red and spicy trip to North Africa; and the third has a base of amba, the Iraqi pickled mango that gives the chicken a totally Middle Eastern curry flavor, hence its color.

ONION MARINADE

1½ cups roughly chopped onions
 1 cup roughly chopped fresh parsley
   Juice of 2 lemons
 ¼ cup canola oil
 1 garlic clove
 1 tablespoon kosher salt

HARISSA MARINADE

1½ cups roughly chopped onions
 ¼ cup canola oil
 ¼ cup harissa (see page 61 or store-bought)
 3 tablespoons lemon juice
1½ teaspoons kosher salt

AMBA (MANGO PICKLE) MARINADE

1½ cups roughly chopped onions
 1 cup amba puree (see page 51)
 ¼ cup canola oil
 ½ teaspoon kosher salt
 2 tablespoons water

● **FOR ANY OF THE MARINADES:** Combine all the ingredients in a blender and puree until the mixture is smooth and about as thick as a milkshake. You may need to add a couple of tablespoons of water to thin the mixture.

● Toss 2 pounds skinless, boneless chicken thighs cut into 1-inch chunks with the marinade and seal in a zip-top bag. Marinate in the refrigerator for at least 4 hours or up to 2 days.

● When ready to grill, wipe off the excess marinade, thread the chicken pieces on skewers, and grill directly over hot coals, turning every few minutes, until the chicken has lightly charred on the exterior and is cooked through, about 8 minutes total.

HARISSA
MARINADE

AMBA
MARINADE

ONION
MARINADE

PERCY STREET
We opened our barbecue restaurant on South Street in 2009 with chef/owner Erin O'Shea, *above*. We can't get enough live fire.

GRILLED FOIE GRAS
Serves 4 to 6

THE FIRST TIME I PURCHASED foie gras in Israel was from a cooler strapped to the back of a bicycle. It was the summer of 2003, and with my brother Dave's help, I was preparing a dinner party for my mother. When her French friend Jeannot heard that I was looking for foie gras, he offered to help. An hour later, the bicycle man showed up outside my mother's apartment.

Foie gras production originated in Egypt over 2,500 years ago and, at one point, Israel was a major producer, providing kosher foie gras to the French and American markets. Production is banned in Israel, but foie gras is still served in restaurants and kebab shops. It's usually goose liver (a bit meatier than the duck liver found in the United States) and perfect for skewering to grill over charcoal. This approach to foie gras is the polar opposite of the refined French techniques I was schooled in. You cut a lobe of foie gras into chunks, and grill them until just before they catch on fire. This may be the most decadent way to eat foie gras, because it treats the liver like a piece of meat rather than a fragile delicacy.

We serve grilled foie gras on laffa bread to soak up the fat. If there's is no foie gras bicycle messenger near you, these marinades are great with chicken livers, grilled chicken, or lamb. Check out Dartagnan.com; their foie gras chunks cost less than whole lobes.

> Kosher salt
>
> 1 pound foie gras, cubed
>
> Laffa (page 212) or store-bought lavash flatbread
>
> Basic Tehina Sauce (page 32)
>
> Carob molasses (see page 65)
>
> Handful pistachios

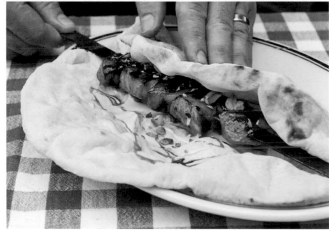

● Dissolve 2 tablespoons of the salt in 4 cups cold water. Add ice. Soak the foie gras cubes in the ice water solution, uncovered, in the refrigerator for 4 hours. This cleanses the liver.

● Heat several metal skewers in a large roasting pan filled with very hot water. When the skewers are hot to the touch, thread the foie gras cubes onto them. Season well with the remaining 1½ teaspoons salt.

● Transfer the skewers to the freezer for 30 minutes. (If the foie gras isn't cold and firm enough, it will melt onto your coals.) Grill directly over hot coals just until the cubes are a bit charred outside. Serve immediately with laffa and tehina sauce, with carob molasses drizzled over the whole plate. Scatter pistachios on top.

DUCK AND FOIE GRAS KEBABS

Serves 6

THIS IS A PLAY on a traditional ground kebab, but since duck breast is so lean, the foie gras stands in for the high fat content that is typical of beef or lamb kebabs. The result is a super-juicy kebab with that certain something extra that only foie gras can bring. Because of the fattiness of the foie, these kebabs have a hard time staying on a skewer, so I make patties and cook them directly on the grill grates. They are great, too, seared in a cast iron pan on the stovetop. I give the meat a nice seasoning overnight before grinding the meat and forming the patties. Although the techniques are Israeli, to me this is a very Pennsylvania dish. You would never see a duck kebab in Israel, but here we have access to beautiful local ducks. And in the fall, when our wild huckleberries are in season, there's no better sauce than Huckleberry Compote (page 71). In fact, the sauce is so good that after dinner, you can serve it over ice cream to finish your meal.

    1   pound duck breast, trimmed and
        cut into 1-inch cubes
    ½   pound foie gras, cubed
    ⅓   cup shelled pistachios
    2   teaspoons kosher salt
    2   teaspoons ground cinnamon
    ½   teaspoon ground ginger
        Pinch sugar
        Pinch ground cloves
    ¼   cup grated onion
    ¼   cup chopped fresh parsley
    ½   teaspoon baking soda

● Arrange the duck breast, foie gras, and pistachios in a single layer on a baking sheet and sprinkle evenly with the salt, cinnamon, ginger, sugar, and cloves. Cover loosely with parchment paper and refrigerate overnight.

● Put the duck breast in the freezer for 20 minutes to firm up. Meanwhile, coarsely chop the foie gras and pistachios with a sharp knife. (If the foie gras is chopped too fine, it will melt out of the kebabs on the grill.) Set aside.

● Working in batches, pulse the duck breast in a food processor until it is coarsely ground.

● Combine the duck, foie gras, pistachios, onion, parsley, and baking soda in a large bowl. Mix well with your hands until well blended. Shape the mixture into patties about 3 inches in diameter. Refrigerate for 1 hour.

● Grill directly over hot coals, flipping often, until lightly charred on the exterior and just cooked through, 5 to 8 minutes total. I like to serve them with Pilaf with Carrots (page 284) and Huckleberry Compote (page 71).

CHICKEN LIVERS WITH BAHARAT

Serves 4

CHARCOAL GRILLING IS A GREAT WAY to tame the sometimes assertive qualities of chicken livers. Just take care to cook the livers only until the interiors are still creamy and pink. We cure the livers overnight with salt and the warm spices of baharat, whose sweet and peppery flavor enhances the livers and amplifies the smoke and char from the grill. I like to pair chicken livers with something mellow to keep their flavor in check, so I serve them with sumac onions and green grapes, which provide a burst of sugar and acid to balance their richness.

1	pound chicken livers
	Kosher salt
	Big pinch baharat (see page 54)
½	cup thinly sliced onion
1	tablespoon canola oil
½	cup green grapes, halved
2	teaspoons minced fresh dill
	Simple Sumac Onions (page 97)

● Toss the chicken livers with ¾ teaspoon salt and the baharat. Transfer to a strainer set over a bowl and let stand in the refrigerator overnight. Sprinkle the sliced onion with several big pinches of salt and let stand in the refrigerator overnight.

● Thread the chicken livers onto skewers, pat dry with paper towels, and brush with the oil. Grill directly over hot coals until a bit charred on the outside and medium-rare on the inside, about 2 minutes per side.

● Arrange the grapes and the skewers on a platter and top with the salted onion slices, dill, and sumac onions.

DUCK HEARTS WITH CAULIFLOWER–TEHINA PUREE

Serves 4

IF YOU HAD TOLD ME we'd be selling 15 pounds of duck hearts at Zahav every week, I'd have asked you to hand over your car keys. But it's true. Duck hearts have become our great gateway offal. Whether it's beef or duck, I believe the heart tastes like the meat of the animal that it comes from—only more so. When cooked medium-rare, duck hearts are super-tender with none of the gaminess that people expect (and fear) from offal.

Although duck hearts aren't available at your neighborhood grocery store, they're worth seeking out from a cooperative butcher. They're a great source of lean protein, are fairly inexpensive, require minimal preparation, and cook very quickly. Seasoned with baharat, the warm spice mix, they are irresistible.

MARINADE AND DUCK HEARTS

¾ cup roughly chopped onion
1 cup chopped fresh parsley
¼ cup canola oil
1 teaspoon kosher salt
1 teaspoon baharat (see page 54)
1 garlic clove
1 pound duck hearts

CAULIFLOWER–TEHINA PUREE

1 small head cauliflower, broken into florets, core chopped
1 tablespoon olive oil
1 teaspoon kosher salt
1 cup Basic Tehina Sauce (page 32)

Chopped celery leaves, for serving

● **TO MARINATE THE HEARTS:** Combine the onion, parsley, canola oil, salt, baharat, and garlic in a blender and puree until the mixture is as thick as a milkshake. You may need to add a tablespoon or two of water to thin. Pour the marinade in a zip-top plastic bag and add the duck hearts. Seal and refrigerate overnight.

● **FOR THE PUREE:** Preheat the oven to 250°F. Toss the cauliflower with the olive oil and salt on a baking sheet. Bake until very tender, about 1 hour. Transfer just the florets to a blender, add the tehina sauce, and puree until very smooth. Set aside.

● Thread the duck hearts onto skewers, wiping off the excess marinade. Grill directly over hot coals until lightly charred on the exterior and rare inside, about 90 seconds per side.

● Spread the cauliflower puree on a plate and top with the duck hearts. Add the roasted cauliflower core pieces and celery leaves to the plate and serve.

LEMONNANA

Serves 1

IN ISRAEL LEMONNANA IS A POPULAR drink often sold frozen by street vendors. We've introduced the drink to American bourbon and created a version that's become the undisputed Zahav house favorite. Perfect for enjoying standing around live fire.

   1 *sugar cube (or ½ teaspoon sugar)*
   6 *mint leaves*
1½ *ounces bourbon*
   1 *ounce lemon juice*
  ½ *ounce Lemon Verbena Syrup (recipe follows)*
  ¾ *ounce water*

● Muddle the sugar cube with the mint in the bottom of a shaker. Fill the shaker with ice and add the remaining ingredients. Shake vigorously and pour into a highball glass.

LEMON VERBENA SYRUP

   1 *cup sugar*
   6 *lemon verbena sprigs (fresh or dried) or*
      6 sprigs lemon thyme

● Combine the sugar and 1 cup water in a small saucepan. Bring to a simmer over medium heat, stirring to dissolve the sugar. Remove from the heat and add the lemon verbena or lemon thyme. Let cool to room temperature, then refrigerate, preferably overnight. Strain and use in the Lemonnana.

POMEGRANATE-GLAZED SALMON

Serves 4

THIS WAS THE FIRST FISH DISH on the menu at Zahav when we opened in 2008. Although we were playing it safe by selecting this popular fish, it turns out that salmon is very well suited to the grill. Its large fillets can be cut into uniform chunks that cook evenly over the coals, and its high fat content prevents it from drying out. A light cure firms up the flesh so that it doesn't slide around on the skewers.

The sauce comes right out of the bottle: Pomegranate molasses is sweetened pomegranate juice that has been reduced to a thick, sticky glaze. It is sweet and tart and a little cloying on its own, but as it caramelizes over the smoky charcoal it becomes an

excellent counterpoint to the rich and fatty salmon. You could make a similar glaze from date or carob molasses. We serve the salmon over Pilaf Coquelicot (page 285)—the poppy seeds in the rice together with the salmon make me think of bagels and lox.

> 1 *small garlic clove, minced*
> 1 *tablespoon finely grated orange zest*
> 1½ *teaspoons kosher salt*
>   *Pinch ground Aleppo pepper*
> 1 *skin-on salmon fillet (1½–2 pounds)*
>   *Canola oil, for greasing the skewers*
> ¼ *cup pomegranate molasses (see page 304)*

● Mix the garlic, orange zest, salt, and Aleppo pepper in a small bowl. Sprinkle the mixture over the salmon on both sides and wrap loosely in parchment. Refrigerate for 4 hours.

● Cut the salmon into 1-inch pieces. Brush the skewers with oil. Thread the salmon pieces on the skewers and grill, skin side down, directly over hot coals. While the skin side is cooking, brush the flesh side with the pomegranate molasses. When the skin is crisp, flip the skewers and brush the skin side with the pomegranate molasses. Continue cooking until the fish is cooked through, about 2 more minutes. Serve.

GRILLED BRANZINO FILLETS WITH CHICKPEA STEW

Serves 4

BRANZINO IS A MEDITERRANEAN FISH with a dense white flesh that becomes almost meaty on the grill. The key to crisp skin that doesn't stick to the grates is simply to leave it alone as it grills. I cook the branzino almost all the way through on the skin side. Left undisturbed, the skin releases easily from the grates and has the crunch of a smoky, salty fish potato chip. Then it needs only a brief "kiss" on the flesh side before it's ready to go.

With the fish, I serve a Persian-style chickpea stew made from fresh green chickpeas and flavored with dill, turmeric, and dried lime. Some of the cooked chickpeas are pureed with olive oil and folded back into the stew to give it a creamy texture. If you can't find fresh chickpeas, you can substitute dried or canned chickpeas or even frozen English peas. Although we use fish fumet to add extra depth to the stew, water works just fine.

Alongside the chickpea stew, I set the grilled fish on a puree of fava beans and labneh (strained yogurt). The puree is half sauce, half dip and could easily work as the sole accompaniment to the fish if you don't have time to prepare the stew.

CHICKPEA STEW

4 tablespoons olive oil

1 cup chopped onion

½ cup diced peeled carrot

2 garlic cloves, sliced

1½ teaspoons ground turmeric

1 whole dried lime (see page 92)

1 cup fresh chickpeas, or dried or canned chickpeas

2 cups Fish Fumet (page 48) or water

1 teaspoon kosher salt

1 teaspoon lemon juice

1 tablespoon chopped fresh dill

FAVA–LABNEH PUREE

½ cup shelled fresh fava beans, boiled for 1 minute and peeled

½ cup labneh (see page 128)

½ teaspoon kosher salt

Pinch ground mace

BRANZINO

2 large, skin-on branzino fillets (about ½ pound each), halved

About 1 teaspoon kosher salt

● **FOR THE STEW:** Warm 2 tablespoons of the oil in a skillet over medium heat and add the onion, carrot, garlic, and turmeric. Cook, stirring occasionally, until the vegetables have softened but not begun to brown, 5 to 8 minutes. Add the dried lime, chickpeas, fumet or water, and salt. Lower the heat to maintain a gentle simmer, cover, and cook until the chickpeas are tender, 30 to 40 minutes.

● Transfer about one quarter of the mixture to a blender, add the remaining 2 tablespoons oil, and puree until smooth. Stir back into the stew. Add the lemon juice and dill, and keep warm while you make the puree and grill the branzino.

● **FOR THE PUREE:** Puree the fava beans in a food processor. Put the labneh in a small bowl and fold in the fava beans. Stir in the salt and mace. Set aside.

● **FOR THE BRANZINO:** Make sure your grill grates are clean, hot, and well oiled. Season the branzino on both sides with the salt. Grill the branzino pieces skin side down directly over hot coals until the skin is crisp and releases easily when you try to flip it, about 3 minutes. Be patient! Turn and cook flesh side down until cooked through, just a minute or two more.

● **TO SERVE:** Spread the puree on a serving platter and top with the branzino. Spoon the chickpea stew on the side.

GRILLED WHOLE EGGPLANT
Serves 2

GRILLING WHOLE EGGPLANT almost turns it into a different vegetable. As the eggplant is literally burned over the coals, its skin gets smoky and somewhere between crispy and chewy, while it shields the flesh, which picks up a deep smoky flavor as it becomes creamy. Once grilled, the eggplant is opened flat on a plate and dressed with herbed labneh, grilled tomatoes, and pine nuts. For a real treat, you can slow-roast a whole brined eggplant directly on top of the coals after they have begun to die down. After several hours or even overnight, the interior can be spooned out like smoky eggplant pudding.

1 large eggplant
¼ cup kosher salt
1 cup cherry or grape tomatoes
1 cup Herbed Labneh (page 128) or Basic Tehina Sauce (page 32)
   Handful pine nuts and pea shoots or basil

● Using a sharp paring knife, make a deep slit down the length of the eggplant to let the brine penetrate.

● Combine the salt with 4 cups water in a bowl and stir to dissolve. Add the eggplant, cover, and let brine for at least 4 hours or up to overnight. Drain the eggplant and pat dry.

● Grill the eggplant over indirect or low heat until the eggplant is soft, collapsed, and creamy inside, about 30 minutes. After the eggplant has been on the grill for about 10 minutes, add the tomatoes and grill until the skins just begin to split, 10 to 15 minutes.

● To serve, open and gently flatten the eggplant on a plate, flesh side up, and top with the herbed labneh or tehina sauce, the grilled tomatoes, and a scattering of pine nuts and pea shoots or basil.

GRILLED JAPANESE EGGPLANT
Serves 4

EGGPLANT ON THE GRILL is like money in the bank. I can't think of anything that is enhanced by time spent over charcoal as much as this vegetable. I like to brine eggplant before grilling, to season it from the inside and mellow its characteristic bitterness. Here thick slices of slender Japanese eggplant are grilled on skewers until they are tender but meaty, then served over lentils.

¼ cup kosher salt
4 Japanese eggplants, cut on an angle into thick slices
2 tablespoons canola oil
2 teaspoons sweet paprika
1 teaspoon hawaij (see page 168)
   Cooked lentils, for serving (page 58)

● Combine the salt with 4 cups water in a large bowl and stir to dissolve the salt. Add the eggplant slices, cover, and brine in the refrigerator for 2 hours. Drain well and pat very dry.

● Thread the eggplant slices onto skewers and brush with the oil. Grill directly over hot coals, turning every few minutes, until the eggplant just begins to char, about 3 minutes. Season with the paprika and hawaij and continue cooking until the eggplant is tender, about 2 minutes more. Serve over the lentils.

BRUSSELS SPROUTS WITH FETA
Serves 4

HERE I USE THE GRILL as part of a multistep cooking process, grilling halved Brussels sprouts on a rack over charcoal to char their cut sides and then gently poaching them in the oven in olive oil and vinegar. This way, the sprouts get the best of both worlds— the deep char and smoke of the grill and the tender, creamy interior from their long warm bath.

Don't be afraid to let the Brussels sprouts get deep, dark brown on the grill—almost burnt. I first saw Marc do this at Vetri, scandalized by how long he seared Brussels sprouts in a pan. I'd have been expelled from culinary school for this violation of golden-brown protocol. But some things can take extreme caramelization without turning bitter—in fact, they benefit from it. Twice-Cooked Eggplant (page 106) is another great example of how detours from classic French techniques can often lead to new and delicious territory. With this method, the Brussels sprouts are hard to overcook and retain a bit of snap along with the smoky, popcorn-y flavor from the grill.

We serve these Brussels sprouts at room temperature with feta and good bread. They are also great with roasted meat or fish.

1	pound Brussels sprouts, trimmed and halved
1	teaspoon kosher salt
1	tablespoon canola oil
3	tablespoons olive oil
1	cup sliced onion
4	garlic cloves, thinly sliced
½	cup dry white wine
¼	cup white vinegar
2	tablespoons chopped fresh oregano
2	tablespoons chopped fresh marjoram
	Feta, for serving

● Toss the Brussels sprouts with the salt and canola oil. Arrange, cut side down, in a grill basket and grill over very hot coals until the exteriors are nearly black, about 4 minutes. Set aside.

● Preheat the oven to 250°F. Warm 2 tablespoons of the olive oil in a large ovenproof skillet over medium heat and add the onion and garlic. Cook, stirring occasionally, until the onion is soft but not beginning to brown, about 5 minutes. Add the wine, bring to a simmer, and cook until the wine has evaporated, about 3 minutes. Add the vinegar and return to a simmer.

● Add the Brussels sprouts, the remaining 1 tablespoon olive oil, the oregano, and marjoram and toss to coat. Transfer to the oven and bake until the Brussels sprouts are very tender, about 1 hour. Serve topped with feta.

GRILLED MUSHROOMS

Serves 4

ALTHOUGH I'VE NEVER SEEN shishlik made from mushrooms in Israel, this dish makes perfect sense to me since big mushrooms, especially the mighty, meaty king trumpets (also known as king oyster or trumpet royale mushrooms), take a marinade well and can stand up to the intense heat of the grill. Often I'll just use creminis; any firm mushroom will work, even large white button mushrooms. I prefer to briefly steam the mushrooms to keep them from drying out, before marinating them in onion, parsley, and allspice (it's the allspice that really makes them taste like meat) and then putting them on the grill.

I sometimes serve them with fava beans, scallions, and Amba Tehina (page 51) for a riff on the flavors of a shawarma sandwich.

MUSHROOMS

- 1 pound (about 8) king trumpet or other hefty mushrooms
- 1 teaspoon kosher salt
- 2 tablespoons olive oil
- 1½ cups roughly chopped onions
- ½ cup roughly chopped fresh parsley
- ¼ cup roughly chopped fresh chives
- ½ teaspoon ground allspice

● **FOR THE MUSHROOMS:** Preheat the oven to 350°F. Season the mushrooms with the salt, toss with the oil, and arrange in a baking dish. Add enough water to cover the bottom of the dish and cover the dish tightly with two layers of foil. Bake until the mushrooms are just tender, about 30 minutes. Let them cool in their liquid, then drain and reserve the liquid.

● Combine the mushroom cooking liquid with the onions, parsley, chives, and allspice in a blender. Puree until smooth. Put the mushrooms in a zip-top bag, cover with the marinade, and seal. Refrigerate for at least 4 hours or up to 3 days.

FAVA BEANS AND SCALLIONS

¼ cup olive oil

 1 pound scallions, trimmed

¼ cup dry white wine

 1 cup shelled fresh fava beans, boiled for
      1 minute and peeled

 2 tablespoons white vinegar

 1 bay leaf

 1 garlic clove, slivered

    Pinch mustard seeds

    Pinch ground coriander

    Pinch ground caraway

    Amba Tehina (page 51)

● **FOR THE FAVA BEANS AND SCALLIONS:** Warm the oil in a skillet and add the scallions. Cook, stirring occasionally, until just softened, about 5 minutes. Add the wine and continue cooking until it has almost evaporated. Add the fava beans, vinegar, bay leaf, garlic, mustard seeds, coriander, and caraway. Cook over low heat until the liquid has reduced and the flavors have married, about 5 minutes more.

● **TO GRILL THE MUSHROOMS:** Thread the mushrooms on skewers, wiping away any excess marinade. Grill directly over hot coals until the exteriors are lightly charred, about 3 minutes. Serve with the fava beans, scallions, and amba tehina.

7

BEN-GURION'S RICE

• *Rice Is Easy, Perfection Is Hard* •

IF I COOKED RICE every day for the rest of my life, I would never outgrow the anxiety in that moment just before lifting the lid off the pot. The feeling of exhilaration when I nail a batch of rice rivals almost any feeling of satisfaction I have ever had in the kitchen, and many outside of it.

> *"Like a watchful father, Avi awaits the sizzle that signals the tahdig—the prized layer of crispy rice on the bottom."*

There were times in my childhood when virtually all I ate was rice. I once thought this was an ironic beginning for a future chef, but now I see it differently. The more I cook, the more I understand what I love about rice. The craft of cooking is about chasing perfection through repetition and ritual—and never quite getting there. It's easy to cook with foie gras and truffles (and at their prices, it had better be). But take a cup of rice and some water and salt and try to make something fundamentally delicious and satisfying. And then try to do it a hundred times in a row. It is a Zen all its own. When new cooks come into my kitchen, one of the first things they are asked to do is make rice. These days, young cooks seem to know everything there is to know about sous vide and reverse spherification. Their knives cost more than my car. But cooking a simple dish of rice can often be a very humbling experience. I remember preparing a staff meal early in my career and making a rice pilaf that was badly undercooked. "This almond pilaf is delicious!" my coworkers said as they crunched on raw rice. The rice had no almonds in it. I still don't know if they were just being polite.

Cooking rice is easy. Cooking it perfectly is incredibly difficult. So many variables can impact the results, from the shape of your pot and the fit of its lid to the starch content of the rice to the calibration of your oven. In cuisines where rice plays an important role, the job of cooking the rice is often the exclusive realm of the master. This is true in Japan, where sushi apprentices work for years before being allowed near the rice. And it is true in Iran, where my half-brother-in-law Avi Mor grew up. In Persian cuisine, rice is the bright center of the universe. It is, literally, the reason for being for many traditional dishes. It would be unthinkable, for example, to make kebabs without having rice to rest them on. Avi was nine years old when his father, a textile merchant, passed away suddenly. With their economic future in question and two siblings already in Israel, Avi's mother decided to move the entire family there. In 1971, the family left their eighteen-room house in Shiraz for a three-room apartment in Hadera near the coast. The youngest of eight, Avi began helping his mother in the kitchen when he was ten. After five years, he was finally allowed to touch the rice. He has spent the last forty years trying to perfect it.

Avi's approach in the kitchen is part scientific, part Jedi master. He juggles a half dozen or more variables with each batch: the type of rice and its starch content, the soaking time, the temperature of the soaking water, how long to blanch the rice in boiling water,

TAMING RICE
For Avi Mor, *above*, rice is the bright center of his universe. The prized golden tahdig, *left*, from the bottom of a perfect pot of Persian rice.

Previous spread: Steve has his defining moment in the Negev desert.

267

GRAIN INTEGRITY
Draining the water as quickly as possible has everything to do with not damaging the individual grains of rice.

"We are drawn to fireworks, even when they burn us. Yet the simple pot of rice sits there on the stove. And says nothing."

how much moisture to allow during the steaming. He adjusts each variable based on the destiny of every batch of rice. Chorosh is a genre of stew, heavy on herbs and dried limes, often made with meat and beans. Chorosh without rice is an impossibility, says Avi. Cholo, the plain rice served with chorosh, should be a bit drier to compensate for the moisture of the stew. Polo, a rice dish unto itself once it's mixed with anything from beans to herbs to dried fruit, should be moist, so it melts in your mouth.

In the kitchen, Avi tends to his rice like a watchful father, looking for the telltale signs: the al dente texture of the blanched grains so that they will become perfectly tender after the final steaming; the sizzling sound that foreshadows the tahdig—the prized layer of crispy caramelized rice on the bottom of the pot; the toasted popcorn fragrance when it has finished cooking. After four decades, Avi is still tinkering, still chasing the perfect pot. He knows that he makes great rice—most of the time. But he also knows that only a fool would consider his learning complete. Even his mother, the undisputed master, would mess up a batch from time to time. If this happened on a Friday evening, it was enough to ruin her whole Sabbath. Avi's children are now older than he was when he first stepped into the kitchen, but he still doesn't let them touch the rice.

When I think of Avi, I always picture him carrying a big pot of rice. He brings rice to every family gathering and tends to it lovingly. He fluffs and seasons it, delicately spoons it onto the serving platter, and carefully removes the tahdig for everyone to fight over. The first time I tasted Avi's rice was in the summer of 2003, a few months before my brother, Dave, died. It was a revelation. When I was younger and plain rice was a staple of my diet, I was made to feel that this was somehow a character flaw. But in Avi's world, the same dish was considered sacred. Rice culture in Iran is rooted in economic reality—an affordable staple that has sustained a large part of the population for centuries. But its significance transcends its nutritional value. There is something akin to a religious practice in the way that Avi approaches rice—it's a daily devotion. By the time I had Avi's rice, I had been cooking professionally for a few years. I thought I was hot shit. But this rice stopped me in my tracks. He was taking perhaps the plainest ingredient imaginable and elevating it into something sublime.

In Israel, rice has played a critical role in the way Israelis eat, and in establishing a national identity. In the years between 1948 and 1951, the population of Israel more

268

than doubled. When Israel declared independence in 1948, the country was inundated with new immigrants, not just European Jewish refugees from the Holocaust, but also Mizrahim, Jews from the Arab and Muslim world, for whom the existence of a Jewish state had made life very difficult in their native countries. In other words, rice eaters. And a lot of mouths to feed for a country surrounded by hostile nations, without currency reserves or access to credit. Israeli independence was followed by a ten-year period of austerity. Food rationing provided only 1,600 calories a day for the average citizen. My father's earliest food memory was as a four-year old on the moshav, the collaborative farm community where he grew up. He and his five-year-old cousin were left alone in the house while the grown-ups were at work. When they got hungry, the only food in the refrigerator was a jar of mayonnaise. They polished it off.

NAILING IT
Making perfect Persian rice is heady—so challenging, and yet so rewarding.

Morale was low during the early days of the state, and the shortage of rice came to symbolize the hardships faced by its citizens. According to legend, the first prime minister of Israel, David Ben-Gurion, challenged the Osem company, one of Israel's largest food manufacturers, to quickly develop a wheat-based rice substitute (Israel grew wheat but not rice). Osem came up with a toasted pasta in the shape of rice grains (sort of like orzo) that was marketed as ptitim (shavings) and became known popularly as Ben-Gurion's rice and later, Israeli couscous. As a boy, my father ate a bowl of ptitim with a bit of rationed margarine almost daily. The austerity period came to an end in the late 1950s, but although some high-tech rice growing is happening today, Israeli couscous has remained a staple, a lasting tribute to the significance of humble rice.

Rice was one of the first foods I loved, and eating Avi's rice marked a turning point in my professional life. When I returned to the United States in the fall of 2003, I took home a new understanding of my craft. The menu I was cooking at Vetri no longer felt simple and rustic. Now I saw Marc's food as a daring tightrope walk, each dish stripped to its essence with nowhere to hide its flaws. Even now, as an experienced chef, I am constantly reminding myself that it takes more guts to leave something off the plate than to put something on it. I am lucky to be working during a time when our profession is celebrated for its role in our society. But one side effect of this culture is an unquenchable thirst for what is new. We are drawn to fireworks, even when they burn us. And the simple pot of rice sits there on the stove and says nothing.

I never tire of eating rice, and I never tire of trying to cook the perfect pot. Rice is an affordable, nutritious, and satisfying staple. It connects us to the past, present, and future. It reminds us that the next pot can always be just a little bit better. It reminds us that simplicity is an elusive virtue that is worth pursuing. It reminds us why we cook.

PERSIAN RICE

"If you're feeling like a rock star, flip the entire (well-rested) pot of rice onto a plate, unmolding it in one gorgeous, golden dome."

WHEN AVI MOR married my half-sister Merav (my father's daughter from his first marriage), my father had been living in the United States for several years. The first time he met Avi's family was on the Sabbath before the wedding. Avi's sister made the rice that day and she had taken it a bit too far. The tahdig had gone from crispy and tender to hard and chewy. But it was too late to do anything about it, so the rice was served. My father was a lone Bulgarian in a crowd of 50 Persian men that he was meeting for the first time. There were 50 suspicious pairs of eyes on my father, watching to see what this outsider would do with the challenging rice. When my father swallowed it down without blinking, he was immediately accepted into the family.

At Zahav, we regard the rice as so special that we serve it with our Mesibah (party) menu, to give you an idea of just how cool it is. The method for cooking it is very different from what we're used to in America.

Instead of steaming the rice in just enough liquid to tenderize the grains, this method calls for blanching presoaked rice in a large amount of salted water until it's barely al dente. The rice is drained and then added to a heavy-bottomed pot that has been lightly oiled. The pot is covered with a lid that is wrapped in a kitchen towel and set over very low heat for the rice to finish steaming. The towel helps regulate the moisture inside of the pot, allowing the rice to take in only as much as it needs. This is similar to the "fuzzy logic" employed by fancy rice cookers. But a rice cooker is much more expensive than a kitchen towel. And far less absorbent.

PERSIAN WEDDING RICE

PERSIAN RICE

PERSIAN RICE WITH
BLACK-EYED PEAS AND DILL

PERSIAN RICE

Serves 6 to 8

LIKE THE METHOD for making rice pilaf (see page 282), the Persian Rice technique provides numerous opportunities for flavor enhancements. Here are three classic varieties: basic crispy rice stained with turmeric; Persian wedding rice mixed with dried fruits and nuts; and a version with black-eyed peas and dill that makes a great one-pot meal. Avi always spoons the finished rice onto a platter and then removes the tahdig separately. But if you're feeling like a rock star, you can flip the entire (well-rested) pot onto a plate to unmold the rice in one gorgeous, golden dome. Party time!

    2   *cups jasmine rice*
          Kosher salt
          Canola oil
          Pinch or two ground turmeric

● Cover the rice with 4 cups water in a large bowl and add a pinch of salt. Let soak for at least 1 hour or up to overnight. Drain well.

● Combine ¼ cup water, 1 tablespoon oil, and ½ teaspoon salt in a bowl and whisk to blend. Reserve.

● Fill a large enameled or well-seasoned cast iron pot about halfway with water and add 1 tablespoon salt. Bring to a boil, add the rice, and boil until the rice is about three-quarters done. The rice shouldn't be crunchy, but it should stick to your teeth when you bite a grain. Start checking after 1 minute, but it may take up to 10 minutes.

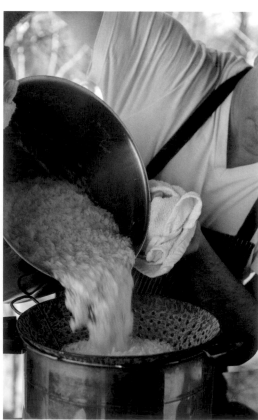

- Drain the rice in a large colander and cool it off somewhat by gently lifting scoops of rice with a spoon to turn and fluff the grains.

- Dry the pot well and coat the bottom and sides generously with oil. Set the pot over medium-high heat and heat until the oil just begins to send out a wisp of smoke. Off the heat, wipe out the pot with a paper towel and coat the bottom and sides with a thin film of fresh oil.

- Sprinkle the bottom of the pot with the turmeric and gently spoon the rice into the pot. Lightly press the surface of the rice with the back of a spoon to even out the surface and slightly compress the grains. Drizzle the reserved water–oil mixture evenly over the rice.

- Drape the top of the pot with a clean cotton or linen kitchen towel and put the lid on the pot over the towel. Pull the corners of the towel up over the lid and secure with a rubber band.

- Set the pot over very low heat and cook, unopened and undisturbed, for 30 minutes. Open the lid and test for the formation of a crust by inserting a knife to the bottom of the pot. If it doesn't feel crusty, replace the towel and lid and continue cooking over very low heat until a good crust forms. Hard to believe, but true: This can take up to another 1½ hours, depending on the heat of your burner and how long you've soaked the rice. Let rest off the heat for at least 20 minutes.

- Carefully unmold the rice onto a platter and serve. (Or, if it doesn't unmold easily, simply scoop the rice into a serving bowl with the crispy shards on top.)

PERSIAN RICE WITH BLACK-EYED PEAS AND DILL

Serves 6 to 8

ADDING HEARTY BLACK-EYED PEAS to rice makes a complete dish. This rice is a perfect accompaniment to meaty stews.

2 *cups jasmine rice*
   Kosher salt
   Canola oil
1 *tablespoon plus 1 pinch ground turmeric*
1 *cup cooked or canned black-eyed peas*
1 *whole dried lime (see page 92),
   optional*
½ *cup chopped fresh dill*

● Cover the rice with 4 cups water and a pinch of salt. Let soak for at least 1 hour or up to overnight. Drain well.

● Combine ¼ cup water, 1 tablespoon oil, 1 tablespoon of the turmeric, and 1 teaspoon salt in a bowl and whisk to blend. Reserve.

● Fill an enameled or well-seasoned cast iron pot about halfway with water and add 1 tablespoon salt. Bring to a boil, add the rice, and boil until the rice is about three-quarters done. The rice shouldn't be crunchy, but it should stick to your teeth when you bite a grain. Start checking after 1 minute, but it may take up to 10 minutes.

● Drain the rice in a large colander and cool it off somewhat by gently lifting scoops of rice with a spoon to turn and fluff the grains.

• Dry the pot well and coat the bottom and sides generously with oil. Set the pot over medium-high heat and heat until the oil just begins to put off a wisp of smoke. Off the heat, wipe out the pot with a paper towel and coat the bottom and sides with a thin film of fresh oil.

• Sprinkle the bottom of the pot with the turmeric and gently spoon one third of the rice into the pot. Layer with ½ cup of the black-eyed peas, another third of the rice, the remaining ½ cup of black-eyed peas, and the last third of the rice. Lightly press the surface of the rice with the back of a spoon to even it out and slightly compress the grains. Add the dried lime, if you like. Drizzle the reserved water-oil mixture over the rice.

• Drape the top of the pot with a clean cotton or linen kitchen towel and put the lid on the pot over the towel. Pull the corners of the towel up over the lid and secure with a rubber band.

• Set the pot over very low heat and cook, unopened and undisturbed, for 30 minutes. After 30 minutes, open the lid and test for the formation of a crust by inserting a knife to the bottom of the pot. If it doesn't feel crusty, replace the towel and lid and continue cooking over very low heat until a good crust forms. This can take up to another 1½ hours depending on the heat of your burner and how long you've soaked the rice. Let rest off the heat for at least 20 minutes.

• Remove and discard the dried lime, and carefully unmold the rice onto a platter, gently fold in the dill, and serve. (If it doesn't unmold easily, simply scoop the rice into a serving bowl with the crispy shards on top.)

PERSIAN WEDDING RICE
Serves 6 to 8

IN MY FAMILY, this celebratory version of crispy rice is served with all the dried fruits and nuts left whole. But chop them up if you prefer. I also love to top this dish with barberries or sweet-tart dried cranberries.

> *Persian Rice (page 272)*
> ½ *cup Marcona almonds*
> ¼ *cup prunes*
> ½ *cup dried apricots*
> ¼ *dried dates*

• Top the Persian Rice with the almonds, prunes, dried apricots, and dates and serve.

FREEKAH WITH CHICKEN AND ALMONDS
Serves 4

I LOVE THIS STEEPING METHOD of cooking chicken. Rather than poaching it in simmering liquid, boiling broth is poured over the seasoned breast and it gently cooks as the liquid cools. The technique guarantees perfectly juicy white meat that is never dry or overcooked. It's a great technique to have in your back pocket for other dishes like chicken salad. For large chicken breasts, you may to need to simmer them briefly before turning off the heat and allowing the chicken to steep the rest of the way.

2	small chicken breasts (about 6 ounces each)
	Kosher salt
½	teaspoon ground cinnamon
½	teaspoon black pepper
	Handful cilantro sprigs, plus more leaves for serving
8	cups My Chicken Stock (page 167)
4	tablespoons schmaltz (see page 167) or olive oil
½	cup minced onion
2	garlic cloves, sliced
2	cups freekah
4	tablespoons sliced almonds

● Season the chicken breasts on both sides with 1 teaspoon salt, the cinnamon, and black pepper. Put in a bowl, cover loosely with wax paper, and refrigerate for at least 1 hour or up to overnight.

● Put the cilantro sprigs and chicken stock in a large saucepan. Bring to a boil over high heat. Pour the hot broth over the seasoned chicken breasts in the bowl. Cover and let stand until the chicken is cooked through, about 12 minutes. Remove the chicken to a plate, reserve the broth, and discard the cilantro sprigs.

● Warm 2 tablespoons of the schmaltz or oil in a large skillet over medium heat. Add the onion and garlic and cook, stirring occasionally, until the onion has begun to soften but not brown, about 8 minutes. Add the freekah and cook, stirring constantly, until it smells smoky and toasted, about 3 minutes. Salt well.

● Add the chicken-poaching broth to the skillet in ½-cup increments, stirring constantly until the liquid has been absorbed before adding the next ½ cup. It will take about 40 minutes for all the liquid to be absorbed and the freekah to cook through.

● Shred the chicken and add half of the meat to the cooked freekah. Add 2 tablespoons of the almonds and stir to combine. Spoon into serving bowls and top with the remaining shredded chicken, remaining 2 tablespoons almonds, cilantro leaves, and the remaining 2 tablespoons schmaltz or oil.

• INGREDIENT •

FREEKAH

FREEKAH (OFTEN SPELLED FRIK) are cracked green wheat berries that have a smoky flavor from the unique way they are processed. After the underripe wheat is picked, it is piled in the field to dry in the sun. The piles are then carefully set on fire (the seeds' moisture prevents them from burning) to complete the drying process, and the burning stalks and chaff flavor the wheat with smoke. Freekah is popular in the Galilee, especially with the Bedouin and Druze, where wheat (not rice) has long been a staple. Picking the wheat berries before they are fully ripe increases their nutritional value.

In the restaurants I grew up cooking in, there was always risotto on the menu, usually finished with tons of butter and cheese. Since we don't mix dairy and meat at Zahav, freekah makes a great substitute because the cracked wheat becomes creamy all by itself. I cook freekah using the risotto method, adding rich chicken stock a little bit at a time and stirring constantly, so that the grains become creamy and tender without overcooking. The result is a bowl of pure comfort food: The combination of the cinnamon and smoky wheat might haunt your dreams.

Freekah is great in stuffings, instead of barley in Stuffed Grape Leaves (page 127), because it absorbs moisture and flavors from the other ingredients without ever losing its toothsome texture. For the same reason, steamed freekah works well in cold salads because it retains its integrity after cooking. Try it instead of bulgur wheat in Traditional Tabbouleh (page 95).

ISRAELI COUSCOUS

Serves 4

I PUT THIS DISH on my opening menu at Marigold Kitchen, partly because it meant that I could actually write the word Israeli on the menu. The funny thing is that Israeli couscous is actually pasta, made from wheat flour but toasted rather than air-dried. And there are several versions of a similar product that predate it. The Lebanese have been eating their moghrabiyeh, Palestinians their maftoul, Hungarians their tarhonya, and Ashkenazi Jews their farfel since long before Israeli couscous became a "branded" product.

Israeli couscous was generally considered kids' food until relatively recently, when chefs like me started serving it with escargots and honey mushrooms. But what I love most about Israeli couscous is the same thing that appealed to me when I was a child: At its heart, it's just a simple bowl of buttered pasta. I add a few steps in the cooking process to elevate it a bit and make sure I don't end up with a stuck-together mass in the shape of the pot. First, I toast the couscous on a baking sheet in the oven with a little oil to bring out its nutty flavor and to prevent the grains from sticking together. Then I cook it risotto style so that the starch from the couscous adds creaminess to the dish. I add mushrooms and kale and finish, of course, with a big pat of butter.

> 2 cups Israeli couscous
> 5 tablespoons olive oil
> 6 cups My Chicken Stock (page 167), or water
> 1 carrot, peeled and grated (about ½ cup)
> 4 garlic cloves, chopped
> ¾ cup diced onion
> ½ cup dry white wine
> 1 cup tomato puree
> 1 teaspoon black pepper

> ¾ teaspoon kosher salt
> 2 cups coarsely chopped maitake or cremini mushrooms
> ½ bunch kale, shredded (about 2 cups packed)
> 3 tablespoons butter

● Preheat the oven to 350°F. Toss the couscous with 1 tablespoon of the oil and spread out on a baking sheet. Bake until the couscous is dark brown and smells nutty, about 15 minutes. Set aside.

● Bring the chicken stock to a simmer in a saucepan and adjust the heat to maintain a simmer.

● Warm 2 tablespoons of the oil in a large skillet over medium heat and add the carrot, garlic, and ½ cup of the diced onion. Cook, stirring occasionally, until the onion has softened but not browned, about 8 minutes. Add the toasted couscous and stir to coat well with the

oil. Add the wine and tomato puree and cook until the wine has evaporated and the tomato puree reduced, about 5 minutes. Add the pepper and salt.

● Start adding the chicken stock to the skillet in ½-cup increments, adjusting the heat as needed to keep the liquid simmering. Stir often until the liquid has been absorbed before adding the next ½ cup of liquid. It will take about 40 minutes for all the liquid to be absorbed and the couscous to be cooked through.

● In a clean skillet, warm the remaining 2 tablespoons oil over medium heat and add the mushrooms and the remaining ¼ cup onion. Cook until the onion has softened and the mushrooms have released their liquid and begun to brown at the edges, about 10 minutes. Add the kale and cook just until the leaves are tender and wilted, about 5 more minutes. Off the heat, swirl in 1 tablespoon of the butter.

● Fold the mushroom-kale mixture into the couscous. Just before serving, fold in the remaining 2 tablespoons butter.

"*At home rice pilaf is the perfect thing to make when you have absolutely nothing to eat in your kitchen.*"

PILAF COQUELICOT

PILAF WITH KALE

PILAF WITH CARROTS

RICE PILAF

"The beauty of the pilaf method is that it manages to pack the rice with flavor while maintaining the integrity of individual grains."

WITHOUT A DOUBT, pilaf is my favorite way to prepare rice. The method takes something as plain as steamed rice and turns it into party time with a handful of ingredients that even a poor, overworked cook would have in his or her home kitchen. The beauty of the pilaf method is that it manages to pack the rice with flavor while maintaining the integrity of the individual grains. Every step in the process is specifically designed to achieve this platonic ideal.

I prefer jasmine rice for its firm texture and the small size of the grains. First I wash the rice to remove excess starch that will cause the grains to stick together. Then I soak the rice to shorten the cooking time, so the interior of the grain finishes cooking before the exterior begins to fall apart. And I toast the rice in oil or fat before adding the liquid; this coats each grain in a protective jacket that helps it retain its individuality. Finally, I cook the rice in the gentle, even heat of the oven, rather than the violent bottom-up heat of the stovetop.

When we first opened Zahav, I imagined that we would make rice in batches throughout the night, which would allow us to serve the freshest rice possible. Before dinner service, we would make up kits of premeasured rice, water, and seasonings to have ready when called upon. Besides being completely impractical in a busy restaurant, I quickly realized that this idea actually did a huge disservice to the rice: Rice needs to rest after it's cooked. The moisture needs time to evenly distribute throughout the grain and the starch needs time to set up—if you handle rice too quickly after cooking, the grains easily break apart and you can end up with a gluey mess. I recommend resting it for at least 15 to 20 minutes, or longer if you have the time and patience. (Avi will sometimes wrap a pot of finished rice in a towel and leave it for hours to cool down completely.)

Another advantage of the pilaf method is it gives you three opportunities to add flavor: toasting the rice; choosing the cooking liquid itself; and fluffing and seasoning the rice before serving. The recipes are far less important than the technique.

At home rice pilaf is a great thing to make when you think you have absolutely nothing to eat in your kitchen. Thinly slice those last few stalks of celery in the bottom of your vegetable bin and sauté them in olive oil with some garlic while toasting the rice. Add a package of frozen peas on top while the rice is cooling (covered) and finish with grated Parmesan cheese. Even leftover orange juice or V8 (or both together) will give you intensely flavored rice. And if you brown some ground beef before you add the rice, you'll have a soulful one-pot meal. Fold a handful of sunflower seeds and raisins (rehydrated in water) from the back of your pantry into a rested pilaf to create an addictive sweet and salty pot of rice fit for royalty. Once you master the technique, you'll likely never settle for plain steamed rice again.

THREE PILAFS

THESE PILAF VARIATIONS are three delicious pots of rice with three distinct personalities. In one, the rice is cooked entirely in carrot juice with a bit of saffron, whose color and flavor reminds me of lobster broth. In the second, minced kale is sautéed with garlic and onions as the rice is toasted to make for a beautiful green rice infused with kale flavor. And in the third version, the rested rice is seasoned with poppy seeds, dill, and walnuts to add fragrance, texture, and flavor to the finished dish.

PILAF WITH CARROTS
Serves 6 to 8

> 2 *cups jasmine rice*
> *Kosher salt*
> ¼ *cup olive oil*
> ½ *cup sliced onion*
> ½ *cup grated carrot*
> 2 *garlic cloves, chopped*
> 2 *cups carrot juice*
> *Pinch saffron*
> *Pinch cayenne*

● Cover the rice with water by several inches in a bowl and add a pinch of salt. Let soak for at least 1 hour or up to overnight. Drain well.

● Preheat the oven to 350°F. Warm the oil in a large ovenproof pot with a tight-fitting lid over medium heat. Add the onion, carrot, and garlic. Season with a pinch of salt, and cook, stirring occasionally, until the vegetables begin to soften but not brown, about 8 minutes. Add the rice and cook, stirring, until the rice is evenly coated and begins to lightly toast, about 3 minutes more.

● Add the carrot juice, saffron, and cayenne. Raise the heat to high, then lower to a simmer. Stir with a fork once or twice, add 1 teaspoon salt, cover, and transfer to the oven. Bake until the rice is cooked through, 15 to 20 minutes. Let stand off the heat, covered, for 20 minutes before fluffing with a fork and serving.

PILAF WITH KALE
Serves 6 to 8

> 2 *cups jasmine rice*
> *Kosher salt*
> ¼ *cup olive oil*
> ½ *cup sliced onion*
> 2 *garlic cloves, chopped*
> 2 *cups (packed) finely minced kale*
> ½ *teaspoon black pepper*
> *Pinch ground Urfa pepper (see page 48)*
> 2 *cups My Chicken Stock (page 167)*
> 1 *tablespoon finely grated lemon zest*

● Cover the rice with water by several inches in a bowl and add a pinch of salt. Let soak for at least 1 hour or up to overnight. Drain well.

● Preheat the oven to 350°F. Warm the oil in a large ovenproof pot with a tight-fitting lid over medium heat. Add the onion and garlic. Season with a pinch of salt and cook, stirring occasionally, until the vegetables just barely begin to soften, about 4 minutes. Add the kale and black and Urfa peppers and cook until the kale is tender, another 5 minutes. Add the rice and cook, stirring, until the rice is evenly coated and begins to lightly toast, about 3 minutes more.

● Add the chicken stock and lemon zest, raise the heat to high, and bring to a simmer. Stir with a fork once or twice, add 1 teaspoon salt, cover, and transfer to the oven. Bake until the rice is cooked through, 15 to 20 minutes. Let stand off the heat, covered, for 20 minutes before fluffing with a fork and serving.

PILAF COQUELICOT (POPPY SEED PILAF)

Serves 6 to 8

> 2 cups jasmine rice
>   Kosher salt
> ¼ cup olive oil
> 1 cup sliced onion
> 2 garlic cloves, chopped
> ½ teaspoon black pepper
> ¼ cup chopped fresh dill

> ¼ cup chopped walnuts
> ¼ cup poppy seeds

● Cover the rice with water by several inches in a bowl and add a pinch of salt. Let soak for at least 1 hour or up to overnight. Drain well.

● Preheat the oven to 350°F. Warm the oil in a large ovenproof pot with a tight-fitting lid over medium heat. Add the onion and garlic. Season with a pinch of salt and cook, stirring occasionally, until the vegetables begin to soften but not brown, about 8 minutes. Add the rice and cook, stirring, until the rice is evenly coated and begins to lightly toast, about 3 minutes more.

● Add 2 cups water, raise the heat to high, and bring to a simmer. Stir with a fork once or twice, add the pepper and 1 teaspoon salt, cover, and transfer to the oven. Bake until the rice is cooked through, 15 to 20 minutes. Top the rice with the dill, walnuts, and poppy seeds. Let stand off the heat, covered, for 20 minutes before fluffing with a fork and serving.

MUJADARA

Serves 6 to 8

THIS LEGENDARY DISH of rice and lentils was said to be the one that Jacob traded with Esau for his birthright. And I can almost understand why Esau did the deal. This one-pot meal has everything: It's high in protein and fiber, has incredible flavor—and it's vegan to boot! Mujadara is the Arabic word for pockmarked and refers to the way that the brown lentils dot the grain. Although mujadara is commonly made with rice, historically it was made with whatever grain was available. On a recent trip to Israel, I ate a meal with a Bedouin family and was surprised to see their mujadara made with freekah.

Caramelized onions are the secret weapon here. With the proper amount of patience, you will be rewarded with something of incredible depth, almost meaty, and sweet in a way that is balanced and not cloying. The warm spices of the baharat in the mujadara help amplify this sensation of meatiness. I like to use beluga lentils because they retain their shape and texture well. Because of their long cooking time, the lentils are cooked separately from the rice and then combined. If you want to cowboy it, you can use brown lentils and cook them together with the rice and onions using the basic pilaf method (see page 282). I like to eat mujadara by itself or topped with sumac and labneh for an incredibly satisfying and healthy meal.

RICE

- 2 cups basmati rice
- Kosher salt
- 1 tablespoon olive oil
- ¼ cup Caramelized Onions (see opposite)
- 1 tablespoon baharat (see page 54)
- Pinch black pepper

LENTILS

- 1 cinnamon stick
- 1 (1-inch) piece fresh ginger
- 1 head garlic, halved crosswise
- ½ onion, unpeeled
- ½ bunch cilantro, leaves picked and stems reserved
- 1 cup beluga lentils

● **FOR THE RICE:** Cover the rice with water by several inches in a bowl and add a pinch of salt. Let soak for 1 hour. Drain well.

● Preheat the oven to 350°F. Warm the oil in a large ovenproof pot with a tight-fitting lid over medium heat. Add the caramelized onions, baharat, pepper, and a pinch of salt and stir to combine. Add the rice and cook, stirring, until the rice is evenly coated and begins to lightly toast, about 3 minutes.

● Add 2 cups water, raise the heat to high, and bring to a simmer. Stir with a fork once or twice, add 1½ teaspoons salt, cover, and transfer to the oven. Bake until the rice is cooked through, about 20 minutes.

Let stand off the heat, covered, for 20 minutes before fluffing with a fork.

● **FOR THE LENTILS:** Combine the cinnamon stick, ginger, garlic, onion, cilantro stems, and lentils in a pot. Cover with about 4 cups cold water, raise the heat to medium-high, and bring to a boil. Lower the heat to maintain a bare simmer and cook until the lentils are tender, 20 to 30 minutes. Drain, and discard the cinnamon, ginger, garlic, onion, and cilantro stems.

● To serve, spoon the lentils over the rice and gently fold to combine. Top with the cilantro leaves.

● INGREDIENT ●

CARAMELIZED ONIONS

I DISCOVERED THE MAGIC of caramelized onions making French onion soup with my mom, long before I became a cook. Over several hours, I would watch as pounds and pounds of sharp onions cooked down to almost nothing and then those soft, concentrated onions would become the base of one of the most flavorful broths I'd ever tasted. Years later, when I cooked at Vetri, huge pots of onions would slowly caramelize all day every day, filling the kitchen with their concentrated sweet-savory fragrance. And today that same scent fills my kitchen at Zahav.

Though most recipes in this book call for just a little caramelized onion, you might as well make a big batch. They can be minced and stirred into soups, are perfect folded into tehina and served with chicken livers (page 54), and can be wonderful added to feta as a filling for borekas (page 205). I love a bit of caramelized onion smeared on a just-baked laffa with plenty of labneh and za'atar. In fact, consider doubling this batch.

¼ cup olive oil
6 large onions, halved and sliced
   Kosher salt

Warm the oil over low heat in a large skillet. Add the onions and a couple pinches of salt. Cook over low heat, stirring periodically, until the onions are completely brown and almost spreadably soft, about 3 hours. Caramelized onions freeze well and will keep for a few months. Makes about 1½ cups.

FIDEOS KUGEL
Serves 4 to 6

THIS BEAUTIFUL PIE is my version of kugel, the noodle (or potato) pudding that originated in Germany hundreds of years ago and still occupies a special place on the Jewish table. Although originally savory, kugels from the Ashkenazi Jewish tradition of Poland are often flavored with raisins, cinnamon, and farmer's cheese. In Israel, the famous Jerusalem kugel, which incorporates caramelized onions and black pepper, walks the line between sweet and savory.

I use Spanish fideos in this savory rendition, inspired by the Sephardic tradition. I briefly toast the fideos on a baking sheet in the oven, then cook them in chicken stock using the risotto method so they absorb as much flavor as possible. When the noodles are cool, I fold in eggs, slow-cooked smoked beef or lamb, dried cherries, and ground Urfa pepper. I bake the mixture in a skillet or baking dish until the exterior forms a golden-brown crust and the interior is creamy and tender.

I use leftover smoked brisket scraps from Percy Street, our barbecue restaurant. In case you don't happen to own your own smokehouse, the recipe works just as well with other leftover meat. In fact, this is a great way to stretch a small amount of meat into a hearty dish to serve a lot of people.

FIDEOS
Our Mexican cooks at Zahav are really familiar with these thin noodles because of the Spanish influence in their native country.

2 tablespoons olive oil, *plus more for the skillet*

1½ cups *fideos*

2 cups *My Chicken Stock (page 167)*

1 tablespoon *Caramelized Onions (see page 287)*

2 cups *chopped cooked meat, such as My Mom's Coffee-Braised Brisket (page 308), The Zahav Lamb Shoulder (page 302), or other cooked meat*

½ cup *dried sour cherries*

Pinch *ground Urfa pepper (see page 48)*

2 large *eggs, beaten*

● Preheat the oven to 425°F. Brush an ovenproof skillet or baking dish with oil and set aside.

● Toss the fideos with 1 tablespoon of the oil and scatter on a baking sheet. Bake until they turn brown and smell toasted, 2 to 3 minutes. Remove from the oven.

● Bring the chicken stock to a simmer in a pot over high heat. Lower the heat enough to just maintain a bare simmer. Warm the caramelized onions and the remaining 1 tablespoon oil in a skillet over medium heat. Add the toasted fideos and stir to coat. Add the chicken stock, about ½ cup at a time, cooking until the stock is absorbed between each addition, and until the fideos are tender, about 12 minutes. Off the heat, add the cooked meat, dried cherries, and Urfa pepper. Stir and let cool.

● Stir the beaten eggs into the fideos mixture. Pour the mixture into the greased skillet or baking dish and bake until brown and crisp on the top, 20 to 30 minutes. Serve hot or at room temperature.

8

MESIBAH

• It's Party Time •

WE MARK TIME sitting at the table. Year after year, on holidays and birthdays and even at funerals, we sit and eat and take note of what is the same and what has changed. We take stock of where we are and where we want to be. And food is the tonic that makes it all easier to swallow. A few glasses of wine don't hurt either.

> ## "I've dedicated my career to bringing people together at table—it's my strongest sense of home."

I've lived in Philadelphia for almost fifteen years now, longer than I've lived anywhere. I was born in Israel and raised in Pittsburgh, but Philly is home. It's where I was during the best and worst times in my life. It's where I met my wife, and it's where my sons were born. It's where I was when my brother died. It's where I met my business partner, Steve, and it's where we've opened ten businesses together in as many years. I came to Philly in 2001, following a girl, of course. The relationship didn't last, but a new one was beginning. The restaurant scene in Philadelphia was taking off and, as a recent graduate of the Florida Culinary Institute, I was hungry to test my skills in the real world. I got off to a rocky start. Terence Feury, the chef of the Striped Bass, fired me almost immediately. The Bass, as we called it, was the legendary Neil Stein restaurant; when it opened in 1994 it helped fuel the Philadelphia restaurant renaissance. I had worked in busier restaurants, but I'd never worked in a place with such impossibly high standards. It came as a shock to me that I could work so hard and still not be good enough. But instead of being discouraged, I was even more determined to work there. I spoke with Terence right before heading out to the Hamptons for a summer gig. Come back in the fall, he told me. But you'll start at the bottom.

I returned to the Bass in September to the garde-manger (cold) station, the traditional entry-level position for inexperienced cooks. It was humbling, but this time I knew what was expected of me, so I put my head down and banged. It was so hard—cooks would regularly walk out before service because they just couldn't take it. The A-team worked dinner on Thursday, Friday, and Saturday, and then brunch and dinner on Sunday. We clocked in from 2 p.m. to midnight, then worked for a couple more hours off the clock. On Saturday night, we left the restaurant at 2 a.m. and had to be back at 7 a.m. to prepare for brunch. And when brunch was over, we had less than two hours to set up our barren stations for Sunday dinner. Terence was always there. He worked harder than any of us, and we worked our asses off for him. He wasn't the fastest cook, but he was the best. He just did not make mistakes. He had spent years in the kitchen at Le Bernardin, finally becoming saucier, and wasn't about to lower his standards just because we couldn't keep up. We cut our herbs inside the walk-in refrigerator so they'd stay fresher. Our mise en place was a field guide of precision knife cuts and classic sauce work. If our brunoise (⅛-inch dice) was less than perfect, it went in the trash. Cutting corners wasn't tolerated. If a cook didn't want to be there, Terence didn't want

293

AMBER #2
The best barbecue
potato chip spice ever.
A bit smoky and sweet,
but the red chiles
Lior Lev Sercarz (see
Resources, page 359)
uses in his spice blend
are reminiscent of
Aleppo or hot paprika.
It's perfect with
shakshouka.

> *"I sometimes wonder what
> my life would be like if I'd
> followed that girl to Vermont
> or a beach with a great break."*

him there, even if it meant more work for him and for all of us. We functioned as a team, and we bailed each other out of the weeds. I loved it. In six months, I was promoted to lead line cook. I worked the station called the middle, cooking half a dozen of the restaurant's most popular dishes and expediting plates to make sure all the food for each table was ready at once. It was a great time to be cooking in Philly. The economy was strong, and the Bass was at the top of the scene. We went through mountains of caviar and foie gras and lobster. People traveled from all over the country to eat there; we did three hundred covers a night.

I was well on my way to being promoted to saucier, one step away from sous chef, when Marc Vetri called. I had been pestering Marc for a job ever since I moved to Philly. With only three cooks in the kitchen of Vetri, opportunities were few, so I jumped at the chance to work with Marc. Terence was pissed, but I think he understood. The writing was on the wall at the Bass. Our paychecks had already started to bounce, and vendors (and the government) weren't getting paid. Terence only stuck around for a few more months after I left and then pretty soon the Feds were there, seizing computers.

Vetri couldn't have been more different than the Striped Bass. At the Bass, we must have had two dozen sauces—pot after pot of careful reductions and emulsions, the distillation of hundreds of pounds of bones and vegetables and herbs and spices into a few drops of precious liquid. At Vetri, the primary sauce ingredients were pasta cooking water, weak chicken stock, and olive oil or butter, thrown in a pan and brought together on the spot. I remember one time we made a dish of salt-crusted branzino, sauced with a quick emulsion of pasta water, vinegar, and truffle butter. "This is the best thing we have ever served here," Marc told me. And I believed him. He could coax flavor out of the simplest ingredients. His food had so much soul. It was amazing to be in a kitchen where the chef was the owner. If you overcooked a rib eye, you felt like you were taking money from his pocket. Vetri only had about thirty seats, but Marc was always trying to figure out how to take tables away, rather than cram more in—anything to make the guest experience more perfect. In those days, Marc drove a beat-up pickup truck and generally carried himself like a poor person, but he would buy $300 custom plates from Italy for his customers. He was constantly reinvesting in

the restaurant, and that was a point of pride for all of us who worked there. He followed his own rules. If he wanted to close the restaurant on Saturdays during the summer, or on New Year's Eve, or for the entire month of August, he just did it. If he wanted to serve spit-roasted goat, he'd build a spit. By hand. In the backyard. One morning, I came into the kitchen and found Marc with a whole goat. Roast this on the spit, he said, and then went off to play basketball or take a nap or something. I had no idea what I was doing. When he got back, he looked at the goat and said, "That doesn't look right." He broke down the undercooked goat into pieces and returned it to the oven to slow-roast in its own fat and juices. Served with polenta, that goat became an instant classic. I have no idea what gave Marc the confidence to put his four-star restaurant in the hands of someone like me, but he is an investor in people. Vetri was Marc's home, and the staff was his family. If Dave hadn't been killed in 2003, I probably would have taken Marc up on his offer to send me to work in Italy. We butted heads a lot, but I realize now that my approach as a chef owes a lot to Marc. And I try to manage people like he managed me, by giving them plenty of room to figure things out on their own.

I sometimes wonder what my life would be like now if I had followed that girl to the slopes of Vermont or a beach town with a great break instead of Philadelphia. I might have been a better snowboarder or surfer, but I wouldn't have worked for Terence and Marc, who have more to do with who I am as a chef than anyone. Terence showed me that there's no substitute for hard work; that success is a collection of a million little things. Marc taught me to do what he did: listen to my own voice. He gave me the confidence to make my own rules. People thought I was crazy to open a modern Israeli restaurant in Philadelphia, but I wasn't listening. I couldn't. Zahav is an extension of who I am. And it's a place for my extended family of coworkers and guests. When Israelis visit Zahav, the nicest thing they can say is that our hummus takes them back home. That is the power of food—the ability to communicate a sense of place that transcends geography. I've dedicated my career to bringing people together at the table. And the table is where my strongest associations of home live, from the Coffee-Braised Brisket (page 308) my mom made every Rosh Hashana in Pittsburgh to the first meal we ever served at Zahav, a Passover seder right before we opened the restaurant.

At Zahav, we serve a family-style meal we call mesibah. The centerpiece is a whole lamb shoulder braised in pomegranate molasses (page 302) that our guests pull apart with their hands from a big platter on the table. Mesibah translates literally as "party time"—because any chance to gather at the table fells like a party to me.

SHAKSHOUKA
At a family breakfast. *Clockwise, from top left*, Shira Rudavsky with Eva, Leo, Steve, and Danny Cook, and Mary Solomonov. High-five with David Solomonov. Mary with Sally Cook.

SHAKSHOUKA
Serves 8

CONSTRUCTION AT ZAHAV TOOK PLACE during the dead of winter in 2008. Since there was no heat in the building, our contractor, Ofer Shlomo, brought in propane-fired space heaters to keep his crew from freezing. The heaters were cylindrical, with flat metal tops—perfect for heating up a frying pan. And so, of course, Ofer made shakshouka. Shakshouka is a simple and quick North African dish of eggs poached in a spicy stew of tomatoes and peppers that packs a punch. It's a great, large-format brunch dish to feed a crowd. Shakshouka is another great example of a dish that came from elsewhere but is now essential to Israeli cuisine. (On a recent trip to Israel, I even had shakshouka at a gas station diner.)

Much of this has to do with economics. Tomatoes and peppers grow year-round in Israel, and eggs are an inexpensive source of protein. Shakshouka became an economical way to create a nutritious and flavorful meal. Shakshouka is a stovetop dish, and that ease of preparation contributed to its popularity. It's also a very fun word to say. This recipe is a very straightforward version, but shakshouka can be bedazzled with all sorts of things, from merguez (or any other sausage) to feta or Parmesan cheese. It's

easily scaled up or down depending on your crowd. But the most important question: What kind of bread will you choose to sop up every last drop of sauce?

½ cup olive oil

2 onions, chopped (about 3 cups)

4 red or green bell peppers, chopped

6 garlic cloves, sliced

2 tablespoons grated dried lime (see page 92), optional

6 tablespoons sweet paprika

2 teaspoons ground cumin

2 teaspoons ground coriander

½ teaspoon kosher salt

8 cups tomato puree

1 tablespoon plus 1 teaspoon sugar

16 large eggs

Serrano chiles, thinly sliced

Fresh cilantro, chopped

● Heat ¼ cup of the oil over medium heat in a cast iron skillet large enough to accommodate 16 poached eggs. (If you don't have a skillet that large, use two pans, dividing the ingredients evenly between them.) Add the onions, bell peppers, garlic, dried lime (if using), paprika, cumin, coriander, and salt and cook, stirring occasionally, until the vegetables have softened but not browned, about 10 minutes. Add the tomato puree and sugar and simmer until reduced by about one-third, 10 to 12 minutes. Whisk in the remaining ¼ cup oil.

● Crack the eggs into the skillet, spacing them evenly in the sauce. Lower the heat, cover, and cook until the egg whites are set but the yolks remain runny, about 5 minutes. Top with serrano chiles and cilantro and serve immediately right from the pan.

"Friends matter most at a big table. Or is it the roast chicken, Zahav lamb shoulder, Persian rice, and grilled fish?"

THE ZAHAV LAMB SHOULDER
Serves 8

ONE NIGHT IN 2006, as the executive chef of Marigold Kitchen, I was preparing a dinner at the James Beard House in New York. By the time we finished up, our crew was hungry and exhausted. We rolled into Momofuku Ssäm Bar around midnight, and several minutes later were presented with an entire slow-cooked pork shoulder, crackling on the outside and soft and juicy on the inside. With the familiarity of a kitchen team that had just worked a fourteen-hour shift, we devoured the whole thing.

The Zahav lamb shoulder was born that night on the drive home. It was also possibly responsible for keeping me from falling asleep at the wheel. Next to our hummus, this is the dish that put Zahav on the map. We brine a whole lamb shoulder and smoke it over hardwood for a couple of hours. Then we braise it in pomegranate molasses until the meat is tender enough to eat with a spoon. Finally, the lamb shoulder is finished in a hot oven to crisp the exterior. This dish is the best of all possible worlds—smoky and crispy, soft and tender, sweet and savory—and it's a celebration all by itself. The use of pomegranate in this dish (and the crispy rice we serve with it) is very Persian, which is a cuisine with a tradition so rich it always makes me think of palaces and royal banquets.

Chickpeas, the underrated star of this dish, recall the humble chamin, a traditional Sabbath stew that's slow-baked overnight. During the long braise, the lamb bones create a natural stock that is absorbed by the chickpeas, creating the richest, creamiest peas you've ever tasted. I've even made hummus with these braised chickpeas—totally decadent!

Preparing the lamb shoulder is a two- or three-day process and thus requires some advance planning. We go through about sixty shoulders a week at the restaurant, and it's still not enough. If you've ever been disappointed at Zahav, chances are it's because we didn't have a lamb shoulder for you. Now, you can make it for yourself.

We smoke our lamb shoulders at Percy Street Barbecue. If you have a smoker, feel free to smoke the lamb. Or just roast the shoulder as the recipe indicates.

Generous ¼ cup kosher salt
2 tablespoons sugar
1 teaspoon fennel seeds
1 teaspoon black peppercorns
1 teaspoon allspice berries
1 head garlic, halved crosswise
1 cup dried chickpeas
1 teaspoon baking soda
1 bone-in square-cut lamb shoulder (about 5 pounds)
½ cup pomegranate molasses (see page 304)
   Persian Rice (page 270), optional

● Combine the salt with the sugar, fennel seeds, peppercorns, allspice, garlic, and about 2 quarts water in a large pot. Bring to a rapid boil, stirring to dissolve the salt. Remove from the heat and allow the brine to cool completely.

● Combine the chickpeas with the baking soda in a large bowl and cover with water by several inches. Let soak overnight.

● Put the lamb shoulder in a large (6- to 8-quart) container and pour the brine over the lamb. (Ideally, the lamb shoulder should be submerged, so weight it with two plates. But if that's impractical, cover the lamb with a clean cloth that's saturated in the brine.) Refrigerate the lamb shoulder in the brine overnight or for up to 48 hours.

● Preheat the oven to 475°F. Place a rack on a baking sheet. Drain the lamb and pat dry. Put the lamb on the rack and roast until well browned on the exterior, about 30 minutes. (Or sear the lamb over a medium-

hot grill for 15 minutes until well browned on all sides and nicely charred in places.) Lower the oven temperature to 300°F.

● Transfer the lamb shoulder to a large roasting pan. Mix the pomegranate molasses with 8 cups water in a bowl and add to the pan. (The liquid should come about halfway up the shoulder; add water if needed.) Drain the chickpeas and add them to the liquid. Place a sheet of parchment paper over the lamb and cover the pan tightly with foil.

● Braise in the oven until the lamb shreds easily with a fork and the chickpeas are tender, about 5 hours. Let the lamb cool in its braising liquid in the refrigerator overnight.

● The next day, preheat the oven to 475°F. Roast the lamb, uncovered, spooning the braising liquid over the lamb every 5 minutes, until the lamb is hot through and glazed with the liquid, about 30 minutes. Serve with crispy Persian rice if you like.

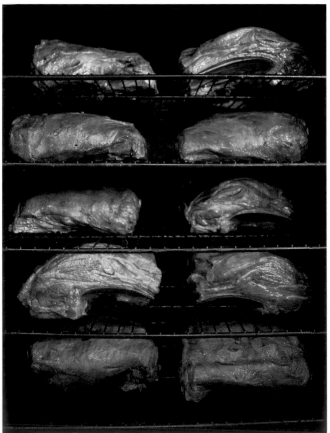

POMEGRANATE MOLASSES

POMEGRANATE MOLASSES is the juice of pomegranate seeds mixed with sugar and reduced to a thick syrup until it's almost candy-like, at once very sweet and very sour from the astringency of pomegranates' natural tannins. It is an important ingredient in Middle Eastern cooking, especially Persian cuisine. I add it to slow-braised meats, like the lamb shoulder on page 302, but it can be used straight from the bottle—as a sauce for ice cream, drizzled onto grilled chicken livers, or poured directly into your mouth. (See Resources, page 359.)

LAMB SHOULDER
Few folks finish the shoulder, which means plenty of leftovers to fry up in a cast-iron pan and serve wrapped in warm tortillas with salsa verde.

WHOLE ROAST CHICKEN WITH LAFFA AND TEHINA

Serves 4

ROAST CHICKEN IS ONE OF MY FAVORITE things to eat, but it's actually difficult to cook well. Either you end up with overcooked white meat or you get a well-cooked bird with pale and soggy skin. Removing the backbone and butterflying the bird (called spatchcocking) is a great way to ensure an evenly cooked and browned chicken. (You can ask your butcher to do this.)

The rub of celery seed and harissa may seem unorthodox, but it's my take on a classic Palestinian combination of bitter and spicy flavors. Although this chicken is cooked in the oven, a butterflied chicken is even more amazing cooked over an indirect fire on a charcoal grill. I like to rest the roasted chicken on an oversized laffa before carving to soak up all of the savory juices. A bed of rice works just as well. Basic Tehina Sauce is the perfect partner for chicken: It is rich where chicken is lean, and won't overwhelm the mild flavor.

1 *whole chicken (about 4 pounds)*

1 *tablespoon kosher salt*

1 *tablespoon celery seeds*

2 *tablespoons harissa (see page 61 or store-bought)*

Basic Tehina Sauce (page 32)

Laffa (page 212) or store-bought lavash flatbread

Simple Sumac Onions (page 97)

● Put the chicken breast side down on a cutting board. Using kitchen shears, cut along one side of the backbone, then the other, and remove it. (Discard the backbone or save for chicken stock.) Flip the chicken over so the breast side is up and press hard on the breastbone to make the chicken as flat as possible.

● Season the chicken all over with the salt and celery seeds. Rub well with the harissa. Cover loosely with plastic wrap and let rest in the refrigerator for at least 4 hours or up to overnight.

● Preheat the oven to 400°F. Place a rack inside a roasting pan. Put the chicken on the rack and roast until cooked through and the spices are browned and fragrant, about 35 minutes (an instant-read thermometer should read 165°F). Serve with the tehina, laffa, and sumac onions.

WHOLE FISH IN GRAPE LEAVES

Serves 2

THE FIRST TIME I EVER SAW a whole fish cooked on the bone was in the kitchen at Vetri. I came from the school of medium-rare cooking, and it was an eye-opener to watch fish cooked well past this point. What I quickly learned was that cooking protein on the bone adds flavor while insulating the meat so that it doesn't dry out. I wrap the fish in grape leaves to keep the flesh moist in the oven. The leaves come packed in brine, and their salt and acidity help to season the fish as it cooks. The grape leaves get super-crispy in the hot oven and make addictive chips to snack on.

We used to have this fish on the menu at Zahav, but filleting it would bury the kitchen every time an order went out. The dish is better prepared at home, where you have the time to give it the attention it deserves and where it will make a big impression on your guests. More guests? Roast more fish!

1   *whole branzino or other similar whole fish (about 1½ pounds)*
    Kosher salt

1   *lemon, quartered*

½   *cup chopped fresh dill*

15   *large grape leaves*
    Olive oil, for drizzling

● Preheat the oven to 400°F. Line a baking sheet with parchment paper and set aside. Salt the fish well (inside and out) and stuff the cavity with the lemon quarters and dill. Arrange the grape leaves in a rectangle nearly as long and twice as wide as the fish and place the fish in the center. Wrap the fish tightly in the leaves, overlapping them to help seal the fish, and transfer to the lined baking sheet. Drizzle oil over the leaves.

● Bake until the fish is cooked through, 15 to 20 minutes. (Poke a knife into the flesh to make sure it's cooked.) Peel the crisp leaves off the fish and set aside. With a knife and a spoon, pull the skin from the fish and discard. Then gently remove the fillets from the bones. Drizzle the fillets with oil and more salt and serve with the reserved grape leaves.

MY MOM'S COFFEE-BRAISED BRISKET

Serves 8

THIS IS MY TAKE ON THE DISH my mother served at virtually every special-occasion dinner of my childhood. And my mom's version was her take on the dish that her mother made. Brisket has a long history on the Jewish table, primarily because it was a very economical cut. Unfortunately, brisket is no longer cheap, but when cooked properly, it's still one of the beefiest and most flavorful pieces of meat you can find. Whether it's first or second cut (the flat or the point) matters less than making sure the meat has a nice layer of fat on one side.

My grandmother made her brisket with carrots, potatoes, and Heinz Chili Sauce, which gave it a traditional sweet-and-sour flavor. My mother added the coffee—she doesn't remember why, but it's pretty brilliant, actually. Unlike stock, coffee is a braising liquid ready in minutes, and its deep, roasted flavors work really well with beef (that's why coffee makes a great addition to barbecue sauce). In my version, I add cardamom to evoke Turkish coffee, and I replace the sweetness of that chili sauce with the deeper flavor of

dried apricots. You'll find braised eggs like the ones in this dish in cholent, or hamin, the Sabbath stew that is cooked slowly overnight and served on Saturday afternoon. They take on an almost creamy texture from the long cooking time, and as the coffee braising liquid penetrates the shells, it colors the eggs and subtly flavors them. I finish the whole dish with grated horseradish for a little bit of pungency to wake up the long-cooked flavors of the brisket.

I make brisket over several days: The first day, the seasoned meat is refrigerated overnight and the next day, it's cooked. The brisket can be served then, but its flavor and texture are far better if it is allowed to rest in its braising liquid for another night, then warmed, sliced, and served the following day.

2	tablespoons finely ground coffee
1½	tablespoons ground cardamom
1½	tablespoons ground black cardamom
1	tablespoon plus 1 teaspoon kosher salt
1	brisket (first cut, about 4 pounds)
¼	cup canola oil

2 large onions, *sliced*

4 carrots, *peeled and sliced*

10 garlic cloves, *sliced*

⅓ cup tomato paste

1½ cups dried apricots

2 cups brewed coffee

8 large eggs in their shells

Grated fresh horseradish

● Mix the ground coffee, cardamom, black cardamom, and salt in a small bowl and rub into the brisket. Cover loosely with plastic wrap and refrigerate overnight.

● Preheat the oven to 475°F. Set a rack inside a roasting pan. Put the brisket on the rack and roast until the exterior has browned, about 20 minutes. Lower the oven temperature to 300°F.

● Warm the oil in a large skillet over medium heat and add the onions, carrots, and garlic. Cook, stirring occasionally, until the vegetables have softened but not browned, about 8 minutes. Add the tomato paste and cook until it reduces slightly, about 2 more minutes.

● Transfer the vegetables to the roasting pan with the rack removed. Add the brisket, dried apricots, brewed coffee, and eggs in their shells. Add enough water to bring the liquid halfway up the side of the brisket.

● Cover the pan tightly with two layers of foil, return to the oven, and braise for 1 hour. Remove the eggs, gently tap them all over to make a network of small cracks, and return them to the braise. Continue cooking until the brisket shreds easily with a fork, about 3 more hours. Let the brisket cool in its braising liquid, then refrigerate overnight.

● To serve, preheat the oven to 350°F. Slice the cold brisket, return to the braising liquid, and bake until warmed through, about 30 minutes. Spoon the broth over the meat. Serve with the peeled eggs and grated fresh horseradish.

YEMENITE BRAISED SHORT RIBS

Serves 6

THIS IS SORT OF LIKE upside-down Yemenite soup—it's the broth flavoring the meat, rather than the other way around. If you don't have homemade chicken stock, you can easily make this with store-bought stock supplemented with an extra tablespoon of hawaij. There are few braising cuts with as much flavor and richness as short ribs. The key to great braised meat is to cook it in advance so that it has time to cool completely in its braising liquid and reabsorb all of its flavorful juices. Then, when you gently reheat it in the braising liquid, the meat will be meltingly tender. For an extra treat, add some small peeled potatoes to the roasting pan during the last hour or so of cooking.

5 pounds bone-in beef short ribs

2 tablespoons kosher salt

1 tablespoon hawaij (see page 168)

2 onions, thinly sliced

2 carrots, peeled and thinly sliced

1 head garlic, halved crosswise

2 tablespoons olive oil

8 cups Yemenite Chicken Soup (page 166), or store-bought stock

● Season the short ribs with the salt and hawaij. Cover loosely with plastic wrap and let stand in the refrigerator overnight or for up to 3 days.

● Preheat the oven to 475°F. Mix the onions, carrots, and garlic with the oil and scatter in a roasting pan. Put the short ribs on top of the vegetables. Roast until the short ribs are well browned, about 20 minutes.

● Lower the oven temperature to 325°F. Add the soup or stock to the roasting pan. The liquid should come about halfway up the ribs; add water if needed. Cover the short ribs with parchment paper and cover the pan tightly with foil. Bake until the meat shreds easily with a fork, about 6 hours. Let cool, then refrigerate overnight in the braising liquid.

● To serve, preheat the oven to 350°F. Remove and discard the layer of fat that has risen to the top of the short rib juices. Cover and bake the ribs until warmed through, about 30 minutes. Slice the ribs and spoon the juices over the meat to serve.

SALT-BAKED LEG OF LAMB

Serves 8

USUALLY I'D WARN YOU AGAINST a recipe that calls for 3 pounds of salt. But what you're really doing here is using the salt to create a super-insulated oven for the lamb. Salt is an even conductor of heat, and the crust traps all the moisture from the lamb so it literally steams in its own juices. The meat is well seasoned, but I promise it's not salty.

There is a romance in treating a leg of lamb this way, and the fragrant and festive spices used to season the meat capture that as well. The dried rose petals and dried lime are very Persian ingredients, and sumac, a floral and sour red spice, is used often in Palestinian cooking. You may be slightly hesitant to cook the lamb past medium-rare, but for this dish I insist. Cooked to a rosy medium and well rested, this lamb is uniformly tender and juicy.

1 *bone-in leg of lamb (about 6 pounds)*

⅓ *cup ground sumac (see page 97)*

2 *tablespoons grated dried lime (see page 92)*

2 *tablespoons ground Urfa pepper (see page 48)*

2 *tablespoons ground cinnamon*

3 *pounds (1 box) kosher salt*

2 *tablespoons dried rose petals (see Resources, page 359), crumbled (optional)*

3 *cinnamon sticks, broken into pieces*

● Score the exterior of the lamb in a crisscross pattern with a sharp paring knife. Combine the sumac, dried lime, Urfa pepper, ground cinnamon, and 1 tablespoon of the salt in a small bowl. Rub the spice mixture all over the lamb, working it into the cuts. Cover loosely with plastic wrap and let stand in the refrigerator overnight or for up to 3 days.

● Preheat the oven to 350°F. To make the salt crust, combine the remaining kosher salt, the crumbled rose petals, and cinnamon sticks with enough water (about 1 cup) to make a paste. Layer about one quarter of the salt paste in the bottom of a roasting pan, covering enough of the bottom so the lamb leg will rest on the salt. Set the lamb leg on top of the salt paste and use your hands to mold the remaining salt paste over the lamb.

● Roast the lamb until 140°F to 150°F on a meat thermometer, 1 to 1½ hours. Let rest for 20 to 30 minutes, then remove and discard the salt crust. Wipe the lamb with paper towels to remove the excess salt and let rest for another 10 minutes. Slice and serve, using the flavorful juices as a sauce.

LEG OF LAMB
Secrets of success?
Cooking the lamb
past medium rare;
letting it rest in its
salt crust; slicing the
leg vertically, then
making cross cuts.

MILK & HONEY

A Glimpse of the Divine

LIKE MY MOTHER (and probably because of her), I am a compulsive sugar eater. Sometimes the most important culinary decision I make all day is whether to choose Reese's or Twix. Savory food is satisfying in a soulful way, but dessert gives us a glimpse into the divine. And it's linked to hospitality because, at its core, hospitality is evidence that our world is basically good.

"A childhood memory: making chocolate truffles with my mom, the kitchen covered in cocoa powder."

My first job out of culinary school was at the Big City Tavern in Boca Raton, Florida. The restaurant was stupidly busy and full of the kind of characters I had read about in Anthony Bourdain's *Kitchen Confidential.* There was a sous chef named Joe Gil, but everyone called him Elvis or Big Daddy. He styled himself like a 1950s greaser, with slicked-back hair and black-rimmed sunglasses that he wore indoors and out. Joe indulged heavily in what I call "the restaurant lifestyle." Once I was working the station next to him and reached up to grab what I thought was my water, only to discover a moment too late that it was Joe's cup of warm vodka. Despite his destructive and self-destructive behavior, the owners of the restaurant kept Joe around. He was just such a goddamned good cook. Joe called me Rabbi, because I was Jewish and he wasn't that creative. He had taken a liking to me because his dad, like mine, was Sephardic. "You know," he explained, "twenty cups of coffee a day and a pastry after every meal."

SWEET TIMES
With my mother in the early 1980s, *above.* She's a really good cook and baking is her thing. Chocolate Babka, *left* (recipe on page 348).

Previous spread: Turning apples into Apple Confit (recipe on page 340).

In Israel, things get done over coffee and pastries. Pastries are truly everywhere: Trays piled with mountains of brightly colored, syrup-soaked confections are part of the landscape. The simplest roadside kiosks sell surprisingly good little sweet cakes and babkas and rugelach. Even the famous Israeli breakfast spread almost always includes a dish of halva for people who need an early morning sugar rush. In the *shuk* (market), a vendor will try to sell you carpets only after inviting you in for some apple tea and perhaps a piece of baklava. Business and personal matters are difficult to keep separate, just as it is virtually impossible to separate hospitality from sweets.

Hospitality has been a hallmark of Middle Eastern culture since Abraham welcomed strangers into his tent five thousand years ago. The philosopher Philip Hallie said that hospitality is not the opposite of indifference; it is the opposite of cruelty. In the harsh landscape of the region, to deny a person hospitality is to potentially put him in harm's way. And true hospitality is measured by how we treat people from whom we have no expectation of reciprocity.

HOSPITALITY
Chocolate babka in Tel Aviv's Carmel Market, *above*. In the old city of Jerusalem, a shop owner's snap of the fingers still brings a boy with the requisite deal-making coffee, *right*.

"In Israel, things get done over coffee and pastries. Brightly colored syrup-soaked sweets abound."

Hospitality is ritualized in the simplest daily routines. When you are invited into an Israeli home, there is always coffee and tea and cakes and cookies. My grandmother never drank coffee, but she always had two types to offer guests (granted, they were Nescafé and instant Turkish, but still). Every household in Israel has a *kumkum* (electric teakettle) at the ready should a guest materialize. At his old house, my father would run into the backyard to pick fresh lemongrass to make tea for visitors. My mother always has a full pot of American-style drip coffee and a Tupperware container full of Chinese chews on the kitchen table in her apartment in Kfar Saba. There's absolutely nothing Chinese about these chewy coconut bar cookies, but she has been making them for as long as I can remember. They keep forever, so they're great to have around when company drops in.

My mother, Evelyn Fisher, is a great cook. I love her coffee-braised brisket (you can find it on page 308), but sweets are her specialty. One of my earliest kitchen memories is making chocolate truffles with her, every surface covered in cocoa powder. The whole family would fight over her chocolate mousse. She used to buy giant boxes of Sour Patch Kids, ostensibly to bribe my brother and me, but I know she just wanted an excuse to eat them herself. I can always tell when she is coming to visit us because my wife starts filling the cupboards with packages of mini powdered sugar donuts and black licorice.

My mom moved to Israel when she was twenty-nine. If I didn't know better, I might think she did it for the sweets. She was born and raised in East Liverpool, Ohio, a small town west of Pittsburgh. Her family never lit a Shabbat candle in her life, but her parents were devoted to Israel. Her father, Alex Fisher, was a pediatrician and part of the volunteer sales force for Israel Bonds, which were conceived by David Ben-Gurion, the country's first prime minister, as a way to bolster Israel's fledgling economy. Ben-Gurion also wanted to ensure that the world Jewish community had a stake in the success of Israel. My grandfather traveled frequently to the isolated Jewish communities in small towns in Ohio, Pennsylvania, and West Virginia, trying to rally support for the new Israeli state. The War of Independence in 1948 had a devastating impact on Israel, and was immediately followed by a huge influx of refugees from Europe and the Middle East. As a conduit for foreign investment, Israel Bonds were a lifeline for the struggling country, allowing Israel to resettle the refugees and invest in infrastructure projects that laid the foundation for generations to come. In times of

GLAMOUR
My mother's parents, Alex and Betty Fisher, lived in East Liverpool, Ohio, and were quite stylish. *Above, ready for a night out in Florida.*

war, sales of Israel Bonds always surged. Since its beginnings in 1951, sales of Israel Bonds have raised $40 billion for the state. Initially, most of the buyers were American Jews. My grandfather knew all the early leaders of Israel—Ben-Gurion, Golda Meir, Yitzhak Rabin. Once, during the Yom Kippur War of 1973, he was summoned to Israel to witness the mutilated bodies of Israeli soldiers on the front lines. They wanted him to understand what was at stake, not just for Israel but for Jews everywhere. It was the only time my mother ever saw her father cry.

In East Liverpool, which had maybe one hundred Jewish families, Israel represented something important—the idea of a place where your identity as a Jew did not make you "other." To my mom, Israel represented home. When she went to boarding school, she had to fight to be able to attend synagogue on the high holidays and not to eat pork at the dinner table. Some of her classmates didn't speak to her because she was Jewish.

She visited Israel for the first time in 1962, when she was sixteen. Her parents hired a guide, who took the whole family through the country in a rented car. Starting in 1968, she returned every summer. In 1975 she decided to stay for the year and got a job teaching English. That was the year she met my father. If they hadn't gotten married, my mother might never have left. But by 1980, my father was fed up with Israel. My mother did not want to leave, but she did not want an unhappy husband either. They moved to Pittsburgh, an hour's drive from her hometown.

For ten or twelve years, she couldn't bring herself to return to Israel. She had a good job teaching English at the local Jewish day school in Pittsburgh, and her two sons were growing up in a tight-knit community. Then, in 1992, she agreed to chaperone an eighth-grade class trip to Israel (coincidentally, Steve's wife, Shira, happened to be a student on that trip). As soon as she got off the plane, a strange sensation set in. Everything had changed. The roads were all different; she didn't know how to get anywhere. But she felt that she was home again. She cried when she had to board the plane back to the U.S. One evening, shortly after returning from that trip, she and my father were eating dinner at Wendy's. "You know," my mom said, "I could really live in Israel again." And my dad said, "Let's go. I'm ready to go back."

"My grandfather, Alex Fisher, sold Israel bonds. He knew Ben-Gurion, Golda Meir, and Rabin."

My parents divorced soon after we moved there, but my mother has lived in Israel for over twenty years now. She might have thought about returning to Pittsburgh if my brother, Dave, hadn't died, since he probably would have enrolled in college here when he finished his army service. But Israel is her home. The country was founded during her lifetime, and now her son is buried there: There's nothing more Israeli than that. I visit her a couple of times a year. We sit at her kitchen table and drink coffee and eat Chinese chews. Dave's old army buddies drop by to visit. So do friends and neighbors and relatives.

FAMILY TIES
Probably in the late 1970s to celebrate my birth and quite possibly my bris, both sets of grandparents, the Fishers, *above right*, and the Solomonovs, were together in Israel.

Like most chefs, I have spent the majority of my cooking career on the savory side of the kitchen. Line cooking runs on adrenaline—it's all about instincts, split-second timing, and, sometimes, improvisation. Pastries are a meditation—time slows down and you must submit to the process. When I got to Vetri, my first job was working the pastry station. Although I struggled, I learned a kind of patience and attention to detail that ultimately helped me become a better cook and chef. We've never had a pastry chef at Zahav. I believe there needs to be continuity between the savory and sweet courses of the meal, a continuity too often lost when the pastry department is an autonomous region. Every cook who has worked the pastry station at Zahav has started on the savory side. I want my line cooks to understand how these disciplines can cross-pollinate. And I want them to experience the simple satisfaction that you get from baking for others (or for yourself). I appreciated this in my first kitchen job, working in the bakery in Kfar Saba, but I understood this much, much earlier—from those hours in the kitchen with my mother.

At Zahav, we welcome guests into our home every night. Many are regulars and old friends. But many are strangers, most of whom we will never see again. We measure ourselves by their experience. We want to find out everything about them. Where are they from and what brought them to Zahav? Are they celebrating a special occasion? Are there foods that they absolutely love or simply cannot eat? Have they visited Israel? We want to know anything that can help us make them feel like they came to the right place. Like the carpet merchant in the shuk, we want to take a business transaction and make it personal. And dessert is our final chance to do this. The Israelites were promised a land flowing with milk and honey. I'm just trying to do my part.

CHOCOLATE BABKA

RUGELACH

MINT TEA

APPLE CONFIT

WHITE CHOCOLATE CAKE

KONAFI

CARROT BASBOOSA

CASHEW BAKLAVA CIGARS

"Pastries are so much fun for a savory chef to make. They offer so many possibilities for fillings and flavors."

CHOCOLATE ALMOND SITUATION

RUGELACH WITH DATE FILLING
Makes 32 cookies

WHILE DRIED FRUITS AND NUTS are traditional, you can fill rugelach with pretty much whatever you like—even peanut butter and Marshmallow Fluff. The possibilities are endless, once you get the dough down. And the dough freezes so well that you can make big batches and use it when you need it. This master recipe has a date filling. Variations follow for peanut butter and Marshmallow Fluff filling, and one I love with apricot jam and pistachios.

DOUGH

- 12 *ounces cream cheese, softened*
- 3 *sticks (¾ pound) unsalted butter, softened*
- ½ *cup sugar*
  Pinch salt
- ½ *cup sour cream*
- 3 *cups all-purpose flour*

DATE FILLING

- 1 *cup dried dates*
- 1 *cup hazelnuts*
- 6 *tablespoons brown sugar*

● **FOR THE DOUGH:** Combine the cream cheese, butter, sugar, and salt in the bowl of a stand mixer fitted with the hook attachment (or use a hand mixer and a big bowl). Mix on low speed until just combined, scraping down the bowl as needed. Add half the sour cream and half the flour. Mix again on low speed until just combined. Add the remaining sour cream and flour and mix once more again until just combined. Refrigerate for at least 1 hour or up to overnight.

● **FOR THE FILLING:** Put the dried dates in a bowl and cover with boiling water by an inch. Cover with plastic wrap and let stand for 10 minutes. Drain the dates.

● While the dates are soaking, combine the hazelnuts and brown sugar in a food processor and process, scraping down the bowl as needed, until it reaches a wet-sand consistency, about 5 minutes. Add the dates

and ¼ cup water and puree until a sticky, smooth, spreadable paste has formed.

● **TO MAKE THE RUGELACH:** Preheat the oven to 350°F, with a rack in the middle. Line two baking sheets with oiled parchment. Divide the dough into 4 equal pieces. (Refrigerate the dough you're not working with.) Roll one quarter of the dough into a 10-inch circle about ⅛ inch thick. To neaten the edges, I like to invert a 10-inch bowl and cut around it. Spread one quarter of the filling evenly over the dough, leaving a ¼-inch border around the edge. Slice into 8 wedges. Roll each wedge into a coil, starting at the thick edge. Arrange on a baking sheet. Repeat with the remaining 3 portions of dough and filling. Bake until light brown, about 35 minutes. The rugelach will keep in a covered container at room temperature for about 2 days and frozen for up to 2 weeks.

RUGELACH WITH PEANUT BUTTER AND MARSHMALLOW FLUFF FILLING

1   *cup peanut butter*
½   *cup Marshmallow Fluff*

● Combine the peanut butter and Marshmallow Fluff in a bowl and stir to blend. Continue with the last step of the rugelach recipe.

RUGELACH WITH APRICOT JAM AND PISTACHIO FILLING

¾   *cup apricot jam*
¾   *cup pistachios, toasted and chopped*

● Combine the apricot jam and pistachios in a bowl and stir to blend. Continue with the last step of the rugelach recipe.

RUGELACH
The dough comes together quickly and once rolled out, becomes a canvas to experiment with fillings such as dates, apricot jam, and pistachio, even peanut butter and Marshmallow Fluff.

MA'AMOUL TARTLETS

Makes 6 tartlets

MA'AMOUL ARE CLASSIC Arabic shortbread cookies stuffed with dates or other dried fruits or nuts, usually shaped into little shells, or rolled and formed by hand. They are popular throughout the Arab world, especially during religious festivals, and are also traditionally eaten by Syrian, Lebanese, and Egyptian Jews on Purim, Rosh Hashana, and Chanukah. I used ma'amoul as the inspiration for this dessert, creating individual double-crusted tartlets stuffed with a rich, fruity date puree. A little bit of coarse semolina in the dough gives it snap. There is something exciting about your fork shattering the tart shell and finding the surprise inside.

DOUGH

1 cup coarse semolina flour or cornmeal

1 cup fine semolina flour

3 tablespoons sugar

¼ teaspoon salt

6 tablespoons (¾ stick) unsalted butter, melted

3 tablespoons milk

2 tablespoons orange blossom water

FILLING

3 cups dried dates

1 large egg

● **FOR THE DOUGH:** Combine the coarse semolina flour or cornmeal, fine semolina flour, sugar, and salt in the bowl of a stand mixer fitted with the paddle attachment (or use a hand mixer and a big bowl). Mix on low speed to combine. With the mixer running, stream in the butter, milk, and orange blossom water. Mix just until a smooth dough forms. Shape into 2 equal balls, wrap in plastic wrap, and refrigerate until well chilled, at least an hour or up to overnight.

· INGREDIENT ·

ORANGE BLOSSOM WATER

ORANGE BLOSSOM WATER is a by-product of the production of orange oil. It's a bit more delicate and appealing than rose water. To me, it tastes like a Creamsicle. It's wonderful in both sweet recipes and such savory applications as Moroccan pastilla (page 144). (See Resources, page 359.)

● **FOR THE FILLING:** Put the dates in a bowl and cover with boiling water by 1 inch. Cover the bowl with plastic wrap and let stand for 10 minutes. Drain the dates and puree in a food processor. When cool, add the egg and puree again to combine.

● Preheat the oven to 350°F with a rack in the middle. Divide each dough ball into 6 equal pieces. Roll each piece into a circle roughly 5 inches in diameter. (If the dough seems stiff, let it stand at room temperature until soft enough to roll without breaking apart.) Press half the dough rounds into the bottom and up the sides of six 4-inch mini tart pans. Spoon the filling evenly into the tartlets and top each with a second circle of dough. Crimp the edges to seal and cut a few slits so steam can escape. Bake until the tartlets are beginning to brown around the edges, about 30 minutes.

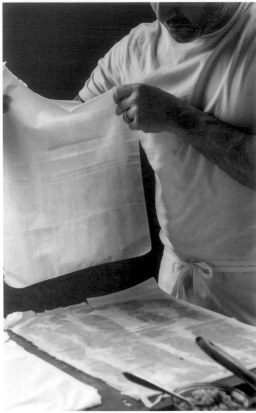

CASHEW BAKLAVA CIGARS

Makes 10 pastry rolls

I DON'T KNOW IF I'D EVER SEEN cashew baklava anywhere else, but I love cashews so much, I had to figure out how to make it. You can substitute any nut you want—peanuts work well. Unfortunately, the baklava most people experience has been made in huge batches and left to drown in syrup for days. Although baklava does require at least a few hours to set up and absorb the syrup, there is a world of difference between fresh and the stuff you see sitting around in deli cases. Adding a bit of cayenne to the filling is a trick I learned from the brilliant pastry chef Hedy Goldsmith of Michael's Genuine Food & Drink in Miami. Urfa pepper is amazing, too. Make sure that your sugar syrup is properly concentrated. If it's too watery or your cigars aren't rolled tightly enough, they can burst. If that happens, let the cigars cool, crush them, and use them as a topping for ice cream.

LEMON SYRUP

1 cup sugar
   Grated zest and juice of 1 lemon

FILLING

¾ cup whole cashews, *lightly toasted*
¼ cup brown sugar
   Pinch ground cardamom
   Pinch cayenne
   Pinch ground cinnamon
   Pinch salt
2 tablespoons unsalted butter, *melted*

DOUGH

3 sheets phyllo, *thawed*
5 tablespoons butter, *melted and cooled*

● **FOR THE SYRUP:** Combine the sugar with ½ cup water in a medium saucepan over high heat and bring to a boil. Continue boiling, whisking, until the sugar is completely dissolved, about 2 minutes. Add the lemon zest and juice and cover. Let stand off the heat for 15 minutes. Strain out and discard the zest. Reserve the syrup.

● **FOR THE FILLING:** Combine the cashews, brown sugar, cardamom, cayenne, cinnamon, salt, and butter in a food processor. Pulse until the mixture is finely ground to a uniform texture.

● **TO ASSEMBLE:** Lay out one sheet of phyllo with a short side closest to you and brush with butter. Place another sheet on top and brush with butter. Repeat with the third sheet of phyllo. Slice the rectangle lengthwise into 2 halves.

● Preheat the oven to 350°F, with a rack in the middle. Spoon 2 tablespoons of the filling in a straight line along the bottom edge of one of the phyllo rectangle stacks. Roll several turns into a cigar shape, slice the cigar free, and place in a baking dish. Repeat this process with the remaining filling. When all the cigars are assembled, brush with more butter.

● Bake until browned and crisp, 30 to 35 minutes. Drizzle with about ¼ cup of the lemon syrup, refrigerating the rest for another use. Let cool completely before serving.

BAKLAVA & KONAFI
In the heart of
the ancient city of
Nazareth, the bakery
Mahroum is run by the
fourth generation of
Arab bakers. Towers
of baklava, *above*, and
sweet konafi, *right*,
are just a few of the
offerings.

CLASSIC KONAFI
Serves 12

KATAIFI IS SHREDDED phyllo dough, used to make any number of traditional confections but especially the ubiquitous konafi. What's wonderful is that it's easy to find kataifi in boxes already shredded. Konafi has a baklava-level importance in the Middle East. In other words, it's huge. My introduction to it came in the little pastry stalls in the Old City of Jerusalem, where I discovered huge round sheet trays of pastry glistening with syrup and stained orange with food coloring. I ate a piece still warm, the filling of sheep's milk cheese oozing out the sides, and washed it down with the sweetest cup of Arabic coffee. Like baklava, konafi is moistened with sugar syrup after it is baked. I hold back on some of the syrup to keep the sweetness in check, but remember that the sugar is not there just for flavor. If the syrup isn't dense enough, the konafi will not hold together. One of the original Zahav desserts is what I call New-School Konafi (page 339), which replaces some of the ricotta cheese filling with dark chocolate. It is not traditional, but it is fantastic.

FILLING

5 *cups ricotta cheese*
¾ *cup sugar*

KONAFI

¾ *cup heavy cream*
½ *cup sugar*
1 *(1-pound) box kataifi, cut crosswise into 1-inch-long pieces*
2 *recipes Lemon Syrup (page 332)*

● **FOR THE FILLING:** Combine the ricotta and sugar in the bowl of a stand mixer fitted with the paddle attachment (or use a hand mixer and a big bowl) and beat on medium speed until combined, about 1 minute. Refrigerate.

● **FOR THE KONAFI:** Combine the cream and sugar in a small saucepan over medium heat and bring to a simmer. Cooking, stirring, until the sugar is dissolved, about 2 minutes. Refrigerate until chilled.

● Combine the kataifi and the cream-sugar mixture in a large bowl and stir gently until evenly distributed. Spoon half of the kataifi mixture into a 9 by 13 inch baking dish, cover with oiled parchment paper, and use a heavy, flat meat mallet or the back of a heavy pan to press the kataifi into a dense, smooth layer. (If it it's not compact enough, it will be difficult to smooth on the filling later.) Refrigerate for 1 hour.

● Preheat the oven to 375°F, with a rack in the middle. Remove the parchment from the baking dish and very gently, using an offset spatula, spread the ricotta filling evenly over the kataifi. Spoon the remaining half of the kataifi mixture evenly over the top, cover with oiled parchment, and gently press until the top layer is flat and even, then remove and discard the parchment.

● Bake until golden brown, about 50 minutes, rotating the pan halfway through. Cool on wire rack. Drizzle with lemon syrup, cut into squares, and serve.

CLASSIC KONAFI

NEW-SCHOOL KONAFI WITH CHOCOLATE FILLING

4   cups ricotta cheese

3   tablespoons unsweetened cocoa powder

1   cup chopped dark chocolate
     (at least 60% cacao)

● **FOR THE FILLING:** Combine the ricotta and cocoa powder in the bowl of a stand mixer fitted with the paddle attachment (or use a hand mixer and a big bowl) and beat on medium speed until combined.

● Melt the chocolate over a double boiler. Stream the chocolate into the ricotta-cocoa mixture with the mixer on low speed. Mix until incorporated. Refrigerate.

● **FOR THE KONAFI:** To make individual rounds, divide half the konafi mixture among 12 oiled ramekins. Then proceed with the method on page 337, dividing the remaining ingredients evenly. Top with candied kumquats.

MOM'S HONEY CAKE WITH APPLE CONFIT

Makes 1 loaf

HONEY CAKE IS TRADITIONAL for Rosh Hashana, the Jewish New Year—the honey carries wishes for a sweet year. This is my mother's recipe. She makes it in Israel, freezes it, and sends it to me. In the mail. I've stopped reminding her that I'm a chef and accept the package gratefully. The cake holds up well and is very easy to make. I love a slice with coffee in the afternoon, but this cake works in savory applications, too—think goat cheese, or beneath a piece of seared foie gras, or—don't tell your grandma—with chopped liver.

For dessert, we serve the cake with apples that have been cooked very slowly in syrup until they are a beautiful, translucent amber color with an incredible jelly-like texture. Treated this way, the apples keep well in the fridge.

CAKE

- 2½ *cups all-purpose flour*
- 2 *heaping teaspoons baking soda*
- 1 *cup sugar*
- ½ *teaspoon salt*
  - *Pinch ground cinnamon*
- 3 *large eggs, lightly beaten*
- 1¼ *cups brewed coffee*
- ⅔ *cup honey*
- 6 *tablespoons canola oil*

APPLE CONFIT

- 3 *apples, peeled and sliced thinly crosswise*
- 1 *cup sugar*
- 1 *tablespoon honey*
- 2 *cinnamon sticks*
- 1 *vanilla bean, split*
- 3 *cloves*

● **FOR THE CAKE:** Preheat the oven to 350°F, with a rack in the middle. Line two 5-by-9 inch loaf pans with oiled parchment paper. Combine the flour and baking soda in a bowl and whisk well.

● In the bowl of a stand mixer (or use a hand mixer and a big bowl), combine the sugar, salt, cinnamon, eggs, coffee, honey, and oil. Mix on low speed until blended. Add the flour mixture and continue mixing just until combined. Divide the batter evenly between the prepared loaf pans. Bake until a toothpick inserted in the center comes out clean, about 30 minutes. Decrease the oven temperature to 275°F.

● **FOR THE APPLES:** Toss the apple slices with the sugar, honey, cinnamon, vanilla bean, and cloves. Arrange in a single layer in a large ovenproof skillet or a baking pan. Add enough water to just cover the apples. Press a sheet of parchment onto the surface of the water.

● Cover the skillet tightly with foil, bring to a simmer over medium-high heat, and transfer to the oven. Bake until the apples are just tender, about 1 hour. Cool to room temperature, transfer to a lidded container, and refrigerate until cold. Serve with the honey cake.

CARROT BASBOOSA WITH HAZELNUT CRUMBLE

Serves 12

BASBOOSA IS A CLASSIC Middle Eastern semolina cake with Egyptian origins. Like baklava and konafi, basboosa is saturated with syrup to help keep the cake moist and preserve it. I wanted to create a less-sweet version that doesn't rely on as much sugar for moistening, so I doubled the butter, added a bit of milk, and folded grated carrots into the batter. This is a great alternative to carrot cake—the semolina gives the crumb texture. In addition to adding flavor and aroma, the carrots help keep the cake moist.

CAKE

2½ cups semolina flour

1 cup hazelnuts, skins rubbed off, toasted

2 cups sugar

1 tablespoon baking soda

1 tablespoon baking powder

1½ teaspoons salt

2 sticks (½ pound) unsalted butter, melted

3 large eggs

1 cup milk

½ cup carrot juice

2 cups grated carrots

Lemon Syrup (page 332)

HAZELNUT CRUMBLE

1 cup hazelnuts, skins rubbed off, toasted

2 tablespoons brown sugar

2 tablespoons confectioners' sugar

1 tablespoon olive oil

Pinch salt

● **FOR THE CAKE:** Preheat the oven to 350°F, with a rack in the middle. Line a 9-by-13-inch baking dish with oiled parchment paper.

● Combine the semolina flour and hazelnuts in a food processor. Pulse until the mixture is as fine as flour.

Combine the hazelnut-semolina mixture with the sugar, baking soda, baking powder, and salt in the bowl of a stand mixer fitted with the paddle attachment (or use a hand mixer and a big bowl). Mix well and then stream in the butter with the mixer running on low. When the mixture is well incorporated, add the eggs, one at a time, beating until each is incorporated before adding the next. Add the milk, carrot juice, and grated carrots and continue mixing until combined. Pour the batter into the prepared baking dish. Bake until a toothpick inserted in the center comes out clean, about 45 minutes.

● Pour lemon syrup over the warm cake and allow to rest 4 hours.

● **FOR THE CRUMBLE:** Combine the hazelnuts, the sugars, oil, and salt in a food processor and pulse until the mixture is ground to a sandy consistency. Transfer to a plate. Cut the cake into squares and toss each piece in the crumble before serving.

CHOCOLATE-ALMOND SITUATION

Makes one 9-inch round cake

IT'S HARD TO BELIEVE this recipe is gluten-free! I especially love it as a great alternative to flourless chocolate cake. And it's very easy to make. Almond flour gives the cake fantastic structure while remaining nice and moist—almost brownie-like in texture. The cake can be made ahead of time and cut into small cubes to serve with tea or coffee, or cut into big wedges for dessert.

8   *tablespoons (1 stick) unsalted butter, softened*

1   *cup sugar*

    Big pinch salt

2   *scant cups chopped dark chocolate (at least 60% cacao; 11 ounces), melted and cooled slightly*

4   *large eggs, lightly beaten*

½   *cup almond flour*

● Preheat the oven to 375°F, with a rack in the middle. Oil a 9-inch round or square cake pan, line the bottom with a round of parchment paper, and oil the parchment.

● Combine the butter, sugar, and salt in the bowl of a stand mixer fitted with the paddle attachment (or use a hand mixer and a big bowl) and beat on medium-high speed until pale and fluffy, about 2 minutes. Add the melted chocolate and mix just until combined. Scrape down the sides of the bowl with a spatula and mix for another few seconds. With the mixer on low speed, add the eggs, one at a time, beating until each one is incorporated before adding the next. Scrape down the sides of the bowl again, then add the almond flour and mix on low until just incorporated, about 10 seconds.

● Pour the batter into the prepared cake pan and smooth the top with an offset spatula (the batter will be very sticky). Bake until a toothpick inserted in the center of the cake comes out clean, about 25 minutes. Let cool in the pan for 10 minutes before turning it out onto a wire rack to cool completely.

POPPY SEED CAKE WITH BLUEBERRIES AND LABNEH

Makes one 9-by-13-inch cake

THE EARTHY FRUITINESS of poppy seeds makes them shine in recipes both sweet and savory; they're equally at home on top of a buttered bagel as in a sweet filling for hamentashen, the stuffed, three-cornered Purim cookie. This poppy seed cake is basically a madeleine batter—almond flour, egg whites, and butter. The butter is browned first to give it a bit more complexity and a nuttiness that complements the poppy seeds. The egg whites keep the cake nice and tender and lend a bit of crispness to the crust.

10	tablespoons (1¼ sticks) unsalted butter
½	cup almond flour
⅓	cup plus 1 tablespoon all-purpose flour
½	teaspoon baking powder
5	large egg whites
1	cup confectioners' sugar
3	tablespoons honey
¼	cup poppy seeds
1	tablespoon finely grated lemon zest
1½	cups blueberries, for serving
1	cup labneh (see page 128), for serving

● Melt the butter in a small saucepan over medium heat. Cook, swirling frequently, until the foaming stops and the butter turns a rich brown color and smells nutty, about 5 minutes. Set aside to cool.

● Whisk the almond flour, all-purpose flour, and baking powder in a bowl.

● Combine the egg whites, confectioners' sugar, and honey in the bowl of a stand mixer fitted with the paddle attachment (or use a hand mixer and a big bowl). Beat on medium speed until the mixture is smooth and thick, about 3 minutes. Add the flour mixture to the egg mixture and fold in gently with a spatula until just combined. Whisk about ¼ cup of the batter into the brown butter until well combined, and then fold the brown butter mixture into the batter. Add the poppy seeds and lemon zest and fold in gently until just combined. Cover and refrigerate for at least 1 hour or up to overnight.

● Preheat the oven to 350°F, with a rack in the middle. Line a 9-by-13 inch baking dish with oiled parchment.

● Pour the batter into the prepared dish and bake until a toothpick inserted in the center comes out clean, about 30 minutes. Let cool in the pan. You can turn it out of the pan before slicing and serving, topped with blueberries and labneh, or serve straight from the pan.

WHITE CHOCOLATE CAKE WITH RHUBARB, LABNEH, AND SORBET

Serves 12

WHITE CHOCOLATE IS SWEETENED cocoa butter and milk solids with the cocoa solids removed. I love it because it can go places that regular chocolate would overpower. It is rich and creamy with a very subtle buttery flavor and is particularly good with fruit. This sheet cake is a great base for poached stone fruit, fresh berries, or in this case, melon sorbet. To enhance the white chocolate in the batter, I melt more white chocolate and whip it with labneh, whose acidity helps create a sauce that highlights the flavor of the cocoa butter.

Finally, I roll pieces of the cake in a mixture of sachlab (ground orchid root) and confectioners' sugar. It smells like marshmallows and tastes like the best powdered sugar donut you've ever had. The cake is wonderful with the melon sorbet and the white chocolate labneh, but I won't tell if your ice cream comes from a container.

CAKE

2	cups all-purpose flour
1½	teaspoons baking soda
¾	teaspoon baking powder
	Pinch ground cardamom
	Pinch salt
10	tablespoons (1¼ sticks) unsalted butter
1⅓	cups sugar
½	cup chopped white chocolate, melted, plus ½ cup chopped
3	large eggs
⅔	cup sour cream
½	teaspoon vanilla

POACHED RHUBARB

½	cup sugar
1	bunch rhubarb stalks, cut into 1-inch pieces (about 2 cups)
1	teaspoon rose water (see page 351)

MELON SORBET

1	pound honeydew melon, cut into chunks (about 4 cups)
5	tablespoons sugar
2	tablespoons light corn syrup
1	tablespoon lemon juice

WHITE CHOCOLATE LABNEH

1½	cups white chocolate, chopped
⅔	cup heavy cream
1	scant cup labneh (see page 128)

Confectioners' sugar, for dusting
Sachlab, for dusting (see Resources, page 359)

● **FOR THE CAKE:** Line a 9-by-13-inch baking dish with oiled parchment. Whisk the flour, baking soda, baking powder, cardamom, and salt in a large bowl.

● Combine the butter and sugar in the bowl of a stand mixer fitted with the paddle attachment (or use a hand mixer and a big bowl) and mix on medium speed until light and fluffy, about 3 minutes. With the

mixer running, add the melted white chocolate and mix until blended. Add the eggs, one at a time, beating to incorporate each one before adding the next. Add half of the sour cream, half of the flour mixture, and the vanilla. Mix until incorporated, scraping down the bowl once or twice. Add the remaining sour cream and flour mixture and continue mixing until just combined. Add the chopped white chocolate and mix for another 30 seconds, just to combine. Pour the batter into the prepared baking dish, cover tightly with plastic wrap, and refrigerate at least 1 hour or overnight, all the better to develop the flavors.

● **FOR THE RHUBARB:** Combine the sugar with ¼ cup water in a medium saucepan. Bring to a boil. Cook, whisking, until the sugar has dissolved, about 3 minutes. Add the rhubarb and rose water and lower the heat to maintain a gentle simmer. Simmer until the rhubarb is just tender, about 10 minutes. Remove from heat and let the rhubarb cool in the syrup.

● **FOR THE SORBET:** Combine the honeydew, sugar, corn syrup, lemon juice, and ⅓ cup water in a blender and puree until smooth. Refrigerate until chilled,

then churn in an ice cream maker according to the manufacturer's instructions.

● **FOR THE WHITE CHOCOLATE LABNEH:** Put the white chocolate in a large heatproof bowl. Bring the cream to a boil and immediately pour over the white chocolate. Stir until the white chocolate has melted and the mixture is smooth. Refrigerate overnight. Before serving, put the white chocolate–cream mixture in the bowl of a stand mixer with the paddle attachment (or use a hand mixer and a big bowl). Add the labneh, and mix until smooth. Reserve.

● Preheat the oven to 350°F, with a rack in the middle position. Bake the cake until a toothpick inserted in the center comes out clean, about 35 minutes.

● To serve, I like to cut cylinders from the cake. Then I dust them with a mix of three parts confectioners' sugar to one part sachlab, as shown. But you can just slice the cake in in any shape, then dust the pieces. Assemble plates with the sugared cake, the ruby-red poached rhubarb, a scoop of melon sorbet, and the white chocolate labneh.

CHOCOLATE BABKA

Makes 1 loaf

THIS BABKA IS SO EASY, baking it almost feels like cheating. Sweet and rich yeasted dough is stuffed with chocolate, then rolled up and baked. It has the kind of balance of sweet and savory that lures you into consuming way too much of it—I have a hard time not eating it as it comes out of the oven. We gild the lily by serving the babka with cardamom-flavored Turkish Coffee Ice Cream (page 354). The sweetness of the cardamom is excellent with the bitter notes of the coffee and chocolate. You can bake the babka in a single loaf or in muffin tins for individual servings. If there are any leftovers (doubtful!), babka makes excellent bread pudding or French toast.

FILLING

⅔ cup sugar

¼ cup all-purpose flour

1 teaspoon unsweetened cocoa powder

Pinch salt

6 tablespoons (¾ stick) unsalted butter, chilled and cubed

⅓ cup chopped dark chocolate (at least 60% cacao)

DOUGH

2 tablespoons active dry yeast (from three ¼-ounce packages)

2¼ cups all-purpose flour, plus more if needed

6 tablespoons sugar

Pinch salt

6 tablespoons milk

½ teaspoon vanilla

¼ teaspoon finely grated lemon zest

2 large eggs, plus 1 large egg yolk

6 tablespoons (¾ stick) unsalted butter, softened

● **FOR THE FILLING:** Combine the sugar, flour, cocoa powder, and salt in a food processor. Pulse until evenly mixed. Add the butter and chocolate and pulse until a crumbly, coarse mixture forms. (It should be chunky, not powdery.) Set aside.

● **FOR THE DOUGH:** Combine the yeast with 6 tablespoons warm water in a small bowl and let stand until frothy, about 5 minutes.

● Combine the flour, sugar, and salt in the bowl of a stand mixer fitted with the dough hook (or use a hand mixer and a big bowl) and mix to combine. Add the yeast mixture, milk, vanilla, and lemon zest. Mix on low speed until combined. Add one of the eggs, the yolk, and the butter. Mix until the dough comes together in a smooth, pliable ball, about 8 minutes. (If the dough seems too wet and resists forming a ball, add a little extra flour, 1 tablespoon at a time.) Turn the dough out into a greased bowl, cover with plastic wrap, and let rise in a warm place until it doubles in size, about 1 hour.

● On a well-floured surface, roll the dough into a rectangle as wide as your loaf pan is long and about ¾ inch thick. Set aside ¼ cup of the filling. Sprinkle the remaining filling onto the dough and roll up like a jelly roll. Freeze until firm and sliceable, about 3 hours.

● Line a 9-by-5-inch loaf pan with enough oiled parchment so that the parchment extends over the edges of the pan. Cut the frozen babka into 1-inch-thick rounds and reassemble the loaf in the prepared loaf pan. Cover it loosely with plastic wrap. Let rise again until doubled in size, about 90 minutes.

● Preheat the oven to 325°F. Lightly beat the remaining egg. Remove the plastic wrap and brush the babka with the egg and sprinkle the reserved filling on top. Bake until the loaf is golden brown and springs back when you press it, 60 to 70 minutes. Let cool completely on a wire rack before serving.

SACHLAB DRINK
Serves 4

I LOVE TO MAKE THIS WARM lovable drink from sachlab (ground orchid root). It's the cold weather cousin of malabi custard. Milk, sugar, and sachlab are simmered until lightly thickened and the sachlab is served hot in a mug, sprinkled with cinnamon and crushed pistachios. It's so pure—perfect on the inevitable chilly nights in Jerusalem.

4   cups whole milk
4   teaspoons sachlab
    (see Resources, page 359)
5   tablespoons sugar
    Handful crushed pistachios
    Pinch ground cinnamon

● Combine the milk, sachlab, and sugar in a saucepan over medium heat. Cook until the milk is steaming, whisking until the liquid thickens, about 5 minutes. Serve hot with pistachios and cinnamon on top.

MALABI CUSTARD WITH MANGO
Serves 8

MALABI IS A CLASSIC milk pudding, typically flavored with rose water and vanilla, originally thickened with ground orchid root (sachlab), and served cold. I like our malabi to be more like a panna cotta than a pudding. I set it with gelatin to make it as ethereal as possible and flavor it with a bit of the precious orchid root that we get from Lior Lev Sercarz (see page 132). A drop of rose water, judiciously applied, is a good substitute for orchid root. Or try another floral note such as orange blossom water or even a few drops of elderflower cordial. I top the malabi with a glossy layer of mango and sometimes passion fruit.

· INGREDIENT ·

ROSE WATER

Rose water was developed in Persia several hundred years ago and is a by-product of the rose oil that is produced to make perfume. It is traditionally used to flavor sweets throughout the Middle East, from baklava to ice cream to malabi. It is quite potent. A little bit goes a long way. (See Resources, page 359.)

1   *cup milk*

2¾   *teaspoons powdered gelatin*

6   *tablespoons sugar*

2   *tablespoons sachlab (see Resources, page 359), or 1 teaspoon rose water*

3   *cups heavy cream*

1   *cup mango nectar*

● Pour the milk into a medium saucepan and sprinkle with the gelatin. Let stand for 10 minutes. Put the saucepan over medium-high heat and cook, stirring frequently, until the gelatin is completely dissolved and a thermometer registers 135°F, about 2 minutes.

● Off the heat, add the sugar and sachlab or rose water and stir until dissolved. Whisking, pour the cream into the milk mixture. Set the saucepan over a bowl of ice water and whisk until cold, about 10 minutes. Divide among eight 4- to 6-ounce bowls. Cover with plastic wrap and chill until set, about 4 hours.

● Bring the mango nectar to a simmer in a small saucepan over medium-high heat. Cook until the liquid has thickened, about 5 minutes. Let cool completely, then spoon a thin layer onto the chilled custards just before serving.

CARDAMOM-VANILLA CUSTARD WITH SQUASH CONFIT AND HUCKLEBERRIES

Serves 4

THIS IS AN INSANELY DECADENT vanilla custard taken to the next level with the addition of cardamom. The fragrance of this spice reminds me of a sweet evergreen forest—its woodsy, piney aroma works incredibly well with vanilla. But be careful not to overdo it, unless you like the taste of cough medicine. The custard goes with just about anything, so it's often on the menu at Zahav, served with a rotating cast of seasonal fruit, from fresh berries to poached stone fruit to brûléed bananas. It's wonderful with the sugary squash confit and fresh berries.

CUSTARD

1½ *cups heavy cream*

½ *cup sugar*

5 *cardamom pods, crushed*

1 *vanilla bean, split and scraped*

8 *large egg yolks*

SQUASH

1 *cup diced peeled butternut squash (about 5 ounces)*

6 *tablespoons sugar*

2 *tablespoons lemon juice*

Handful huckleberries or blueberries, for serving

● **FOR THE CUSTARD:** Combine the cream, sugar, cardamom, and vanilla bean in a saucepan over medium-high heat and bring to a boil, whisking occasionally. Remove from the heat.

● Put the egg yolks in a heatproof bowl and whisk well. Add a spoonful of the hot cream mixture to the egg yolks and quickly whisk to combine. Continue adding the hot cream mixture to the egg yolks a couple tablespoons at a time, whisking well after each addition, until the outside of the bowl feels warm to the touch. At this point, add the yolk mixture to the hot cream mixture and whisk energetically until smooth and combined.

● Cool the mixture quickly, setting the bowl in a larger bowl filled with ice and a bit of cold water. Stir to speed the cooling. Refrigerate overnight, then strain.

● Preheat the oven to 325°F, with a rack in the middle. Place four 4- to 6-ounce ramekins inside a baking dish. Divide the custard evenly among the ramekins and transfer to the oven. Pour enough boiling water into the baking dish so that it comes halfway up the sides of the ramekins. Cover the pan tightly with foil, then bake until the edges are set but the custards jiggle a bit in the middle, 30 to 35 minutes. Cool on a wire rack and refrigerate until cold.

● **FOR THE SQUASH:** Arrange the squash pieces in a single layer in a baking dish. Combine 6 tablespoons water, the sugar, and lemon juice in a small saucepan over high heat and bring to a boil. Pour the boiling syrup over the squash, press a square of parchment paper onto the surface of the squash, and cover tightly with two layers of foil. Bake at 325°F until the squash is tender but not falling apart, about 30 minutes.

● Strain the syrup from the baking dish into a saucepan. Bring to a boil over high heat and cook until it has reduced by half, about 8 minutes. Let cool completely, then pour the syrup through a strainer over the squash.

● Spoon some squash cubes and syrup over each custard, top with the huckleberries or blueberries, and serve.

TURKISH COFFEE ICE CREAM
Makes 1 quart

FOR ME, THE BEST ICE CREAM is coffee ice cream. It is a perfect balance of bitter and sweet. Our version uses Turkish-style coffee and a bit of cardamom to add Arabic flavor. Because the coffee is so finely ground, we don't strain it all out before we freeze it, which gives the finished ice cream a nice speckled look and texture.

2 cups heavy cream
⅔ cup milk
¼ cup ground Turkish coffee
5 cardamom pods
6 large egg yolks
¾ cup sugar

● Combine the cream, milk, coffee, and cardamom in a medium saucepan over medium-high heat and bring to a boil. Remove the saucepan from the heat and let the mixture steep for 10 minutes.

● Combine the egg yolks and sugar in a large heatproof bowl set over a pot of simmering water. (The bottom of the bowl shouldn't touch the water.) Whisk until the sugar is dissolved and the mixture falls from the whisk in ribbons when you lift it out of the bowl, about 2 minutes. Add the cream mixture and stir with a rubber spatula, scraping the sides to prevent coagulation, until the mixture reaches 180°F.

● Strain out some of the coffee grounds, pour into a container, cover, and refrigerate overnight. Churn in an ice cream maker according to the manufacturer's instructions.

· INGREDIENT ·

CARDAMOM

Native to India, the cardamom plant produces tapered pods that contain intensely flavored black seeds. By weight, it is an expensive spice, although you don't need much of it to make an impact and it will keep for a long time in pod form. Of the several varieties of cardamom, green is the most widely available. On its own, cardamom's sweet, resinous flavor can be overpowering. But as an accent to things as different as the peppery condiment schug or Turkish Coffee Ice Cream, cardamom is a flavor enhancer that can make the flavors around it sparkle.

ACKNOWLEDGMENTS

FROM MICHAEL SOLOMONOV: I am a product of the fantastic people in my life.

This book would not be possible without Steven Cook. Let me back up a little bit. Zahav and the success of our entire restaurant group would not be possible without Steven Cook. We have been to hell and back together and I am grateful to go through all of it with not only an amazing mentor and partner, but alongside my best friend.

My wife, Mary, deserves an entire book written about how incredible she is. For all the years of putting up with a chef as a spouse, she has never stopped being encouraging and generally wonderful. And her heart becomes seemingly larger with our two boys, David and Lucas, whom we have been blessed with raising.

To Marc, Jeff, and the Vetri family—literal family and the *"familia"*—I don't know what would have become of me if it weren't for the time that I spent at Vetri. In a bizarre way, I feel like cooking was almost secondary to the experience, even though Marc shaped my cooking style. I would like to thank Terence Feury for his mentorship at Striped Bass and his invaluable friendship, for firing me and rehiring me, and for teaching me how to cook.

To my parents for inspiring and continuing to inspire me through absolutely everything. Thank you to Ava, Michael, Rebecca, and Alex and Kelsey Maxwell and Aline Fisher for their unconditional love and support. I would like to thank the Armisteads for allowing me to weasel my way into their incredible family.

A big double-handed high five followed by a hug and a kiss to Dorothy Kalins for producing such an incredible book and assembling the team. Dorothy, creating this book has helped me define the cuisine that we cook at Zahav. To be able to have a clearer perspective on my life's work after this process is an unexpected gift. Also I want to thank you and Roger Sherman for your friendship.

A big thank-you to Don Morris for creating such a beautiful book and being so incredibly easy to work with. Watching you and Mike collaborate was an absolute privilege. Michael Persico, I hate you for ruining my life by teaching me to surf: Now I don't want to do anything else. Your photography is mind blowing, and I am proud to call you a friend. It feels like just yesterday we were stuck in a blizzard together. Thank you for all of your hard work. I'm so grateful to our friend and food professional, Joy Manning, for diligently testing and worrying through each and every recipe.

Heartfelt thanks to Rux Martin for believing in this project and being so supportive and trusting. And mastering the ingredients; and cooking the recipes! And a big thank-you to David Black for working so hard to put all of this together. Getting to know you has been a privilege and I look forward to working together in the future.

I would like to throw a shout-out to Sarah Rosenberg, thanks for all of your hard work and friendship and love. Jenny Hatton, Clare Pelino, and James Narog, we are lucky to have worked together. To Erin O'Shea, Felicia D'Ambrosio, Tom Henneman, and Bobby Logue—I thank you for all of your continued support, partnership, and friendship. To Amy Henderson, Yehuda Sichel, Emily Seaman, Dean Hilderbrand, Okan Yaziki, Brian Kane, and Eilon Gigi, you guys

are rock stars! I love you and I am honored to be able work with you. I would like to acknowledge the late food historian Gil Marks for his *Encyclopedia of Jewish Food*, and Ron Maiberg for being one of the first people to put a name to Israeli cuisine. And also a big ole thank-you to Sara Corse, Carl Mason, and Wade Hinnant for keeping me sane and always being in my corner.

To the past, present, and future staff of Zahav restaurant, thank you for your tireless dedication to getting the "custies fired up." You have all literally made my dreams come true.

FROM STEVEN COOK: I first met Mike Solomonov at a coffee shop on Fairmount Avenue during the summer of 2005. We had mutual friends (including my wife, Shira) and were cooking in the same city but had never met. We had even lived right next door to each other for a year. True story. At the time Shira arranged this meeting, I was just finishing up my first year as a rookie chef/owner at Marigold Kitchen, a tiny BYOB in West Philly. Although things seemed to be going well on the outside—great reviews, a steady and growing customer base—on the inside, I was struggling. Owning your own restaurant can be a very lonely business.

I'd like to say that I knew instinctively that Mike and I would make a great team, but my head was elsewhere. I thought I was done in the restaurant business and I was looking for someone to replace me in the kitchen.

Mike was my exit strategy. What I found instead was a partner, in the truest sense of the word. Ten years and ten restaurant openings later, we've shared almost every experience imaginable in this business, good and bad, and I am thankful each day to be able to work with and be inspired by my friend and my brother. I can only hope that the generosity, warmth, humor, intelligence, and passion that I get to see every day comes across in these pages.

My own cooking career was short, but not without people who made a lasting impact. I am grateful to my first chef, Kiong Banh, for teaching me professionalism and how to be a gentleman in the kitchen, and to Vernon Morales, for setting the bar high every day and challenging me to constantly raise my standards. I must also thank Howard Gellis and Sal Gentile, who hired me right out of school and showed me the ropes of high finance for six years before I bolted for the restaurant business. None of our restaurants would be possible without the education and support they gave me—not just how to crunch numbers, but also how to do business with honor, integrity, and reason, and not for the last dollar.

In the ten years since I've been in the business, I've had the good fortune to have a number of great partners, especially Erin O'Shea at Percy Street Barbecue and Tom Henneman, Bobby Logue, and Felicia D'Ambrosio at Federal Donuts. And of course, none of this would be possible without the hard work and enthusiasm of all of the Zahav managers and staff, past and present, for making the restaurant (and this book) come alive every night. You are hospitality personified and I am beyond proud to work with you.

This book would not exist without Dorothy Kalins, who had a vision for what it should be even before we could see it. The worst part of being self-employed is not having someone to tell you what to do and when to do it. But Dorothy made sure that was never an issue. Her vision never wavered, and her gentle (yet firm) touch brought this book to life (also, her willingness to schlep props back and forth to Philly during what seemed like a perpetual snowstorm).

The best thing about being your own boss is getting to pick the people you work with. At our restaurants, the number-one criterion is simply that you have to be nice. This book was no different. The dream team of designer Don Morris, photographer Mike Persico, and recipe editor Joy Manning (who, not coincidentally, was the first professional critic to understand what we were trying to do at Zahav when we opened in 2008), made this process fun from beginning to end. I cannot imagine a more gracious, talented, professional, generous, and supportive group of collaborators. And oh, yes, nice too!

Writing a book is a dream come true for me, and for that I thank Rux Martin for holding her breath and trusting a first-time author with so much on the line. She (and everyone at HMH) took a leap of faith that there could be magic in this book. And thank you to David Black for helping us to find just the right publishing partner. Also at Houghton, big

thanks to art director Melissa Lotfy, production editor Jacqueline Beach, and managing editor Marina Padakis. Thanks, too, to copyeditor Deri Reed for saving us from ourselves. Finally I want to thank my family for all of their support, particularly my parents, who always encouraged me, even when their nice Jewish boy abandoned a high-paying Wall Street job to pursue his dream in a restaurant kitchen. And thank you, Dad, for emailing me a link to every blog post that has ever mentioned one of our restaurants.

To my wife, thank you for giving me the courage to put myself out there each day without the fear of failure. Shira was the first person to read the words in this book and, if it is any good, it is undoubtedly much better because of her. And so am I.

PHOTOGRAPHY CREDITS

All photographs by **Michael Persico** with the exception of family photographs and images from the photographers and sources listed below.

Steven Cook: *24–25, 27, 45 bottom, 68, 120, 121, 122, 126 bottom, 197, 320*
Michael T. Regan: *10–11, 15, 19, 22, 65 top, 66, 78, 116-117, 119, 123, 158, 161, 173 bottom, 194, 196, 234, 264–265, 290–291, 292, 321*
Roger Sherman: *141, 160, 235, 236, 267, 334, 335*
Karen Shakeridge: *17, 155, 295*
Jay S. Simon/The Image Bank/Getty Images: *30*
Zhaojiankang/Dreamstime: *31 left*
Tonny Anwar/Dreamstime: *31 right*
Darko Plohl/Dreamstime: *45 top*
Tor Eigeland/Alamy: *50*
Mrakhr/Dreamstime: *65 bottom right*
Dennis Donohue/Dreamstime: *97 left*
R. Koenig/AGE: *172*

RESOURCES

I've highlighted many delicious ingredients throughout the course of this book. Happily, many of them are readily available in good markets everywhere. Here are my favorite sources.

TEHINA

Excellent-quality sesame seeds and sesame butter are now available here. Our main source is **Soom Tahini,** page 28, imported by the three Zitelman sisters. You can order directly from them: **soomfoods.com** or **amazon.com.** Try their chocolate tahini!

SPICES, HERBS, RICE, GRAINS & MORE

For the most incredible spices and spice blends (and cookies), you must visit **La Bôite à Epice.** Lior Lev Sercarz, page 132, is truly a master at his craft. I depend on Lior's Amber #2 blend, Shabazi blend, hawaij, dried rose buds, orchid root (sachlab), za'atar, and so much more. Visit his gallery shop at 724 11th Avenue, New York, NY, but call first to make sure he's there: (212) 247-4407. Or order from **laboiteny.com.**

Terra Spice Company has a richly comprehensive array of spices, oils, and fancy cooking products. Chefs and culinary professionals are well served here. PO Box 921, North Liberty, IN, (574) 222-2462, **info@terraspice.com.**

Kalustyan's in New York stocks thousands of spices, such as dried limes, sumac, rose petals, ground Urfa pepper, baharat, fenugreek, and black garlic. Plus, they have a hundred kinds of rice; the boxed shredded phyllo dough called kataifi; nuts like pistachios; prepared ingredients such as amba (mango pickle); harissa; date, carob, and pomegranate molasses; orange blossom water; rose water; and labneh. Order online at **kalustyans.com.** Even better, visit their magical shop at 123 Lexington Avenue, New York, NY. Or call (800) 352-3451.

MEAT & MORE

DeBragga, an amazing meat purveyor that also sells retail, is our source for the square-cut Colorado lamb shoulder that we are almost famous for. **debragga.com**

D'Artagnan is our go-to source for specialty meats and such great poultry, as well as products both fancy and rare. **dartagnan.com**

We rely on **Pat La Frieda's** beef, especially their dry-aged ground beef and hanger steak, available at **lafrieda.com.**

PHILADELPHIA SOURCES

How lucky we are that just a few blocks from Zahav, in our Society Hill neighborhood, The Food Trust runs the Sunday **Headhouse Farmers' Market** in the historic brick buildings at Second and Lombard Streets. Many of our favorite farmers and purveyors can be found there from May to December.

You must explore **Reading Terminal Market** at 12th and Arch Streets, in the heart of Philly. Dozens of my favorite vendors, such as Valley Shepherd Creamery and their handmade cheese, Iovine Brothers Produce, Border Springs Farm Lamb, and of course, The Cookbook Stall, make up this old-school/new-school marketplace, operating since the mid-nineteenth century. Open every day, but check hours at **readingterminalmarket.org.**

I have been shopping at **Di Bruno Brothers** since I moved to Philly. They have amazing cheeses, cured meats, olives, and high-quality legumes. If you happen to be in the Italian market, ask for Emilio and tell him I sent you! 930 South 9th Street, (215) 922-2876, **dibruno.com**

POTTERY

We were lucky enough to discover **Liz Kinder,** a world-class Philadelphia potter who invited us into her Fishtown studio and let us borrow for photography every plate, platter, and bowl our fingers touched. You'll find Liz's singular work throughout the book, and especially on pages 124–125. Liz wants me to say she's always up for studio visits. Call (267) 235-5820 or e-mail liz@lizkinder.com. See her work at **lizkinder.com**, potsonhand.blogspot.com, and throwingandtantrums.blogspot.com.

Let's be real here for a second. If you don't want to scour the earth for crazy ingredients (like the transglutaminase, meat glue used on page 56, or the pink salt to cure basturma) or don't have time or whatever, do what my wife does—order it on **amazon.com.**

INDEX

INDEX

INDEX

INDEX

INDEX